JOEL SELWOOD

All in

Hardie Grant

BOOKS

Published in 2023 by Hardie Grant Books, an imprint of Hardie Grant Publishing

Hardie Grant Books (Melbourne)
Building 1, 658 Church Street
Richmond, Victoria 3121

Hardie Grant Books (London)
5th & 6th Floors
52–54 Southwark Street
London SE1 1UN

hardiegrant.com/books

Hardie Grant acknowledges the Traditional Owners of the country on which we work,
the Wurundjeri people of the Kulin nation and the Gadigal people of the Eora nation,
and recognises their continuing connection to the land, waters and culture. We pay our
respects to their Elders past and present.

A catalogue record for this
work is available from the
National Library of Australia

Joel Selwood: All in
ISBN 978 1 74379 942 0

10 9 8 7 6 5 4 3 2 1

Cover design by Luke Causby, Blue Cork
Edited by Geoff Slattery
Front cover image by James Braund
Back cover image AFL photos
Typeset in 11/18 pt Sabon LT Std by Kirby Jones
Printed in Australia by Griffin Press, an Accredited ISO AS/NZS 14001 Environmental
Management System printer.

JOEL SELWOOD

I never intended to write a book. But when the end of my career drew near, people close to me encouraged me to do so. One argument convinced me it would be worthwhile: the book wasn't for me. It was so Joey and any other children we are lucky enough to have would know my story.

Contents

Chapter 1

A grand finale

IT WAS GRAND Final night and my wife, Brit, and I – and Geelong's 2022 premiership cup – were on the way to our place in Barwon Heads, on Victoria's Bellarine Peninsula. We were lucky to make it home after an exhausted Brit and I had found ourselves stranded at a service station with a 24-hour cafe a few kilometres from home, unable to re-start our car.

We had left the celebrations at the club early as Brit was 18 weeks' pregnant and we were keen to get home. When we got to our car, parked in a street nearby, I realised I had left the keys in my locker. I rang Harry Taylor, who grabbed them from the locker, jogged to where we were waiting, jumped in the car, and away we went. Without another thought we dropped him back at the club. He still had the keys in his pocket but the motor was running so it didn't matter. But once we had stopped, it was a different issue.

We only realised our dilemma after we'd stopped at APCO service station, a few kilometres from home, to fill our empty stomachs. Like all modern cars, we needed the keys to activate the push-button start. We wanted to get home as quickly as possible, and I was lucky to convince a P-plate driver also at the cafe – she told me her name was Emily – to drive me home to get the spare key and bring me back. I hadn't given her much choice, to be honest. I told her I needed her help and was making my way to the passenger seat before she had a chance to think!

Emily, who worked at the Barwon Heads Pub, did not recognise me. She wasn't in the best of moods after enduring a tough shift but she asked me how my day had been. 'It was actually pretty good,' I said. She then asked me what I had been doing; I told her I had played in the game at the MCG that day. It took her a moment before she recognised me and started swearing to herself. I loved that and appreciated her timely and kind gesture even more. She became the first person in Barwon Heads to have a photo with the premiership cup.

A memorable finish to a perfect day!

After a good night's sleep, the next morning we packed the cup back in the car. We were heading back to Geelong to celebrate the victory with players, coaches, staff, friends, family and the many thousands of fans who had gathered at St Mary's Football Club, in the shadows of GMHBA Stadium. Brit, with a big smile on her face, surprised me: 'Do you want me to drive down the main street?' Such a thought had never entered my mind. I laughed out loud: 'Why not?'

Moments later, we drove up Hitchcock Avenue with Brit tooting the horn. I hung out the car window with a big grin on my face and the premiership cup in my hands. The footpaths were overflowing, a mix of holiday makers and locals enjoying the school holidays, all delighted with the Cats' victory. The crowd roared approval, sharing our joy. Being understated has been ingrained in me but this was a time to savour. Geelong were premiers, again. Finally, eleven seasons after our 2011 victory, I was now a premiership captain.

* * *

On Grand Final morning, Brit and I had woken early after sleeping in adjacent rooms – 726 and 727 – at Albert Park's Pullman Hotel; the club had given us all the option of staying in town after the pre-Grand Final parade. I felt so confident we could defeat Sydney in the Grand Final later that afternoon, but that feeling made me slightly uneasy as I walked into the next room to say hello to Brit. We had not slept in the same bed for about a month as I had become paranoid – or sensible, depending on your perspective – about the prospect of catching COVID or some other bug Brit might pick up at her work as a teacher. I could sense Brit was more anxious than me. She was one of about a dozen people who knew for sure the Grand Final would be my last game, win or lose, but that thought had not entered my mind at all. My only focus was on winning.

The day before, as I moved from a speedboat that had taken me along the Yarra River into a waiting car during the pre-Grand Final parade, I had met my manager and friend, Tom Petroro. Tom was one of the handful who knew the next day's match would be farewell time. 'Happy tears only,' I said, as we embraced.

Tom had been my manager for 16 years – through my whole career. In many ways we had grown up together. But in recent weeks, as we discussed my retirement, his care went to another level as he checked in on me and Brit constantly to see how we were feeling. Seeing him that morning made me realise that other people were more nervous for me than I was. Even Brit kept asking me whether I was happy or sad. I was neither. I just knew we had a Grand Final to win.

Although my possible retirement loomed as an obvious question leading into the game, the media had been respectful on the issue. I batted away a fair pre-game question from Channel 10's Rob Waters about whether this would be my last game. My answer was truthful but non-committal. 'I play every game like it will be my last,' I said. Those words did not mean I was immune to emotional surges or any distractions. I had always been able to deal with peripheral issues heading towards any game, without expending any reserves of football energy.

Despite my self-confidence, Brit knew me better than anyone. She knew I was better off alone at the hotel. She took the unusual pre-game step of booking herself in for an early-morning hair appointment, across town in Essendon, having spent the previous afternoon out shopping. It was an excuse to get out of my hair rather than to do anything glamorous with hers. I was so grateful for her consideration. She assumed her presence would only make me nervous. But I was excited. And that made me nervous, in a good way.

My routine had changed a little over the years but the pattern I followed this Grand Final day had been pretty well established. As I packed my gear for my last game of footy, not much was ordered; in fact, the process was pretty loose. One thing was constant: I always packed Speedos to wear under my shorts. This year Tom Atkins, a St Joseph's product who emerged as a rookie via the VFL, had organised a bunch of Speedos that carried the initials VF, honouring our mate Vic Fuller, who was a volunteer at the club for 50 years before he collapsed while standing in the race at GMHBA Stadium as we trained 20 months earlier. I adored Vic, as everyone at the club did, for his quick wit, honest feedback and football truisms. His wife, Nola, and his family remain firm friends. All of us would be wearing the Vic Fuller Speedos as we ran onto the ground. I also pack my boots. Nowadays many players just pack toiletries and nothing else, relying on the property steward to bring everything they need. I couldn't do that. I need to take my own boots, so I know they are with me. Always a towel, too. For me, that's being ready.

Even though it was Grand Final day, some long-held habits remained. I watched the North Melbourne breakfast on Fox Footy before switching to the pre-game show on Channel 7. I then headed downstairs to join my teammates (15 had stayed overnight in Melbourne) for a bite to eat. Mitch Duncan joined me at a table in a large room on the first floor reserved for players and football department staff. We reminisced about me driving him and Allen Christensen – 'Bundy' – from Geelong to the 2011 Grand Final. He reckons I sorted out him and Bundy, keeping their minds at ease ahead of their first Grand Final.

This time Mitch and I were veterans and friends, two of 10 players in the Cats' Grand Final team aged above 30, a fact that had led to some derision through 2022, after the disappointment of 2021's finals campaign. To win a flag we had to become the oldest team (by average age) in the last 20 years. Our average age was 28.6; in 2015, Hawthorn had won with an average age of 27.8. We also were beyond the 2015 Hawks' average games played – 166.6 vs 165.8. The conversation between us was relaxed as I tucked into the breakfast my teammate Sam Menegola had introduced me to: Vegemite on toast with bacon and eggs on top. He had perfected this unusual mix, while I battled to get the balance right.

Mitch still remembers me rebuking him in his third pre-season when he did not push hard enough to reach a cone in a drill. 'Too good for that now?' I had snarled at him. He never forgot it, nor, he reckons, did he not ever push hard towards a cone again.

In that first Grand Final we played together, we defeated Collingwood by 38 points in what was the last game for Cameron Ling, our captain. The result meant both Mitch and I had both become premiership players for the first time before we had turned 21 – him in 2011, me in 2007 – but that Grand Final was 11 years ago, a lifetime in football terms. I had been the skipper since, a period in which the club lost one Grand Final and five preliminary finals.

Those losses had hurt. In 2019, after we lost the preliminary final to Richmond, the doubts crept in. I wondered whether my time as skipper should end. Would it be better for the club if someone else took the reins? After each of our finals exits, I battled to come to terms with the result; I am a really bad loser. That one, however, had me reflecting, taking on board what the outside world was saying about the club's need to change its approach. I was my harshest critic. The drive home that night took two hours and I contemplated every scenario – past, present and future. I was so dirty, I sat at home for a few days, hibernating, not communicating with Brit or anyone else.

The wins were different. It would take until I was in the car with Brit, away from teammates and the cameras, before I would let out a guttural scream of pure joy. For me, showing such an explosion of emotion was unacceptable elsewhere. My moment had become our moment from the moment our relationship had begun in 2015.

* * *

When it was time to go to the ground, I found my regular seat up the back on the right-hand side of the bus even though I realised my hold on that spot had become problematic. Sam De Koning had been cheeky enough to sit there when we returned from training the day before, which had me thinking, 'What is going on here?'

I stared out the window while most of my teammates put on headphones. The bus was quiet. Occasionally there's a group playing cards. I always let people do what they want to do before games because the truth is that 90 per cent of what occupies a player's mind at this time is simply what role they need to perform. They don't need another idea entering the mix. As the skipper you just hope no-one is tightening up because of the occasion so I just try to be relaxed, and to show it. In any case, I had total trust in my teammates and how they prepared themselves.

AFL rules require us to drop our mobile phones into an allocated box a couple of hours before any game. This time, most of our phones were flooded with messages of goodwill, or that last call for tickets. Some check, some respond, some don't. Those who had travelled from home rather than stayed at the hotel had arrived about 45 minutes before the bus. The trip from Geelong was so much quicker than for Friday night games. Poor Jeremy Cameron; he usually arrives in the rooms 80 minutes before games. On this day he was there 180 minutes ahead of the first bounce, having spent the night before retrieving a mate who had become lost on the way to his place at Freshwater Creek.

I jumped in the shower as soon as I arrived at the MCG. The pre-game shower was a habit I had started about four years earlier. It is something of a cleansing ritual, helping me to make the switch from day-to-day life to becoming an AFL player with a job to do. There's a lot more time than usual to kill before a Grand Final as we arrived at the ground two-and-a-bit hours before the bounce. I made sure I was in the queue for the physios to get my ankles strapped and a rub down from the masseurs. I usually do Spot the Difference in the *AFL Record*. This time I stood and watched the TV as Robbie Williams entertained the growing crowd. As the queue began to dawdle outside the physio area, we realised the physios and masseurs had disappeared. Lo and behold, a bunch of them were at the top of the race watching Williams in action. They were more interested in the big act than doing their job. It made me laugh.

* * *

Chris Scott, our coach since replacing Mark 'Bomber' Thompson in 2011, is not a hot gospeller but the gathering as a group for the pre-match address is football at its purest – individuals getting together to become a team. Throughout the year our motto had been to always be looking at the next moment to bring on the heat. It was simple but effective – on this day, it was a reminder of what had brought us all to that point. The coach had not deviated from that message all season, and nothing changed on Grand Final day.

In our narrow qualifying final win over Collingwood three weeks earlier we had moved away from that mindset and played safe football. Post-game, during our debrief, we used an analogy that was somewhat appropriate for a team from the surf coast. We likened our performance that night to swimming between the flags, keeping ourselves and our opponents in waist-deep water. This time we wanted to head into more dangerous waters, and drag Sydney out with us.

Even 355 games into my career I always tune-in to the pre-match address and look to take something from the coach's words to weave into my pre-match on-ground rev-up. Usually I'll mention a milestone or clarify a point Chris had made to knit it all together. This time my message was brutal. It was to drown the opposition. If they are going to swim outside the flags with us, let's make sure we get on top of them and push them under.

I felt relaxed but my subconscious must have been working overtime. Before we ran onto the ground, I startled defender Jed Bews: 'Mate, I don't know why but I need to brush my teeth.' I'd never done that before. Jed giggled, as he does, and looked at me like I was half-mad. That was weird but I knew my body was strong. I also had a job to do. I was looking forward to carrying

Levi Ablett, my old teammate Gary's son, through the banner. Levi, who was then three years old, had been diagnosed with a rare degenerative disease.

That idea had come about earlier in the week when our chief executive, Steve Hocking, the club's events manager, Carly Flakemore, and I thought it would be a nice gesture to the Ablett family and also, we hoped, a great experience for them and Levi. We had lived with the trio in the hub at Southport in 2020. They were part of the gang.

Gary wondered how it could happen when I called him with the idea. I stressed the point there was no pressure on him and his wife, Jordan, to take up the offer. This was not a publicity stunt, I told Gary. It was both a thankyou to his family and a chance for him and Jordan to see their boy on the MCG in front of 100,000 people. I knew that if it came off, it would be emotional and memorable for the family. Gary loved playing football. But he especially loved playing football for the Cats. I wanted him and Levi to be in the moment.

There were some logistical hurdles to overcome, so I rang Gary's mate Jason Davenport, who was on our rookie list in 2006 and then played 28 games for Port Adelaide, to work through any issues, aware that Gary was to appear at an event before the Grand Final. We soon realised that a designated car spot under the MCG was all that was needed to ensure Gary would be there on time. He had a car spot arranged at the tennis centre but can you imagine Gary Ablett Jr walking from there to the MCG at 1.30 pm on Grand Final day with Geelong playing? Not ideal. Happily, the AFL made that happen. All that was left were a few tips on how to hold Levi.

I grabbed Levi from Gary then forgot what I was doing as I leaned in to hug my former teammate, and Levi's head clashed with his dad's shoulder. It was the only moment of uncertainty I experienced all day, but Levi's smile took over as he laughed when I twirled him around for a look at all the mayhem around, the players, the crowd, the banner, the noise.

I wasn't feeling tense. Steve Hocking had asked me on Friday if I was feeling okay and I was. Brit had not pushed the issue, but I knew she understood – in many ways better than me – the magnitude of the moment. I had made the decision before the end of the home-and-away season but when the finals arrived, my mind was consumed only with winning.

* * *

I started on the bench but as soon as the ball bounced, I could see the boys were on. Tom Hawkins broke the shackles with two goals from boundary throw-ins and the ball seemed to follow me when I ran onto the ground as I picked up 12 touches in that first quarter. Some of them I gave straight back to Sydney but our pressure was high. Despite our 35-point lead, we had not been content at quarter-time. After starting with 6.2 we had kicked three behinds to finish the quarter and those misses left me on edge. It was a wasted opportunity, but we still had a six-goal lead at half-time.

We went into half-time stirred up as Sydney kicked two of the last three goals of the half. We were tapping the ball on rather than being strong with the ball and either attempting to find a teammate or copping the inevitable tackle. I had been guilty, tapping the ball to Bews and watching it roll through his legs, leading to a Sydney goal. Immediately afterwards Atkins tapped the ball on, and Sydney was able to attack in open play. This was just what we wanted to avoid. It was time to straighten up. We were onto each other to play every minute: to bring on the heat.

In the stands Brit was on edge, telling my old schoolmate Brock Bouch, who was sitting next to her, the same story every Geelong supporter was hoping for. If the Cats could kick the first two or three goals in the third quarter, the game would be over. In the rooms we knew that too. I told everyone to settle for five or six minutes before going into their half-time routine because we had extra time. The long break on Grand Final day is longer than usual, at 27 minutes. Knowing that detail was important to me as the captain. The coach is big on that too. Before the game we had ticked off every what-if scenario, even what would happen if there was a draw. Not everyone needed to know that sort of detail but Chris and I did.

Although I did not presume the game was won, at half-time I asked my old teammate Harry Taylor, who had returned from Western Australia to the Cats as head of medical services at the start of the season, to bring a spare pair of my boots to the bench. On Brownlow night earlier in the week I had caught up with the AFL Auskicker of The Year, Archie Stockdale, and told him I hoped I'd see him again on the dais on Grand Final day. I was squeezed onto a bench inside the locker room next to Isaac Smith, Paddy Dangerfield and Blitz (Mark Blicavs). Each time we played at the MCG we would sit together to dissect the game, as well as clearing our heads.

Then we went back to work.

A ferocious tackle from Blitz soon after the break gave us the ascendancy in a passage of play, in which we had no right to break even, let alone win. That made me realise Sydney were going to have to do something extraordinary to win. I was pumped. I jumped off the bench and had to be restrained to make sure I did not enter the field of play. I was deep into my match-day zone. We kicked the first three goals of the third quarter within six minutes and six unanswered goals for the quarter to lead by 74 points at the last break.

The game was over, and we knew it when we reached the final huddle. When I said: 'We've won this', I noticed Paddy's eyes widen. He was so entrenched in the game he had not looked at the scoreboard. My comment shook him for a second. It was then the words of my first senior coach, Mark 'Bomber' Thompson had delivered in my first Grand Final (2007) at three-quarter-time resurfaced in my head. We then led Port Adelaide by 90 points, and Mark told us that we had it won, but that what we did in the next 30 minutes was important because it was what we would remember forever. I repeated Bomber's exact words. It was my turn to pass on such thinking. The only way to enjoy the last quarter was to play football in the right way, the way we had played all season, with humility and respect for the opposition. And to win the quarter.

I had dreamed for so long about leading a team that would play every minute, humming, in synergy, excelling – to win a Grand Final. It was amazing to dominate an opposition for pretty much 80 of the 90 minutes that had been played to that point.

As Chris spoke, I looked around the stands trying to bottle the feeling. One message registered: I was about to start the last quarter of my career. In the stand, Brit had started crying midway through the third quarter. She later told me she was overcome by a sense of gratitude: that it all had worked out so well.

But I had other thoughts: when should I take my rotation, so I would be on the ground when the final siren went. Eventually, after six or seven minutes, I sat down on the bench in the middle of Mark Blicavs and Sam De Koning for my last rest. I decided to sit there for four or five minutes rather than the standard three minutes as I was determined to finish the game – and my career – well.

As I sat there, all of a sudden, my breathing began to quicken, my heart was racing, and I began thinking, 'fucking hell'. In that moment my body took me to a place I had never been before. I have been fortunate to avoid what sometimes comes to others when pressure builds. I wasn't scared or upset. My body, I guess, was telling me to enjoy this last spell on the ground. Sam, however, noticed the change in my demeanour as emotion took hold of me. He said: 'You're not finishing.' I told him to just get out there and fucking play. But his words hit me, creating a raw connection in that moment. Blitz put his arm around me and pulled me towards him, a satisfied hug. I jumped on the phone to Chris: 'I'm really fucking proud of you,' I said. His first reaction was to laugh but he quickly shot back: 'Go out there and enjoy yourself.'

'Hell yeah,' I thought, as I ran out to enjoy those last 15 minutes. Little did I expect to kick a goal, just my seventh for the season. Mitch Duncan had been looking for me all quarter, but this was all luck as the ball bobbled from a stoppage and Brad Close tapped it to me. The ball twirled off the outside of my right boot from 45 metres out and kept tracking through the goals. It was, possibly, the most spectacular of the 175 goals I kicked in my career. Normally in that circumstance I would play the percentages and look for someone in a better position, but this was surely not a normal circumstance. I just flushed it. I fell to the ground and covered my face with my hands as Paddy Dangerfield dragged me off my stomach and my teammates mobbed me.

To most my reaction seemed a retirement statement but it was not as contrived as that. Nothing was controlled. Maybe the subconscious took control and the body followed. I was also in shock that I had kicked the goal! Now Mum was grabbing for the tissues in the stands too. Jeremy Cameron summed it up when he yelled: 'How the fuck did you do that?'

It was a question I could not answer.

Chapter 2

Early days

I LAID A FOUNDATION for my career through family and country values.

My maternal grandmother, Margaret Crapper, was the first to notice a problem with my running technique when I was a toddler. As soon as I found my feet, I was on my toes, folding them under my feet like knuckles and racing around the tiled floors at home in Bendigo. Nan suggested to my mum, Maree, that someone should check it out.

We visited an orthopaedic specialist in Bendigo who identified me as an idiopathic toe walker and suggested I wear a splint. Fortunately, he explained my condition in plain language: it refers to 'a normal child who walks on their tiptoes for no known reason'. Luckily, with specific exercises and a little outside help, it is fixable. So, from when I was 18 months old until I turned three, I not only had to wear nappies but a contraption that pushed the front of my foot up and my heel down.

It was only because Mum hung onto the brace until after I had left home that I had any sense of what helped me correct the habit. I had no recollection of the device and it did not stifle my activity. I still trailed my twin brothers, Adam and Troy, who are four years older than me, around the house, kicking and catching balls as much, if not more, than they did. You soon learnt not to take yourself too seriously at our place because if you did, you missed the next opportunity to laugh or learn. With Scott born 20 months after me there were four boys in the house with two loving parents working hard to raise them. Life would throw them enough challenges without any of us trying to complicate it.

My dad, Bryce, had stopped playing footy in his early 20s because he worked on Saturdays at the local TAB after working during the week at the menswear store in Williamson Street (a shop then owned by former Carlton champion and Eaglehawk product Rod Ashman). Mum worked part-time in administration at hospitals and schools. She had played A-grade tennis in Bendigo but put that on the backburner too, for us. All her time and energy was put into home, but her competitive spirit was never far below the surface. In May 1988, she waited to give birth to me in Bendigo's St John of God hospital alongside another expectant mother who also had two boys. Mum felt as though she was racing the other mother to have a baby first. She did not know the 'competitor' but she lost the 'race' against her rival, who produced a girl, April, born five hours before me. I was named Joel, after the singer Billy Joel!

Mum also carried some football pedigree as three cousins of her grandfather Robert Crapper – brothers Frank, (North

Melbourne), Harry (Melbourne) and Fred Crapper (Richmond) – all played VFL football, combining for 41 games between them in the 1930s. Mum's dad, Bill, loved footy but he wasn't a star player. What made him a popular figure around Raywood, 30 kilometres north of Bendigo, where he and his wife, Margaret, ran a sheep and wheat farm, was his gentle soul, great sense of humour and prodigious work ethic. Unfortunately, he died before I had a chance to get to know him.

Unable to commit to organised sport, Dad took up running. By the time we were old enough to notice he would wake at 5.45 every morning, run for an hour and then get us ready to attend St Therese's, the local Catholic primary school. Dad didn't just run without aim. In 1986 he ran his first marathon. By 1997 he became a Melbourne Marathon Spartan when he finished his 10th and final Melbourne Marathon, having achieved his best time in 1994 when he finished 45th, running the bitumen from Frankston to Melbourne in 2.43.31.

Life at that time was fun from the moment I woke up until I went to bed, although, subconsciously, I was learning to toughen up. One of Troy and Adam's favourite tricks was to stir up the plover birds nesting over the back fence. The twins would then run and hide under the trampoline as the birds swooped. What excited them was blocking my entry as I arrived late to join them under cover. Left out in the open, I ducked and weaved, terrified by the swooping birds while the twins laughed their heads off. They kept me honest then, and later, during my AFL career they liked to wind me up by saying that the plovers had taught me to duck.

When I first attended AFL Auskick in primary school the coordinators pushed me straight up a grade, then another, then another, as I was more than holding my own. When I got to the level Troy and Adam were at, they pushed back and told Mum I was not welcome to play alongside them. But that was the only place I couldn't be in their sphere because at home it was a free-for-all. We lived on a relatively large block and Dad had an inspired idea to use the space available to build a tennis court. It was a big move but he helped the contractor; it soon became our field of dreams.

We played every sport imaginable on that concrete block – from tennis to basketball to football to cricket to scooter soccer (this was a game involving scooters and soccer; it wasn't named after my brother Scott's nickname). We even grabbed Nan's wheelchair one Christmas and held time trials around the perimeter. 'Boisterous' is the ideal description of our behaviour. The games weren't restricted. Anyone from the neighbourhood was welcome. We would also swarm around the area playing sport. Often we would take our football matches to a park across the road and before school we would all gather to ride our bikes on the four-kilometre trek to school.

Every game we played was for a sheep station. We weren't aware of it at the time, no matter what the game, we just wanted to get better, be quicker and be winners. Losing was not a good feeling. I'm sure these hours were critical in developing the finished football product.

Obviously wearing a splint in those growing years did not affect me because I soon began to win races at school and in Little Athletics. My best event was hurdles. Near the end of primary school, it was clear I had some talent over the hurdles, so Dad approached Adrian Sexton, a coach who had trained hurdlers, to refine my ability. Unfortunately, Adrian told him he wasn't coaching any more, but Dad gave him a videotape showing me running and asked him to take a look. Soon enough the phone rang and Adrian – whose son Michael would later play in Carlton's 1995 premiership team wearing No.14 – said: 'When do we start?'

Quality coaching taught me proper technique. Athletics training tends to be repetitive but I revelled in the environment. Not many of my mates did athletics but I did not care because I really enjoyed running. Adrian's lessons included basics like how to warm up effectively. He was a great coach and a true gentleman. We just clicked. A friend and good local hurdler Sascha McPherson joined me on the circuit as we attended regional and state titles all over Victoria. My races would spread from short hurdles to 800 metre flat races. One of my main opponents was Mornington Peninsula's Nathan Jones, who would be drafted by Melbourne a year before me and become one of the Demons' greats.

Running was not just getting out there and going for broke. I loved working out different tactics to win, particularly in longer races. Did I need to go out fast to stop being beaten in a sprint home or would I be better off tucking in behind the pace and kicking hard at the end? My analysis of the opposition varied but the objective of winning was a constant.

By this stage the twins were playing in the under-12s with St Therese's and there was no doubt my heart was in footy too. I would earn a Mars Bar working as a boundary umpire for their games, but I wanted to play. Whenever I could, I would have a footy in my hands and I knew after playing so often against my brothers that I could play. Our backyard scraps meant that they knew as well that I was better than half their teammates, despite being four years younger. Adam reckoned I was his triplet not his younger brother when I would join them at the park for their drills work.

But I was held back by Mum and Dad who had a rule that they didn't want us playing until we turned nine. Dad had seen too many junior footballers burn out or lose their love of the game by starting too early, but I didn't keep my desire to play a secret. In a practice match at Sunbury when the twins' team was a couple of players short, my chance came. I had headed to the game with Paul Francis, the coach, and his son Daniel, who was a good mate. We were there to be goal umpires. I was still just eight years old and was still hurdling but I did not hesitate to throw on the jumper to play in the under-12s. I slotted onto a wing and we were trailing at half-time. But the game changed when my brothers encouraged the coach to put me into centre bounces. They knew I could get the ball myself.

Dad was not surprised when he heard of my performance. His attitude to sport was outstanding. He knew I had some serious football talent but he never revealed that to me. He told me to ensure I could kick effectively on each side of my body, so I practised in the park across the road until I could. Unlike with athletics, Dad did not employ a specialist coach to help. He left it to the junior coaches although he was well aware what was happening, and when to say something. He was always on a footy club committee.

I attacked the task in a slightly obsessive manner but Mum and Dad never worried because they knew I could switch off too.

I was relatively laidback, just enjoying myself in those moments rather than focusing on a specific goal. That would come later. My left foot was always there but being two-sided was not a weapon, especially when you think of players like Hawthorn's Sam Mitchell and Collingwood's Steele Sidebottom. It just gave me confidence to know that I was never trapped.

The four boys would also join Dad when he participated in cross-country runs around the area on Sundays. As he warmed up, we would go for shorter runs, learning how to control our breathing so we could build endurance. These were great days, jumping in the Ford Falcon as we waited for Dad to finish while we listened to Rex Hunt calling the footy on the radio.

Dad was also teaching me life lessons – that winning wasn't the only thing that mattered. He coached my basketball team – which included a future NBA star and Australian Olympian Matthew Dellavedova, who won a championship with the Cleveland Cavaliers – and he developed a rotation system that meant every player would spend time on the bench and the same amount of time on court, regardless of their performance. I didn't like it much but I understood why it was a good idea. It was all about fairness. He also noted that I liked to bring teammates into the game, ensuring everyone had a chance to score at least once. An under-10s game sticks in Dad's mind. I found a teammate in space so he could score his first points for the season. He raced to the sidelines to give Dad a high-five, before giving one to each of his teammates on the court. Meanwhile, we allowed the opposition to score!

* * *

I was a Geelong supporter. Although we rarely attended AFL matches, I was a diehard Cats' fan following the footsteps of Dad's brother, Roger. I also wanted a different team to support than the twins, with Troy barracking for Fitzroy and Adam being a Hawks' man; otherwise I would have had to wear their hand-me-down jumpers. Despite my one-eyed view of footy, I had enough sense to list Sydney's captain and star midfielder Paul Kelly – who also wore No.14 – as my favourite player. I was also not too disappointed when, as a seven-year-old, I watched Geelong lose to Carlton in the 1995 Grand Final as I was happy that another Bendigo product, Michael Sexton, had won a premiership medal. It didn't register that it was the Cats' fourth Grand Final loss in seven seasons.

At this time, I left primary school for Catholic College Bendigo (now Catherine McAuley College) and I stopped playing for St Therese's having played in a premiership with St Therese's Gold at Bendigo's Harry Trott Oval and joined the under-13-and-a-halfs at the same club as the twins, Kennington Sandhurst Dragons.

I just loved playing footy. Even at that age, I knew how to help my teammates get into the game, kicking it low and hard to some – such as leading forward Sam O'Brien – and high to others, helping them get in the best position to win the ball. The opposition didn't always make it easy for me. In a game at Dower Park in Kangaroo Flat, three opponents were sent to tag me at the same time, surrounding me as best they could.

Troy reckons he noted other aspects of my personality at this time. I would drag people my age who had not played or weren't able to play, for whatever reason, into the huddle to sing the song when we won. He even noticed me sitting out lunch time games to be with some kids who might have liked football but didn't play. He claims now that he saw something about the way I approached footy that surprised him and made me a little different from the other good players in the region. He knew I had the talent but later told me I did things that made him believe I felt there was more to sport than just winning.

I wasn't thinking that way consciously. I just followed in Mum and Dad's footsteps – to treat people fairly and to make everyone welcome. That's how I saw people around me acting and I liked what I saw, and I also took in the family values my parents espoused: work hard, stay humble, try to do the right thing and accept the consequences if you make a mistake. Why wouldn't I do what they did?

We weren't always deadly serious. Sometimes Scott would play junior football alongside me. He started calling me 'Toni' and I would call him 'Frank' because it felt weird to call each other Joel and Scott when our teammates were yelling out 'Selsy'. Selsy didn't feel right to us so we used each other's middle names (mine is actually Anthony). I insisted to Scott it would have to be Toni with an I' as that had more of a mobster feel to it!

Not only did I enjoy the game. I enjoyed training, particularly running, and soon enough the pathways began to open up. In 2000, the Selwood name helped me get picked in the School Sport Australia State Team trials after Troy and Adam had performed so well in the 1996 series. I must have impressed the coach, Paul Stevens, and team manager, Andrew Harrison, during training sessions that determined selection. I was named captain of the Victorian Under-12 schoolboys' team in the National Schoolboys

Championship in Darwin alongside future Sydney premiership players Nick Smith and Josh Kennedy, North Melbourne's Leigh Adams and the Tigers' Daniel Connors and Steven Morris. We played on TIO Stadium and an oval next door and dominated to win the championship. During one of those games, Josh Kennedy's dad (four-time premiership Hawk John Kennedy Jr) sidled up to Dad on the sidelines and said he was struggling to work out whether I was a left- or right-footer. I must have improved that part of my game.

Representative football wasn't unusual for our family. The twins' Victorian under-12s team in 1996 had been pretty handy, with Luke Hodge, Luke Ball and Gary Ablett Jr all playing. It was an education sitting behind the goals, watching these future stars, even at that age. One game, when the Vics thrashed the ACT at Cramer Street Preston, has stuck in my memory. Gary Ablett Sr came down to the rooms after the game. He was then everyone's hero and I managed to squeeze next to him to get a photo with him and his autograph. His presence turned the rooms into a circus.

Watching my brothers play in that championship was the moment I decided that making a career out of football was what I wanted to do and from then on, I was chasing the twins, watching and learning. They could fight, those two. An errant foot or fist would occasionally make a hole in some part of the house. But they never made me uncomfortable. They were fast becoming my idols, as I watched them emerge as potential AFL players.

By the time I became a teenager and was hanging out with friends such as Brock Bouch and John Leyden, we were always active, riding our bikes far and wide or going for runs on tracks such as The Power Lines, a renowned local track which took us up and down hills through the Bendigo countryside. We were getting fitter with no real purpose; we just enjoyed the challenge. But when I played footy, I could see clearly that there might be something special in the way I played: I could get to every contest, literally, and opponents could not keep up. Xavier Ellis, who became a premiership player with the Hawks, became my teammate for the first time in the Vic Country under-15s. He described my style as playing 'kamikaze football' as I attacked every contest as though winning the ball was my right.

Before I was drafted, Michael Lovett, the editor of the *Footy Record* wrote an essay for a book called *The Australian Football Quarterly*, headed 'The next in line'. Michael interviewed me, and Mum and Dad. What was amazing in the article were some lines from Garry Bryan, my under-15s coach at Sandhurst, who embarrassed me when he said: 'He's a cross between James Hird and Nathan Buckley.' He went on to describe what he saw as my attributes. 'He has the ability to sum up any situation on the field. For example, if he had the ball and he saw a kid with lesser talent calling for it, he would float the ball so the kid could mark it ... he had an impact on my ability to coach because he would conform to team rules. Joel would spend equal time on the bench and would be rotated through midfield, defence and attack and he was a pleasure to coach. He wasn't selfish and he has got terrific leadership skills.'

There was a game in my teenage years for Kennington Sandhurst when I did use my ability to its full extent. We needed some luck to get over the Sandhurst Marist Dockers as they had a much stronger team. I was also lining up against my mate Jarryn 'Gears' Geary – who later played 207 games for St Kilda and captained the club for five seasons – so I was highly motivated and decided to take matters into my own hands. At each contest I would win the ball then kick the ball to the boundary, get to the next contest, then do the same thing as I worked the ball down the ground. It was a selfish ploy, but it worked. I kicked seven goals and we won the game nine goals to eight with Jarryn also kicking seven of his team's goals. Jarryn still shakes his head and laughs about that game.

That was not my usual style. I loved to share the fun and would happily come off the ground to give teammates (and opponents) more of the ball. That might sound arrogant but I wasn't. As I said, we were a family who didn't take things too seriously. I was just loving football and the results were quickly forgotten. My parents reinforced the better parts of my attitude. Although Mum enjoyed the social side of football clubs, she was quiet when the ball was bounced, retreating to the car to watch all the games because she did not want to be distracted. On the way home she would often praise me for helping out teammates.

From then on life was football, athletics and basketball with work as a lifeguard at the local pool giving me an income. I still liked school, though I wasn't an academic and most of my time was spent hanging out with my mates or my brothers or playing football. Being captain or co-captain of the football team felt natural because I was the best player, but leadership was not something I saw as a natural pathway.

Dad would occasionally drag us along to help him out with the mowing round he did on weekends to earn some extra cash.

He was always relaxed, but he rolled his eyes when Adam and one of his friends, Elliot Bowen, painted on the back of his trailer, 'You Grow It, I Mow it' for a laugh. He rolled with the punches and we enjoyed pitching in to help.

My parents treated us all as individuals. As they drove us around to different sports, they got a clear insight into our personalities. Scott was more laidback than me about his footy, although he was just as active and was very talented. He did not decide to go after a career in the AFL until Mum and Dad sat him down as a teenager and made it clear there was no pressure on him from their perspective to try to follow the same path as his brothers. Dad reckons Scott's response to them was: 'Are you for real?' He was clearly just as keen as the twins – and me – to become an AFL player.

By then our house had become a drop-in centre for footballers staying in the region to play for the Bendigo Pioneers in the TAC Cup competition. Elliot Bowen was a classic. He had moved from Echuca to live with his cousin in town but after one game Mum took pity on him and invited him around for dinner and to wash his footy gear. Soon enough he was sleeping on Troy's floor and would stand in front of an open pantry and yell out to Mum: 'Have you been shopping this week, Maree?' or 'You're out of biscuits, Maree.'

Mum loved his personality because, despite his cheek, he was also respectful and appreciative, but he wasn't the only young talent who made our place their second home. Mum would occasionally say: 'I'm tired you lot, go home' but most of the time she just drove into the driveway after a day's work, wondering whether she would be feeding six or 16 that night.

Perhaps that was the time when I became comfortable around footballers.

As Troy and Adam moved into their draft year (2002) my eyes opened even wider. Troy was considered a certainty to be selected but Adam wasn't as he had missed the AFL under-18 National Championships due to injury. That meant Mum and Dad played down the experience, more concerned with ensuring Adam was prepared for any potential disappointment. The twins were tight but they also lived different lives, being put in different classes in primary school and then spending most of their secondary school years at different schools. I was sharing a bedroom with Scott and we were like twins too, in the sense that we were very close. We were a bit nicer to each other than Troy and Adam were at times!

After watching recruiters come and go in the lead-up to the 2002 draft the pair were gone in an instant, the Brisbane Lions drafting Troy with pick No.19 and West Coast using pick 53 to snap up Adam after Geelong had passed at pick 52. I was rapt and Mum hid her disappointment well given both her boys were heading to opposite corners of the country. I was only 14 but all of a sudden, the house had been emptied of my idols. My dream of playing AFL was now beginning to fully form.

Chapter 3

Resilience and challenge

MY KNEE HAD become painful late in the 2003 season, some months after I had captained the Vic Country under-15s team in Coolangatta.

A doctor in Bendigo referred me to a local surgeon and in November 2003 I had an arthroscope. He noticed a piece of floating bone from my femur and decided then and there to screw it back on. There was no real involvement from the football community in my treatment. We just acted on the surgeon's advice without thinking too much about what might lie ahead.

I was on crutches for six to eight weeks and was not allowed to put any weight on the leg but other than that the rehabilitation process was not very scientific. Nowadays I would be in a leg brace and given a strength program. Not then. I hopped around school and waited impatiently to resume football.

I had the screw taken out in a procedure by the Bendigo surgeon and then went to Melbourne to see Professor Julian

Feller, a leader in the field of orthopaedic surgery. He thought at that stage the knee was likely to heal. For close to two seasons, playing football for Sandhurst, Bendigo Pioneers and Vic Country teams, I managed the injury by applying packs of frozen peas to the knee. If it became really painful, I would ice it all night, without knowing I was living on borrowed time. Professionalism and patience was a big thing to ask at 16. But I wanted to be the best underage player in the country. How could I achieve that sitting on the sidelines?

I played the same way every week, moving from contest to contest, and with a fierceness that probably surprised some opponents. Winning the ball was my right rather than my desire, and I also learnt to play with some discomfort.

Selection in the 2004-2005 AIS/AFL Academy was exciting because it meant I would tour Ireland with the best young players in the country. Most of the squad was set to be drafted at the end of that season but with me being a bottom-aged player, as I was born after the April cut-off, I was not eligible to be drafted until the end of 2006.

Caulfield Grammar, a renowned APS school (Associated Public School) in the south-east of Melbourne had also tried to recruit me on a scholarship but Mum and Dad were reluctant to lose another son from the house so soon after the twins had been drafted.

We toured the school and I was keen, particularly when the school's football director, Richmond and Hawthorn premiership player Barry Rowlings, dropped in the conversation that Brendon Goddard and Chris Judd – who had just won the 2004 Brownlow Medal – had attended the school before being drafted.

That didn't impress Mum. She was more focused on whether the school could provide me with anything more than a country lifestyle while attending Bendigo Secondary College with friends and Bendigo Pioneers players. In the end she would have let me go if she had been convinced it was the best thing for me but she wasn't and nor was Dad. They thought a country upbringing had its benefits too.

Their decision made me angry. I didn't yell or scream. That wasn't my style. Instead, I sooked. Mum knew I would move on quickly as soon as I was around my mates in Bendigo, Brock Bouch, John Leyden, Jarryn Geary and Brenton Hall, who had moved down from Mildura, and she was right. I came to accept I was to spend the last two years of my schooling at Bendigo Secondary College. There was plenty of sporting talent at the school but the facilities were pretty basic. We had half a dozen ovals covered in kangaroo crap and the goalposts were probably 30 years old, but we didn't care. It was on these ovals that I had started playing at NAB AFL Auskick on Sunday mornings with skills followed by games. It was generally cold and frosty but I could not wait for Sunday to arrive.

My knee was annoying me. It had now been causing me pain for two years as it would catch and lock up. I carried an ache, but I refused to accept that a sore knee would stop me from having an AFL career. Sure, there were times when I questioned the impact the injury might have. Was I going to be slower and, if so, how much slower? Was I going to be able to be as good as I hoped I could be? Would my growth be stunted?

* * *

Ireland beckoned. Mum and her sister-in-law Narelle joined the crew of players, parents and recruiters to the under-17 International Rules series under the guidance of Kevin 'Shifter' Sheehan and the newly appointed AIS-AFL Academy coach, Alan McConnell. Shifter is not only the AFL's talent guru but proved himself an excellent tour guide with a talent to connect across generations. McConnell had coached Fitzroy in their last seasons and was then an assistant at Geelong before getting the Academy job. He eventually became the GWS Giants' first football employee.

This was a bonding trip but also about developing a group of promising young players, identified in the AFL's pathway. The game plan was very basic. I had hardly kicked a round ball before I was on the plane; the team had been selected on the basis of football talent rather than their suitability to the hybrid game.

Despite being bottom-aged – this was an under-17 series – I was named captain for the first Test in a team that included future AFL stars Xavier Ellis (Hawthorn and West Coast), Grant Birchall (Hawthorn and Brisbane), Marc Murphy (Carlton) and Travis Boak (Port Adelaide). I was rapt to get that honour but thought the number of Vic Country boys in the squad might have helped my elevation as I was able to mingle easily with a big section of the group. Shifter (who played 102 games at Geelong from 1974 to 1982) probably enjoyed handing the honour to someone who had played junior football at his old club, Sandhurst. One thing I did know was that I could speak to parents and teammates equally, and I wasn't intimidated if someone in the group had a big ego. That didn't impress me.

I just allowed individuals to be themselves although, in the back of my mind, I thought that blokes with a bad attitude would only go so far. At that stage I let it be their issue.

Things didn't start well: we were thrashed in the first Test, in Crossmaglen in County Armagh in Northern Ireland, 73-32, after the Irish kicked seven six-pointers – goals in our terms, slotted into the net under the crossbar, as in soccer. The bus driver got us lost getting there, and Shifter jumped out of the bus and co-opted Mum and Narelle to lead the way in their hire car, as they had a map. The ground had animal droppings all over it and the British Army base next door regularly flew a helicopter over the ground, upsetting the locals.

I played well, and Shifter and Alan decided to make me captain for the second Test. The decision was not only based on my performance but apparently the manner in which I had responded to the loss. Shifter recalls saying: 'I think we have another Michael Voss here' when he and Alan discussed whether I should continue as skipper given the usual system was to rotate the role. Voss led the Brisbane Lions to three premierships, so it was a wild compliment, which I wasn't aware of at the time. They just announced that I would be continuing as captain, and no-one raised an eyebrow. I spoke to my teammates about the need to respond from the loss and to hit the training track with a desire to improve. We were representing Australia after all.

We had great fun, even though we lost the series. After that first thrashing, we fought back to win the second Test 56-44 in Dublin, then lost the third in Killarney when Ireland kicked a late six-pointer to win 39-31. Despite the disappointment of losing, my performances were good enough to be awarded the

Ron Barassi Medal, as best player in the series, an honour I shared with Ireland's Ray Cullivan. AFL recruiters who attended the camp also earmarked me as a future leader.

My friendship with Xavier Ellis, who grew up in Gippsland but went to Melbourne Grammar, strengthened on that trip and his parents, Geoff and Angela, hit it off with Mum too. Xavier could rib me about taking football so seriously and I could shock him by teaching him the odd reality of life my older brothers had taught me. We complemented each other well and he was a little taken aback when I handed him my headphones to get him to listen to Al Pacino's inspirational speech from *Any Given Sunday*. That's how I thought captains acted but he was happy to remind me that the way I played was more important. He also knew I could have the piss taken out of me, something he did frequently.

Mum also became friends with Travis Boak's mum, Chicki, and we were all shattered when Roger, Travis's dad, died of cancer at the end of that year. Such was the connection the group developed, when I put out a call for players on the trip to head to the funeral in Torquay, a bunch of my Irish tour teammates made the trip to form a guard of honour out of respect for the Boak family.

Later that season I was named among the best players in each of the Vic Country games in the AFL Under-18 championships, racking up possessions in the middle. We lost each game but I knew I belonged at that level. I was able to manage my knee with exercises and ice and I was named on the half-back flank in that carnival's All-Australian team and made the TAC Cup Team of The Year.

Both Adam and Troy were playing regular senior football for the Eagles and the Lions, and I would be picking their brains constantly on what was required to take the big step to join them as an AFL player. I also had a manager lined up – Stride Sports' Tom Petroro was assigned to look after me. Stride was then a fledgling management company after they had started the business with former Flying Start colleagues a couple of years earlier. The twins had joined Flying Start so I looked to follow suit, but Ricky Nixon was busy with the best players in the game, not a kid from Bendigo.

By now I was well entrenched in football's pathway, so the decision was made to get my knee checked out in the big smoke. I headed to Melbourne with Tom Petroro, along with a bunch of referrals, to have the knee checked out by renowned surgeon Hayden Morris. Troy had told Graeme 'Gubby' Allan at the Brisbane Lions about my knee problem, and he suggested to Tom that we visit Dr Morris.

His diagnosis was that I had a case of osteochondritis dissecans (OCD), a joint condition in which bone underneath the cartilage of a joint dies due to lack of blood flow. Doctors find it hard to assess why this happens despite it having been around for 150 years. It is more common in children and adolescents. The thinking is that, in the knee, it is caused by repetitive trauma, causing the joint to break away from the femur.

My joint was more affected than most and putting in the screws had not worked. Dr Morris operated on me in the first week of September, cleaning up the knee and leaving some of the joint behind with the thought that it would regenerate the area.

The season ended with the family watching Adam play for West Coast in the 2005 Grand Final. He was one of five 21-year-olds in that Eagles team that lost to the Swans by four points in that drought-breaking premiership for Sydney. That's the game that will always be remembered by Leo Barry's match-saving mark, and Steve Quartermain's commentary: 'Leo Barry, you star!' At the time I didn't imagine being out there myself. I just took in the spectacle, and watching my brother play in a Grand Final was huge.

* * *

Bendigo Pioneers had not won a game in 2005 and I didn't enjoy being part of a team that went winless. Occasionally I would drive our coach, Mark Ellis, mad asking him about how we might improve certain players to make us more competitive. He would tell me to focus my energy on getting drafted. He carried dual concerns – to find a way to get his team winning while preparing young men to play senior football. I understood that but I also wanted to ensure any new players were made to feel welcome, especially if they arrived from outside Bendigo and might be standing back, finding it all a bit daunting.

With 10 Kennington Sandhurst Dragons' players on our list I was looking forward to the new season. I expected to continue to manage my knee as there was no clear reason that 2006 would not be like 2005. I had a few issues emerging with my hamstrings but I was still shocked when Mark told me I would not be playing round one.

Bendigo's regional manager Ray Byrne, the former Carlton and Collingwood player, had made the call because he thought I was a certainty to be drafted and was determined that no risks would be taken with me, but Mark was not looking forward to breaking the news to me. I did not accept the decision well, telling him with a deal of passion that I would be fine. I made him laugh inside when I said earnestly: 'I'm an honest man', but he would not budge. We lost to the Murray Bushrangers, a game I thought we could have won. I was back for round two, and we won that game, the Pioneers' first victory since August 2004. My season – and our season – was up and going.

I was still being managed but I wasn't completely convinced it was necessary. All I wanted to do was play and I figured the body would endure whatever was put to it. Growing up with brothers I learnt to hide pain and find a way to keep going. Leading into a match against North Ballarat – our archrivals – in round six, I popped my cartilage at training. I thought to myself: 'I am buggered here', but I told Mark I was fine to play as I knew the Vic Country squad was soon to be picked.

As I lined up in the middle of Queen Elizabeth Oval in Bendigo with my knee hurting, I noticed James Frawley (who would play 241 games for Melbourne, Hawthorn and St Kilda) wandering towards me. I knew he was strong, but I was used to being tagged as I had not been left alone for most of my junior career. Tagging never concerned me as, to be brutally honest, I was too good for most of my opponents to contain, particularly given the tags were not super tight.

However, the more Frawley clamped down on me the more frustrated I became. I gave away half-dozen free kicks in the first half. Mark dragged me. I was a liability and he knew it, so he made me sit next to him on the bench for the rest of the game. I was seething. Suddenly, the knee issue had become serious. I had pushed it to the point I could push no more.

We were a long way from Dr Morris's practice, at that time situated in East Melbourne, which made travelling to Melbourne for these check-ups something of a grind, but it had to be done. The joint Dr Morris had left behind when I went under the knife in September had not regenerated so in June 2006, he operated on the knee a second time. He tried to increase my confidence by telling me that Carlton's Andrew Walker, the number two selection in the 2003 national draft, had overcome a similar issue. Such reassurance didn't help me much. Every time I saw Walker play, I could not escape the feeling that he didn't seem to be going that well. I was probably wrong: he ended up playing 202 games for the Blues and probably should have won the Mark of The Year in 2011.

This time Dr Morris drilled eight holes (the size of pin pricks) in the knee where the bone was flapping off and pulled out cracked bone and any other floating fragments in what is referred to as a microfracture technique. Underneath the dense bone is marrow. Dr Morris called the technique 'drilling for oil'. The holes in the cartilage would stimulate growth as marrow leaking out would convert to cartilage which would provide a cushion and remove the pain I had been experiencing. That was the theory anyway.

If I was honest with myself, I was a little scared. But belief in my ability to solve 'the knee issue' mostly overruled any doubts. Mostly! As I sat in the hospital bed immediately after this operation

I momentarily lost faith everything would be okay. After being discharged from hospital I lay on the couch at home and cried.

Naturally Mum and Dad thought the tears were a result of me thinking that an AFL career was doomed. But it wasn't that as much as being worn down by the constant focus on my knee that included surgery, trips to doctors, pain, missing football, and a realisation that I would likely need to manage the injury forever. It was pure frustration. I just wanted to have a kick with my mates in a game I was good at, and I couldn't. That did not seem fair.

My disappointment at how the year was panning out became obvious when I became emotional on the phone with Vic Country coach Leon Harris as I realised my knee problem would stop me from playing in the championships. During our conversation he told me to stop worrying as I was going to get drafted at the end of the season and not playing would set me up for future success. His comment made me stop in my tracks. Instinctively I'd known I was heading towards being drafted but hearing someone else tell me with such certainty was the first time the penny actually dropped. I was going to play AFL. If, of course, the knee did not get in the way.

The surgery put me back on crutches for another eight weeks, a common sight for my schoolmates who, by now, did not think much of it.

During my enforced break, Mark made me an assistant coach of the Pioneers and because I could not run, I focused on my fitness and helping teammates. I was told to keep the leg as stiff as possible but I would do weights at home and then, as soon as I could, I developed a rigorous routine in the university gym nearby.

I was not exactly organised when it came to training. Both Brisbane and the Eagles had been kind enough to provide me with a program – via Troy and Adam – but I went my own way as my chest and biceps grew. But I was not completely silly either and started, with religious application, my career-long exercises to activate and strengthen the vastus medialis oblique (VMO), one of the four big muscles in the thigh, a process critical to drive the rehabilitation of my knee. The exercise was repetitive but I knew its importance and my athletics training helped me stick with such drills.

I swam one day and did weights the next. I was anal about keeping my leg stiff in the pool, always swimming with a buoy so only my upper body was doing the work. Brenton Hall or Jarryn Geary or John Leyden would join me in these workouts, but often they would just laugh at my fanatical approach. I was bench-pressing 120 kilograms while they would put just 70 kilograms on their bar. Chin-ups were a favourite, wearing a 50-kilogram weight belt as I pushed myself. Apparently, I would tell Jarryn – who was a hard trainer himself – that I was determined to be ready to play AFL in round one the next season. This was a killer instinct I seemed to be born with. I just went at it like a bull at a gate. In my mind you either did something properly or you didn't do it all.

My optimism about playing in round one wasn't just false bravado. I watched Carlton's Marc Murphy and Melbourne's Clint Bartram play AFL a year after I had toured Ireland with them – and they played in round one of their debut season! Xavier Ellis had told me he thought I was ready to play immediately and was adamant I would have been the number one pick in his draft (an honour bestowed on Murphy, while Xavier was pick three).

He even invited me to watch him train with the Hawks so they would know who I was. He was hoping it would sway them to pick me in the draft. They had pick six.

I resumed walking after about 10 weeks then began running as July rolled around and my knee was given the all-clear in August by Dr Morris, two months after my final operation. I could now run with confidence again. He thought the surgery had succeeded in alleviating the issues that had kept me off the field and the biggest danger I faced would be bad luck. The knee would still need constant management.

Although I was desperate to play, I did enjoy being Mark's assistant and watching my teammates play well too. I'd surprised my Academy coach, Alan McConnell, when I had rung him mid-year for advice on how I could support the coach as we weren't winning too often, winning three in 2006 after being winless in 2005. He just assumed I was ringing to ask him how he could help my progress as he had never heard that question from a junior before, but I was clearly learning some good habits off the field.

By this stage I could have put my hand up to play but with the Pioneers out of finals contention, no risks needed to be taken. I just enjoyed watching Adam reverse the result from the year earlier and become a premiership player with the Eagles after another great contest against the Swans in the 2006 grand final.

I figured I would show my wares when invited to the AFL Draft Combine in October, and any doubts the clubs may have had about my fitness would be erased. The work had been done. But I would need to be lucky to land at the right place at just the right time.

I had no plan B. That wasn't my style.

Chapter 4

Drafted to the Cats

THERE WAS NO doubt in observers' minds at the start of 2006 that I was likely to be chosen within the first 10 selections during November's AFL draft, but it did not really enter my mind when I would be picked or where I would end up. One thing was obvious, if the predictions were right, I was unlikely to be at Geelong as they seemed destined to finish in the top half of the ladder having reached a preliminary final in 2004 before sixth place in 2005. That form line suggested they were likely to have a pick outside the top 10 in the next draft.

Had there been little concern about my knee, most recruiters would have had me among their top selections alongside the versatile Bryce Gibbs, midfielder Travis Boak, and talls such as Scott Gumbleton, Lachie Hansen, Ben Reid, Nathan Brown, James Frawley, Mitch Thorp and Matthew Leuenberger.

Talls were all the rage, as St Kilda's Nick Riewoldt had just won his third best and fairest and had been named All-Australian for the second time before he had turned 24. Such a player was hard to find but could set the club up for future success.

The recruiters were still aware of me but some had reservations about my knee. Mark Williams, then Port Adelaide coach, tried to suss out how I was tracking from Adam when he sat next to him on a bus as part of the International Rules tour of Ireland in that October/November. Adam, who knew Port Adelaide was probably the destination Mum and Dad were least keen on, told Williams he didn't think the knee was too good. It wasn't because we had a set against Port Adelaide, who had pick five. It was more that for Mum and Dad to have three boys all playing for AFL clubs outside Victoria seemed too much to bear.

Geelong recruiter Stephen Wells preferred to focus on my footy skills and, most importantly, on my decision-making. He saw me as someone who knew where the ball was going and who would make good decisions under pressure. Ray Byrne, the Pioneer's divisional manager was later quoted as saying: 'I had never seen a kid prepare in the TAC Cup like Joel. He had a fantastic football brain. He could sort it out within 10 minutes of a game who should be where and [doing] what.' Stephen thought I was not only skilful but made teammates better. He was less focused on my competitiveness.

I didn't really need to prove much to recruiters at the Draft Camp (now called the Draft Combine), a multi-day event the AFL runs before the draft to gain some objective measures on key prospects. Events range from time trials to vertical leaps and there are also medical checks and interviews. I didn't have many interviews as a likely high pick and the interviewing was not as formal then as they are now; clubs were happy to engage with me informally. For me, the camp was more about proving to myself I was ready.

It was not to be. I had a shocking camp. I did finish top 10 in one test, a standing vertical jump of 65 centimetres, but it was not exactly career-defining. I ran 3.14 seconds for the 20-metre sprint when three seconds was par. Jarryn Geary beat me and I had never lost to him. My agility was poor too and I began to wonder what the hell was going on. I had trained for the camp and suddenly I was not performing. I was seriously stressed.

I was banking on salvaging some pride in the three-kilometre run but when I trailed in, managing 10 minutes and 50 seconds, well off the pace – and again behind Jarryn – I was devastated. I had no answers for what had happened except that it seemed I had let the pressure get to me. I thought I was immune to such failure after having put so much into my preparation. All these flops did not reassure the doubters that my knee would not affect my football.

Just before the draft I again went to see Julian Feller to discuss what my future in football might look like as the clubs were keen to find out, in particular Collingwood, who had picks eight and 10. Julian was Collingwood's go-to orthopaedic surgeon. He told me the knee looked good after the operations and clubs should not be wary about picking me, but he also said he was 'not sure what I would be like at age 28'. He had repaired former Collingwood midfielder Paul Licuria's knee in 1994 and 1995 so told me I would need to devote myself to looking after my knee in the same fashion as the diligent Magpie, who had overcome two knee reconstructions before he turned 18. The dedicated

Lica went on to play 192 games and win two best and fairest trophies at the Magpies.

Dr Morris's message to clubs was a little more reassuring although there were no guarantees. Each club checked me out themselves in groups of four. North Melbourne recruiter Neville Stibbard was desperate to recruit me, but North's medical staff was not convinced, reporting to their football department that I would be on a modified program for the foreseeable future. They had drafted David Trotter with pick nine in the 2003 national draft and he'd struggled with hamstring injuries, managing just seven games in three seasons at Arden Street, so they were wary of using their top 10 pick on me or anyone with question marks about their durability. However, they later would complain that Geelong had some inside word on my knee during the draft camp. It was true that then-Cats' club doctor Chris Bradshaw had made plenty of phone calls about me, but any information was available to all.

Essendon and the Brisbane Lions wanted a tall and although Carlton tried to create some intrigue when their recruiting manager, Wayne Hughes, said they had not forgotten me, they appeared set on choosing Bryce Gibbs as pick one, having 'won' the 2005 wooden spoon. I accepted each clubs' rationale – I had no other option. I was also hearing through Troy and Adam the doubts clubs had in my knee. Injury had restricted Essendon champion forward Matthew Lloyd to just three games in 2006, so Scott Gumbleton, a key forward who had not shown any signs of being susceptible to injury as a teenager, was their clear preference. Brisbane had pick four but they needed a ruckman as triple-premiership ruckman Clark Keating had retired and

Jamie Charman needed support. The Lions did their medical assessment when I visited Troy in Brisbane, and he tried to reassure them about my diligence, but they were always going to pick a ruckman.

With Carlton, Essendon, North and Brisbane out of the equation, Port Adelaide, Hawthorn and Geelong had the next three picks. The Cats had been on an upward trajectory after several years drafting quality crops, but in 2006 they had a terrible season, underperforming to finish 10th, with 10 wins and a draw. Chief executive Brian Cook led a whole-of-club review which led to changes being made to the football department. Mark Thompson wasn't happy with the public nature of the process, but he remained as senior coach. Tom Harley was made captain, replacing Steven King. Neil 'Balmey' Balme made the switch from Collingwood to become football manager, Steve Hocking, who had been on the selection committee, became head of operations. The club also commissioned the Leading Teams program, with Gerard Murphy in charge, to introduce its 'team-first' focus.

The senior players had decided enough was enough after reaching the preliminary final in 2004, then experiencing a heartbreaking loss to eventual premiers, Sydney, in the 2005 semi-final – the 'Nick Davis match' – before all went off the rails. They were ready to embrace a new style of leadership, playing with flair and, most importantly, communicating openly. The review also meant the leadership group had a bigger say in decision-making and that Bomber would have enough resources to concentrate uniquely on coaching. Clearly Cook had viewed 2006 as an aberration but the slide meant they had picks 7, 25, and 57 with the potential to choose Tom Hawkins as a father–son selection in the third round.

Geelong physiotherapist Nick Ames had delivered a positive prognosis on my knee, telling the list team that my knee *may* have an impact on my career and even shorten it but they should not rule me out. The club had also heard via Matthew Knights, who was coaching the Bendigo Bombers and would later become an assistant at Geelong, that he'd seen me training around town, which instilled them with some confidence. Essendon must have known this too because they would later say that if they had two selections available, they would have picked me after Scott Gumbleton. Reflecting on that time, Essendon's long-serving list manager, Adrian Dodoro, said, in 2020: 'The rules changed around the compensation picks and if we had ended up with (pick) two and four, I can assure you that, ... we would have taken Joel Selwood as well. At the time, Joel had a knee problem and there were question marks around that and there were medical concerns around durability. As luck would have it, he's gone on to have an absolutely amazing, durable career and unfortunately Gumbleton didn't.'

Geelong's networks suggested they had a one-in-three chance of drafting me, so Stephen Wells paid me a visit. I had just spent a week in Perth with mates from high school staying with Adam and was then heading to Brisbane to visit Troy when Stephen arrived at our home, so he only stayed for half an hour, introducing himself to my parents and asking me about my knee. I told him it was fine. Hawthorn recruiting manager Gary Buckenara also had dinner with Mum and Dad at the All Seasons Hotel in Bendigo, but eventually the Hawks had too many concerns about my knee, and Collingwood, which had the pick after Geelong, had shown some interest. The joke was that Mum would only put out chocolates for recruiters from Victorian-based clubs when they visited us. In fact, Collingwood seemed to be where I was destined to play; they had picks eight and 10. In a coffee catch-up 10 days out from the draft, their recruiting manager, Derek Hine, told me they were likely to select me if I was still available. Unbeknown to me they became less confident the night before the draft after internal debate about my knee.

The Cats continued to toss up whether they would pick me or Torquay's Travis Boak and as the draft drew closer, they were still undecided, with some preferring Boak and others me. It was a huge decision. Although the club physio's report had eased their doubts somewhat, they knew it would be the recruiters who would carry the can if I broke down. The story goes that Stephen Wells told his wife, Maiva, as he left for the draft that if he was able to pick Joel Selwood, he'd have had a good draft. Given he was guaranteed to get Tom Hawkins, he was already in a pretty good position. In the end Stephen went to the draft confident Geelong had two live options in the top 10, me and Travis Boak, although the word was that Travis would be gone before pick seven.

Kevin Sheehan had rung Mum to invite me and my parents to the draft but again Mum and Dad decided we'd be better off staying at home and celebrating – or commiserating – around friends. I knew I would be happy wherever I landed but Mum was hoping Port Adelaide would not use their pick five to select me.

Stephen Wells did have a good draft. And so did my parents. Mum breathed a sigh of relief when Port Adelaide chose Travis

Boak; that meant I was staying in Victoria. As forecast, Bryce Gibbs went to Carlton, Scott Gumbleton to Essendon, Lachie Hansen to North Melbourne and Matthew Leuenberger to the Brisbane Lions. After Port snared Boak, Hawthorn chose Tasmanian forward Mitch Thorp then the Cats read out my name. I was off to the club I had always supported!

At home champagne flowed and the barbecue was fired up as friends and family arrived. The phone started to catch fire as well-wishers and new teammates started contacting me. But by mid-afternoon most were more interested in listening to the races on the radio rather than my future.

Daniel Connors (Richmond, pick 58) and Andrew Collins (Carlton, pick 73) had been drafted from the Pioneers but I was aware that Jarryn Geary had not been picked so it didn't feel right to get carried away. Gears was later grabbed by the Saints at pick 58 in the rookie draft. What a steal!

It was hard to reconcile the draft in 2006 to today's slick affairs. Back then I was sitting in the backyard at Paperback Court listening to a crackling radio rather than being at an official function. Unless someone really loved football, they did not take all that much notice of what was happening in the AFL at that time of the year. The draft has certainly come a long way. Now we are discussing draft prospects not only the day after the Grand Final but throughout most of the year. Although players are better prepared than ever, they are, in general terms, still a long way off being ready to have an impact in the AFL. By definition, most of the high picks go to clubs which have performed poorly, which only heightens the pressure and expectations on those picks to turn a club around. It's unfair to 18-year-olds to carry that weight, even though most are eventually going to be good players. Very few players can step into the fray like Collingwood's Nick Daicos did in his first season, although we shouldn't forget other early goers Luke Hodge, Chris Judd, Marc Murphy, Cyril Rioli, Sam Walsh and co. These are the exceptions; a player usually needs two or three years before he is pushing for regular selection or is seriously influencing games.

Geelong's joint vice-captain Cameron Ling rang me to welcome me to the club. I surprised him with my response. I told him I had worked out that a lot of the media focus would be directed at Tom Hawkins – who had already been on *The Footy Show* before being taken by the Cats with their father–son pick, pick 41 – which would allow me to get to work quicker and keep me away from the spotlight. I thought I could have an impact straight away. My attitude was clear: being drafted was just a step towards playing in a successful team. Lingy, who by then was about to begin his eighth pre-season, had never heard that sort of thinking from a draftee. I know now he thought: 'Okay, let's see him back his words up with hard work.'

Being able to use a pick in the third round to grab Tom Hawkins was a real bonus, as had been the case with Matthew Scarlett (pick 45, 1997) and Gary Ablett Jr (40, 2001). Tom's father, Jack, played 182 games for the Cats between 1973 and 1981. The next year the father–son bidding system was introduced as the League was concerned at the windfall some clubs were gaining through father–son selections. From that point on, a player such as Tom Hawkins would likely cost a club a top-10 pick, with Essendon, for example, having to use pick

10 to grab Joe Daniher in the 2012 national draft. As well as me and 'Hawk', Nathan Djekkura (pick 25) and Simon Hogan (57) were drafted to the club along with a few rookies.

* * *

Hawk wasn't around on my first day at Kardinia Park, so it was just me, Nathan and Simon who were to be shown around the club. I was introduced to Gary Ablett while he was playing cards on a computer in the property room. He said, 'You'll have to get my phone number. Actually, I'll get your number.' I walked away thinking, 'What a nice bloke.' In truth, it took a fair while before he did ring me!!

We started with a three-kilometre time trial around Eastern Gardens on a rolling track around Eastern Beach in East Geelong. Lingy, as he would continue to do for as long as we were teammates, broke our hearts going up a hill that tracks alongside the East Geelong Golf Club towards Corio Bay. We had him for speed but not endurance. He was also tactically smarter. I was pleased to finish inside the top 10; it restored my confidence in my body.

Hawk and I moved in with a host family in Highton – Bernie and Hillary Jenner and their four children, Andrew, Yvette, Juliette and Felicity, who were hardly ever around. Hawk and I already knew each other a little, as he had become mates with Xavier Ellis while boarding at Melbourne Grammar, but we soon became firm friends and fierce competitors. The pool table, the small cricket pitch and the swimming pool became sites of great battles between us. Everything was competitive and our bond grew quickly.

One tennis match we had sticks out. We decided to play on a typical 40-degree January day at a local court. Hawk forgot to bring a water bottle and after I had lost the first set he suggested we call it quits. There was no way I was agreeing to that, so we played a second set, which I won. He was gagging for a drink but there were no taps around and I wasn't sharing my water, so he said he'd settle for a draw. That was also not on my agenda, so we played a third and I wore him down to win the match. He was more technically proficient than I was at most ball sports, but I knew how to win. I drained him that day.

We would often play golf at the Balyang par-three course in Newtown down near the Balyang Sanctuary, close to the Barwon River. It still annoys Hawk that I managed a hole in one on that track, rolling the ball in on the 50-metre 15th to achieve something he hadn't. Stupidly, we would even race our cars home from training if we left at the same time. I'm not proud to say I once took a shortcut across a grass patch near St Joseph's College to get ahead of him. He was shocked at what I would do to win. I refused to give up.

It was soon clear that I had arrived more prepared for what lay ahead than Hawk. He didn't seem to realise his world was about to change whereas I was already ready, mainly because of what my brothers had shown me during their four years in the system. Hawk's sweet tooth also caused him trouble. He was about 107 kilograms and his inability to resist Hillary's banana muffins didn't help. I tried to stop him, but I couldn't. It was tough on him because I would eat just the same as he did.

All along he made me laugh and we complemented each other so well. I was intense and focused, and he was the opposite. That difference in personality drew us closer. On the track it was rather different; during that pre-season, I was out to get better through each session. Hawk was out to survive.

I was allocated No.14, as the first picked player in the draft got the lowest available number. Paul Koulouriotis, originally drafted to Port Adelaide, had worn the 14 guernsey in his one senior game with the Cats in 2006 before being delisted. He had worn number 36 in 17 previous games with the club, having joined Geelong via the pre-season draft after a stint at Port Adelaide that saw him play three matches. By coincidence 14 was the same number one of my favourite players Sydney's Paul Kelly, had worn in his 241 games with the Swans. Hawk received his dad's number 26. Nathan Djerrkura got 18 and Simon Hogan 34.

My number 14 locker was next to Tom Lonergan's 13. Tom had been lucky to survive the previous year when he lost a kidney in the round 21 match against Melbourne, in just his seventh senior game. He showed enormous courage as he ran back with the flight of the ball and was collected, fairly, by Melbourne's Brad Miller. He had his entire blood supply replaced twice via transfusions as doctors fought to save his life. The club kept him on the rookie list but he looked like a skeleton when I first laid eyes on him. He would have weighed no more than 60 kilograms. He was working hard but I thought football was all over for him. Nine years later I was still rocking up to the sight of his jocks hanging off his locker door. He was such a character!

It was quickly clear to me our team was talented, and change was happening. We were becoming tougher on each other as we learnt, via Leading Teams, how to give feedback. Bomber was the boss but my interaction with him was minimal. Bomber's real connections were with the older players, who had been with him since 2000. He loved them and their loyalty to each other was strong.

However, he was not shy about pumping me up in public, which was always nice to hear. I thought he might have been too complimentary when he praised me in a radio interview the day after our round 14 win over Essendon. 'He's incredible,' Thompson said. 'He is the best young kid we've had at the club by a mile. I mean we've had Gary Ablett, Jimmy Bartel, Cameron Ling, Joel Corey, those sorts of guys, but he is the best we have had. He is going to be pretty special.'

Training loads on the track had stepped up but the change didn't really impact me because it was all new to me anyway. I also found anything to do with training fun. Some at the club thought I had an insatiable work ethic but that was a function of enjoying the opportunity to do what I loved and do it full-time. At eight o'clock every morning, before training, I would literally be standing next to midfield coach, Brendan McCartney, ready for action. He would drop a Sherrin from a walkway above the rooms or bounce it off the roof or off a net or roll it along the ground to me time after time. It was just repetitive work, all aimed at developing firm, one-touch hands. I doubt anyone has done more touch sessions than I did in my first few years. Brendan would never say no even though some sessions could last up to an hour. We also did enormous amounts of bag work to perfect the technique I needed to master to remain protected while entering a contest and we also worked on maximising speed out of congestions. It was hard, physical work but I never became tired of it.

Our one-on-one sessions were brutal. I would battle Cameron Ling, Jimmy Bartel, Joel Corey, Max Rooke, James Kelly and Gary Ablett. Watching Rooke and Ling go at each other was exciting as their competitive natures made their battles last-man-standing affairs. Often these drills were as simple as a ball being thrown haphazardly with two players fighting to fetch it. I wanted to win every contest. Although there was no deferring to seniority, I was respectful once we left the track and ate up every word I heard.

Sometimes tempers would be frayed as none of us liked getting beaten or being reminded that running flat-out to the next cone during interval running sessions was not optional. The culture was black and white. It was more important to be respected than to be liked. That suited me fine. In fact, it was my good fortune to arrive in a group fed up with not having reached the pinnacle. They were ready to drive each other. That's what happens at clubs at certain points in their evolution. My arrival was good for the older players as well. My presence drove them even harder than they may have anticipated when challenged by a first-year player. They were most receptive to my approach – being the youngster who wanted to win every session.

On Tuesdays, 90-minute wrestling/grappling sessions were held in the well-worn gym. Knockout tournaments we labelled as King of the Ring finished some sessions. Grappling with Steven King who was over 100 kilograms, and me less than 80 kilograms, was a test. I tried my best to find a way to beat him, but it was impossible.

Our game plan was shifting to encourage faster ball movement with Bomber reviving the 'Speed Kills' motto that drove

Essendon to the 1993 premiership, when he was captain. The idea was for all players to be in constant motion. We would use game-day simulation sessions to perfect the process of creating overlap run and carry. If a teammate had the ball, he would receive support on his left or right or behind, and the ball would be flicked around to put a teammate into space. It was also about developing quick decision-making rather than using leg speed, as only Gary Ablett and David Wojcinski were super-fast. We could go this route because my teammates' skills were finely tuned.

It was both hard to get a touch and hard not to get a touch with the way we moved the ball in these sessions. Because the skills were at such a high level unless you made a good decision with or without the ball, your moment would be lost. It was during the first of those intra-club matches in 2007's pre-season I left the field for the first time with a cut on my face after clashing with Tim Callan.

Players were also given responsibility to teach parts of the game to their teammates, so for a five-week patch Jimmy Bartel might discuss how he would break a tag while Cameron Ling passed on the tricks employed to apply a tag. It was called Advanced Skill Development (ASD) and worked on the principle that you could only master a topic if you knew how to teach it. The trust it showed in player knowledge made us focus even more on the game's intricacies as players would also be given responsibility to prepare sessions. ASD fitted into the review's overall emphasis on empowering players.

Apparently, I'd made a strong impression early on because Cam Mooney told Tom Petroro within the first week, I would captain the club one day, something former AFL Game

Development executive (and future Giants chief executive) Dave Matthews had told recruiters when I was drafted. One recruiter had also told *Herald Sun* journalist Jay Clark he could see me captaining the club within three seasons.

Despite all that talk I was still not even sure I would be chosen for round one.

At this time there were some road humps for the club. Stevie Johnson's arrest, when he was found drunk in the backyard of a house in Wangaratta over the Christmas break, was the most high-profile incident. I watched on as the leadership group suspended him for five matches for his actions after much discussion between the leadership group, Neil Balme and Leading Teams.

I liked Stevie and he made the young draftees feel very welcome when they arrived. He had Hawk and me over for barbecues and would look out for us, but his punishment did reinforce to me that if I messed up badly off the field, I could have football taken away from me.

Leading Teams' approach wasn't hard for me to navigate as I was young and relatively unknown. It became apparent that individuals were being forced to confront some realities that may have been danced around in previous years. I did not have to endure any one-on-one peer assessments because I was new but watching others go through the process was a 'money can't buy' footballing education.

The well-publicised Gary Ablett assessment was fascinating. In a direct feedback session at a community camp in Swan Hill, teammates told Gary he could be the best player in the game if he worked harder. Such an edict put a fair bit of pressure on a

22-year-old who had played his 100th game in the last round of 2006. But Leading Teams ensured informal mechanisms existed to help players deal with such challenging messages. In Gary's case Bomber's assistant, Ken Hinkley, an excellent communicator who knew the person as well as the footballer, became the future champion's bedrock.

The leadership group was a relatively new concept for the Cats. Max Rooke was new to the revamped group, with Cameron Ling, Matt Scarlett and Tom Harley having shared the vice-captaincy under the skipper Steven King in 2006. I had unknowingly impressed Harls after being drafted when I returned his call even though he had not left a message, and said: 'I just missed a call from this number.' He impressed me too, when he took Simon Hogan, Nathan Djerrkura and myself out for an informal lunch on our first visit to the club. He had my respect from that point on. The all-of-club review promised to give the leadership group greater 'responsibility in assisting the likes of pre-season, match committee, core club KPIs and values, and delisting and trade activity'. The review made 21 recommendations and all but one was implemented.

As the season approached, Rooke had an idea for everyone to write down their goals for the season on a piece of paper. The submissions would then be burned, with the ashes put in an urn which would then be sealed with wax. Those ashes contained the team's spirit, the Geelong spirit. We assembled in the meeting room next to the old locker room and Max declared he had written that we were going to win the premiership that season. His bold statement of intent had a big impact on the group and was much braver than the aspiration I had written: to play a senior game. Max's idea nearly became rather infamous when the smoke from the urn containing the ashes set off the sprinklers in the rooms. Not to worry, a potential crisis was averted.

Our values were set too: Honest, United, Ruthless and Disciplined – we called it the HURD mentality.

* * *

I was among the best in our NAB Cup match against Richmond which led to me being picked to play as a pressure forward in round one, against the Bulldogs at Docklands. I had achieved two goals in one – to play a senior game, and to do it in round one. We lost to the Bulldogs and I only had eight touches but my career was away and running, albeit with Ken Hinkley joking that he would put up an electric fence from that point on to keep me out of the forward 50. If I was to be in the team, in Ken's view it was as a midfielder. Hawk made his debut in round two and we belted Carlton as expected. Blues' coach Denis Pagan compared Tom, who kicked three goals, to a young Tony Lockett.

By round four I was out of the team, which created doubt in my mind. Brendan McCartney reassured me a rest was required. I travelled to Tasmania for our match against Hawthorn as an emergency. I shared a room with Hawk and I kept him awake all night with my snoring. He did not touch the ball in the first half and at the break Bomber was in a rage, even though we were in front. He said we were playing like the Geelong of old. Some players were slipping over too, enraging him even further. He was holding a boot as he focused on Tom's lack of impact then threw it at him. No-one said anything as it flashed past

Hawk's face but I was in the corner feeling bad about disrupting his preparation. Hawk, who reckons he had never been yelled at like that during a game before, was shocked. He was still a big country kid who had high hopes pinned on him but he would take time. His body needed refining as did his competitiveness as he had gone from Finley to boarding school through to the AFL with a beautiful naivety, and wasn't ready for the rigours of being a key forward in the AFL. He played nine senior games and played in Geelong's VFL premiership in that first season. In the VFL Grand Final, Tom Lonergan, who kicked six goals, won the Norm Goss Memorial Medal as best on the ground.

We would never share a room again. The club decided that players could have their own room on interstate trips if they paid half the bill. That was another shift towards a more professional approach. We still laugh about that game but no-one was laughing then as we lost by four points to the improving Hawks, a team that had won just 13 of their previous 44 games through 2005-2006.

North Melbourne then upset us on a sunny Sunday at Kardinia Park. Ken Hinkley's 'electric fence' edict was in play: I was back in the team playing in the midfield. We played a shocking brand and the Kangaroos led by 45 points when they kicked the first two goals after half-time. The crowd was restless and although we got within 10 points late in the game it was too little too late. Their skipper Adam Simpson, a premiership player at the Kangaroos who became a premiership coach at West Coast, had 41 touches and 10 clearances and Bomber told the media post-game he wasn't sure who was supposed to be playing on him.

I managed 25 touches and although I was disappointed in the result, I was happy to be given more than 70 per cent game time. But my performance was seen by Bomber as an indictment on the senior players. Bomber praised me publicly to make a point to my teammates: 'The mindset of Joel Selwood was just incredible. For a person playing his third or fourth game of footy, he led the way. It's just a young kid coming out with a dream to play AFL footy and he played a certain way and to me he looked like he inspired the rest of the group.'

A soul-searching session in the rooms followed the loss. We all acknowledged we could blame no-one but ourselves and the responsibility to win lay with all of us. Bomber asked us what we wanted him to say to the media and we told him to be honest. Paul Chapman was forthright accusing his teammates of picking and choosing and not playing as a team when he later spoke to journalist Scott Gullan. We had entered the season with such expectations but had won just two of the first five games, against teams that would finish 14th and 15th.

That game against the Kangaroos and the week that followed is now seen as a turning point in the club's history, but I was oblivious to most of what was happening. I was tied up during the week as I attended the funeral of Dad's father, Murray Selwood. Soon after the funeral in Bendigo I received a call from Balmey that I had been nominated for the AFL Rising Star award. But I know now that the leaders had discussed my performance and it had helped them understand they needed to return to a simple focus: the contest. That meant to display hardness at every contest while bringing pressure and defensive work across the whole ground. It was doubling down on what we were doing at training. They felt I had displayed those qualities against North Melbourne.

My role during games was simple. I would play between 60 and 70 per cent game time, and apart from aiming to win the ball at stoppages, I was expected to run up and down the ground as hard as I could. Brendan McCartney was my conduit for any messages from Bomber.

Our game style was great for a young midfielder because the team was expected to share the ball around, which meant possession tallies were high and you would often have the ball in your hands. Even the defenders would flick the ball around before running it out of defence. It was a little harder for a young forward to get his head around as the ball arrived so quickly and from different angles with often a few too many extra handballs thrown in.

Richmond felt our full fury the following week – we won by 157 points as we began a winning run that saw us lose just one more game on the way to the finals. Cameron Ling and I were rested for our shock home-ground loss to second-placed Port Adelaide in round 21. Jimmy Bartel also missed it due to appendicitis. The loss made no difference to our top-of-the-table finish and Geelong's first minor premiership since 1992.

The mission that Max Rooke had presented to us in the pre-season now felt real, and after only playing one game in the first nine rounds due to a hand injury, our new skipper Tom 'Harls' Harley, had slotted into defence and was doing an amazing job on and off the field in connecting the various personalities in the team. Stevie Johnson had returned from exile in ripping shape and had become the best mid-sized forward in the game, finishing the home-and-away season with 41 goals from just 17 games after his return in round six. I'm not sure his penalty would have had the positive effect it did without Stevie accepting that the suspension was warranted and also, with Tom Harley's support, working in a stubborn, determined fashion to resurrect his career.

It's funny what you remember from such years but my appearance in the VFL mid-year sticks in my mind after I was dropped following our win over Port Adelaide in round nine. It would prove to be the last time I would be dropped in my career. Along with Josh Hunt I had made way for Harls and Paul Chapman who were returning to a very strong side in round 10.

I played against the Northern Bullants without doing enough to force a recall. The following week, before I lined up against Werribee, my teammate Brent Prismall provided me with some words of wisdom. He said the way you play VFL is to get as many give-and-gos as you can. I took Brent's advice and had 34 touches by half-time and ended up playing only a half before catching a plane to Adelaide as a carryover emergency for the game against the Crows. I took Max Rooke's spot the next week after he had been suspended for a front-on bump on Adelaide veteran and hard man Mark Ricciuto. Max was only back for one more home-and-away game that season. After badly tearing his hamstring in round 13 he was off to Germany in July for radical treatment. My VFL career ended at one and a half games.

The finals came along quickly. Mum, Dad and Scott were with me when I was presented with the inaugural Ron Evans Medal as the AFL's Rising Star winner in the week before the finals. Collingwood's Scott Pendlebury was a close second. Ron Evans was a former chair of the AFL Commission, and a winner of the Coleman Medal during his years at Essendon. During my speech I forgot to thank the Evans family and later rang Ron's widow, Andrea, to tell her how honoured I was to be the first winner of the Ron Evans Medal.

I was not one to reflect or to dwell on what a run I was having. I would have been happy for the season to keep going because I just loved playing football and I was not tired. I had won a $10,000 NAB investment account as the Rising Star winner but I hardly saw any of the dollars. I was tight with my cash, but I also had no real need to spend money. I had never seen much growing up, but I never needed it to have fun and never felt as though I was missing out on anything. The Rising Star win did not distract me from our main goal – we had a qualifying final to win against North Melbourne at the MCG.

Our aggressive forward Cam Mooney, a former Kangaroos premiership player, started a fight during the warm-up and I thought: 'Shit, what is going on here?' Not much, as it turned out. We overwhelmed them to win by 106 points – with Cam booting five goals – to set up the week's break and a preliminary final. Collingwood were our opponent after they knocked West Coast out of the race in extra time in the semi-final in Perth.

Nine Cats were named All-Australians – a record – and we were expected to win the preliminary final. Geelong, the town, was already covered in blue and white in anticipation but we just fell in, by five points, in a tense encounter. I had to admit the moment got me. I was making mistakes that I hadn't made before, which was really weird. It was the loudest crowd I'd ever played in front of. Perhaps the fact Geelong had not won a flag for 44 years crept into my subconscious.

Although we led throughout, had it not been for Brad Ottens' ruck dominance, Joel Corey's goal-saving smother, three majors from Mathew Stokes in the first quarter and Gary Ablett's stoppage goal late in the last quarter, we would have lost and been seen as chokers.

By Grand Final eve I knew we were going to win it, our mood evident when we all laughed hysterically after Neil Balme solemnly told us as we took off on the bus for the Grand Final parade that David Johnson, later our player development manager, had been arrested and locked up the night before in Geelong, for being drunk in a public place and resisting arrest. David was one of the nicest blokes on the list and his season had finished early after the Cats had won the VFL premiership. He was embarrassed and remorseful. As young men do, we found great humour in his misfortune and embarrassment. Ironically the news relaxed us, which was Balmey's point, I think.

The lesson I learnt from the preliminary final was front of mind: get rid of the ball quickly in the Grand Final. We were never going to lose once Brad Ottens ran down Port Adelaide's Michael Pettigrew late in the first quarter. It felt like I was a goal-assist player that day and given 24 goals were kicked I probably wasn't alone. My first season ended sweetly: I was a 19-year-old premiership player for the team I barracked for. We had won the Grand Final by 119 points – a record margin – and Geelong had won their first premiership since 1963.

My family and many of my schoolmates from Bendigo were in the rooms sharing the moment before a whirlwind series of celebrations began. My brother Adam joked that he had hoped he would hold the title of 'most premierships won by a Selwood' for longer than 12 months. Bomber told reporters winning the flag had come after years of hard work. I didn't think much about that. But I did think that the timing of my arrival at Kardinia Park might have been timely, for both me and the football club.

Chapter 5

One that got away

2007 TURNED OUT to be a big year for me. I was the first player to win a premiership and the Rising Star Award in the same season (Melbourne's Luke Jackson did the same in 2021) and my profile lifted, earning me attention from sponsors.

Things had become real: regular games, the attention of sponsors, the potentially tempting trappings of success. But I had to face a key question: how was I going to stay on track? The answer was clear – solid foundations had been laid and I needed to stick with them.

Striking any marketing deals was best left with Tom Petroro and his assistant Kathryn Cotsopoulos. Stride had quickly built a good stable of players with Travis Boak also one of their clients. The Stride team was young, which suited me – they became like siblings rather than work colleagues.

The shoe and apparel maker ASICS approached me to be their ambassador. I offered to pay for their boots, but Tom and

Kathryn struck a deal that landed me six pairs of boots and the prospect of a bonus if I won the Rising Star award. Tom wasn't chasing a boots deal but when I realised that ASICS boots suited me the best, he started a conversation about how an arrangement could work for both parties. Meanwhile, NAB had decided they needed an Auskick ambassador, so my name was linked to NAB's AFL Auskick promotions off the back of my Rising Star Award. The thinking was I could demonstrate the pathway to the big time, starting with Auskick as I had done. I had loved Auskick as a child and I loved the Auskick promotional work during my career. From 2009, this included me mentoring the NAB Auskicker of The Year. One child is nominated in each round based on an entry form where they describe their footy skills and, more importantly, their love of the game. Each year's winner is chosen during Grand Final week. Friday night's half-time segment with a footy-loving child chatting with Channel Seven's Hamish McLachlan has never grown tired. My involvement was never a chore because I loved being around children and their parents – anyone who loved football, really.

It wasn't in my personality to just accept a deal and forget that my input was important to its success. It wasn't as though I was particularly strategic at that point – I just felt if people paid me to do something, I would try to do the job properly and with some humility. No matter what it was, once I agreed to do something, I was all in.

That meant checking in with Kathryn before any appointments if I did not yet know the names of the people representing the sponsors so that I could engage positively with them. If I was to be the mentor of the NAB Auskicker of The Year, I needed to get to know the child and their family. It felt more real to give them my phone number and get to know them. I genuinely liked forming these connections.

This became very public in 2022, when Jedd Busslinger, who was the Auskicker Of The Year in 2012, mentioned our connection in media appearances before he was selected by the Western Bulldogs with pick 13 in 2022's national draft. I had kept in touch with Jedd through all those years and converted him from being a West Coast fan to following the Cats. I was also able to give him the odd tip along the way. It will be fascinating to watch his career.

Obviously, Jedd wasn't the only player's family with whom I interacted. Every Auskicker family provided me with a great experience and connection. Will Le Deux's mum, Jasmin, was surprised when I left the house keys for her and her two kids to stay the night at my unoccupied place when they travelled to Geelong from Nagambie for Will to train with us as in 2016 as the Auskicker Of The Year. The fact he was related to Hawk helped me make the extra effort but my thought was as simple as saving them the long drive back, and I liked the connection I had with the Le Deux family.

I really enjoyed the opportunity to meet a wide range of people inside and outside the club, and from all over Australia. The money wasn't a big deal although it was clearly something that I wanted to be managed properly. I probably earned close to $160,000 in my first season – without considering individual sponsors – including prize money and bonuses for games played. I did not see much of it at the time as Tom Petroro managed my income, allowing me $200 spending money a week, which was heaps, as everything I needed was provided by the club anyway.

I had bought my first car from Mum and Dad – a white Ford Falcon that had done plenty of country kilometres – and apart from the odd social occasion and a game of golf here and there, I didn't have much of a need to spend money. Even with Tom managing the big-ticket items, I was a little anal with my receipts, making sure all was ready when it came time to do my tax. Any socialising was generally to pubs in Geelong although it wasn't as if we were tearing the town up; we adhered to club rules to not have a drink seven days out from a game.

None of that felt unusual. I had just developed good habits. My pigeonhole at the club would be clean most of the time as I was quick to respond to any fan mail. By contrast, big Hawk's pigeonhole would be stuffed and overflowing. I wouldn't have been surprised if his first payslip was still sitting there when the season finished.

Between training sessions and games, I didn't enjoy sitting around, so I always played table tennis, four square and cricket matches in the changerooms, lingering, competing and loving it. Formal study wasn't for me, but if there was a chance to do some community work or engage with a sponsor, I would do so enthusiastically. It also surprised some of my teammates that I had a knack for remembering people's names and what they were about. I was just as comfortable speaking to players' parents or partners or siblings or anyone around the club for that matter – from a board member to a trainer. It was a characteristic I recognised in myself when I was made captain of the AIS/AFL Academy when we toured Ireland. It wasn't forced, just part of who I am.

Over time I sensed my teammates improved in that area too, recognising that a club was not a closed shop when it came to players interacting with others inside and outside the building. Relationships were what mattered to me, even then. Harls had set the example on that front, while Jimmy Bartel came up with an excellent idea to connect players with former Cats who had worn their number. Seeing the smile on the face of 1963 premiership skipper Fred Wooller – who wore Jimmy's number 3 – when we had catch-up days with former players made the day worthwhile on its own.

In reality I had always loved football clubs and recognised what it meant to be engaged with the people who loved footy as much as I did and what effect that connection could mean to them. Having such an approach meant I could walk down the street and not seek to avoid contact. In Geelong you would bump into supporters all day, every day. It was better to be able to say g'day than to avoid any connection. I now know not everyone is like that – we all gain energy differently – but such interaction has always enlivened me.

* * *

Winning the premiership had been a thrilling experience, but it wasn't my style to reflect much on what had happened. My approach was simple. Play the season out, have fun or relax during the off-season, then return to training with a desire to improve. That uncomplicated approach did not change much through my career.

So, on day one of pre-season training, I was back at Brendan McCartney's desk at 8 am for touch sessions, wanting to get better, wanting to have a bigger impact in the team, wanting to develop as a player in 2008. I had fleeting thoughts about wanting to be the best player in the competition, but it was not at the front of my mind or any particular motivation. I was not even among the top 10 players at the Cats. It was a tough school. As well as the All-Australians, we had the Brownlow Medallist (Jimmy Bartel), the Norm Smith Medallist (Stevie Johnson) and Gary Ablett had won his first best and fairest.

I had an urgency within me that put no limits on how good I could be. Even before I was drafted, when running around Crusoe Reservoir in Bendigo, I would want to do it quicker. That driven competitor hadn't left me after one year in the AFL. What I knew quickly was that I was not as talented as Gary Ablett so I would have to work harder than Gary.

I would later describe these habits as my 'lonely hours'. I didn't care if anyone was watching me or not. I just did them habitually, without exception. After night games I would do cold water immersion at the club or drive right up to the pool on Eastern Beach and stand there, waist deep in the frigid water in the middle of the night. I still did my VMOs every day, regularly swam, cycled, did yoga, hot and cold baths, prehab and recovery exercises. I was not as conscious about what I ate. In reality I ate to make myself happy. That didn't mean eating junk food, but if I was tempted by lollies or biscuits, I knew I could get away with it as I was expending so much energy. Your mind does need to relax in some areas. When I think back to the pasta meals I used to hoe into before games I shudder, as I would overeat. I would weigh up to three kilograms heavier than my normal weight heading into a game at times because of the water I drank to stay hydrated and the carb-loading I had done. I just thought that was the right thing to do at the time. When we entered the hub during 2020, I soon realised what I ate was on show, but I didn't change much of my diet. I felt as though what I was doing was working and I could still literally eat anything before a game and feel comfortable as long as it was reasonably healthy. I did begin to change things up – chicken and vegetables had a run for a while – but I was never obsessive about my diet.

Whenever I was out of town, I would find a gym in which to work out. On Christmas day each year I would go for a run with my brothers after catching up with friends from Bendigo the night before. The Christmas day runs would start off as a jog but by the last kilometre, it was on for young and old. One of my quirks was that I would always train on Grand Final day if we weren't playing, which eventually became too often for my liking. I would normally be working at the game at an AFL Auskick function and can remember rising at 5.30 am to run around Albert Park lake in darkness so no-one would recognise me. Even if I had post-season surgery, I would need to do some form of exercise.

I was not an isolationist in any way – I enjoyed company and always found time to be around my mates, particularly those from Bendigo who have all remained a key part of my life. I was one of the lucky ones able to combine a social life with the discipline required to perform consistently.

As I noted, not everybody found the requirements of professional football as compelling as I did. Nathan Ablett is an example. He missed just one game through 2007 and was a strong performer in the Grand Final, kicking three goals but he retired in January 2008, aged just 21, after taking a break late in the year. In hindsight, Bomber reckoned the decision to make him attend the family day after we won the flag was wrong. Nathan was a reclusive character and he had to stand around all afternoon signing autographs. That event was, Bomber thought, enough to make Nathan realise professional football wasn't for him. He was a beautiful person and had so much talent but he was so shy, which made being recognised as a professional sportsman difficult, and with his name and frame, he was never going to just fade into the background.

I thought our team in 2008 was better than in 2007. Although we were challenged by Fremantle in round six, winning by a point, we ended up losing just one match in the home-and-away season, a rather spectacular defeat in round nine as Collingwood downed us by 86 points. That result had stopped us from forming bad habits, for a while at least. The only close-run match was against Hawthorn in round 17 when more than 86,000 watched us win a classic by 11 points at the MCG. The Hawks led us in the last quarter which was unusual, and were just five points down with less than four minutes left when Luke Hodge made an uncharacteristic error when he used his right foot to switch the ball through the centre and hit Geelong's Ryan Gamble on the chest, with Stevie Johnson kicking a goal from the turnover. After this match, the Hawks went on record that they thought they could beat us if they had another crack. They had 395 disposals to our 420 but only one other team had managed that number of disposals against us through that season. In hindsight we should have taken more notice of the way that match swayed both ways. We were so confident we were on the right track to win another flag we didn't notice any of the warning signs.

The Fremantle win in round six had exposed the talents of Harry Taylor, who took the first of many match-saving marks in the last seconds to secure our victory. I had originally been upset when Stephen Wells selected Harry with pick 17 in the 2007 national draft when they could have picked my brother Scott, who went to West Coast five spots later. Scott was just 17 and had been named an All-Australian after the AFL Under-18 national championships. He too was in the AFL-AIS Academy and had already earned a reputation for his outstanding work ethic.

I wanted Scott to join me at Geelong although I didn't think at the time that our list was already full of quality midfielders. Now I was the only Selwood left in Victoria and this Taylor bloke from Geraldton, whom I had never heard of, was crossing the country in the opposite direction to Scott to come to Geelong. Then he rocked up to training wearing zinc cream!

I kept my reservations to myself and made sure I welcomed Harry warmly, introducing him to everyone and making sure he knew exactly what he needed to know. Then I picked him up and took him down to Torquay and around the surf coast to give him a feel for the region, given he had said after being drafted he wasn't aware where Geelong was on the map!

From our first conversation it was clear to me how much he loved football and I sensed he was driven to be as good as he could be post-haste. Soon enough I realised I had found a teammate around my age (he was then 21) who wanted to train as hard as I did and was prepared to do the extras to get better.

We would swim together on Saturday mornings at Geelong College or cycle through Geelong up and down the Thornhill Road hills, rarely telling the conditioning team. After training we would be talking footy together in the grey ice baths and spa under the old stand. Harry kept his thoughts in journals to help process them. I just kept my thoughts to myself and only shared them if needed. People saw Harry as an analyser of the game. We both saw the game in much the same way although I don't have the notes to prove it.

Our winning run after the Collingwood loss had been remarkable, with 10 of our 15 consecutive wins – including finals – by margins of 56 points or more. The sight of Bomber eating a sandwich while the team was 68 points up midway through the third quarter against the Eagles in Perth in round 13 was slightly ridiculous. He was not being arrogant, although the media did dine out on it.

Earlier, I became one of seven Cats picked to play for Victoria against the Dream Team in the Hall of Fame tribute match in May at the MCG. The match was part of the game's 150th anniversary celebrations. I was determined to wear the Big V despite carrying a sore collarbone. Later I found out I had actually suffered a broken rib the week before. It turned out to be the last State of Origin match until 2020, when a match was arranged pre-season to support Victoria's bushfire appeal. I loved wearing the Big V and being around top players but the game was no longer played with the intensity that made State of Origin games famous in the 80s and early 90s. Club football had become the priority and I never really yearned to play another game. Bomber was coaching and one of his assistants was the recently retired Chris Scott, who had become an assistant to Mark Harvey at Fremantle in 2007. Scott Pendlebury and I were the youngsters in the squad, but the Bulldogs' Bob Murphy and Sydney's Ryan O'Keefe were the two Vics I connected with best, even though they were half a dozen years older. The rib was fine but a little sore whenever someone inadvertently hit the spot throughout the rest of the season.

After every match, on a Monday, we would vote on who had displayed our HURD qualities the most during the round and present the Spirit of Geelong award to that player. This was a coveted honour, one which drove the group. I had won a few as the award evolved into simply who was having the biggest crack in a game or at training rather than sticking best to our trademarks. However, our strength that season became, when we reflected later, our weakness, as each individual's desire to be the best saw us drift away from the defensive basics that made us work as a team. We were only a small percentage off the mark but in elite sport that is enough to make you vulnerable. We didn't address the issue because we were only faintly aware it was happening, given our run of wins and their ease. That double makes any flaws easy to overlook.

That solitary loss against Collingwood had straightened us up for a period, before bad habits began emerging as each of us felt like we needed the ball more for us to get better. Seven times that season the team accumulated more than 450 disposals which was crazily high even for a team that prided itself on sharing the ball around. We all wanted us to get better and to get better we thought we had to do it all ourselves, without knowing that it was hurting us. There is no doubt an arrogance crept in among some players, with celebrations being organised prematurely. This, of course, became clearer with the value of hindsight.

We had such a belief that our team was not just good, it was exceptional. By the 15-minute mark of the first quarter in most of our matches we felt the game was won, regardless of what the score was at that point. We were process driven and our game style was refined – we moved the ball quickly and maintained possession and we were tough in contests. Training still felt more difficult than playing. The hardest thing was keeping your spot which meant no-one backed off. Add to that equation we also had several champions playing at their peak including Ablett, Bartel, Scarlett, Harley, Johnson, Enright and Corey, all to be named All-Australians.

After strong finals wins over St Kilda and the Bulldogs, we rode into another Grand Final as red-hot favourites against the in-form and talented Hawks. We soon found ourselves in the fight of our football lives. At half-time, I was angry. The Hawks were keeping the ball off us and walking the ball through for behinds to relieve forward pressure, which frustrated us. Paul Chapman kicked the first goal of the second quarter after a minute, but then we reeled off 11 consecutive behinds – two rushed – while Hawthorn kicked three goals. Most of the misses were ridiculous, with Cam Mooney's set-shot miss from point-blank range on the half-time siren getting all the post-game coverage. Cam shouldn't have been singled out as he was far from alone in making errors in front of goal. We had scored 6.12 to Hawthorn's 8.3 and what should have been a half-time lead was a three-point deficit. You could sense the understandable elation in the Hawthorn camp as Cam's shot missed. Meanwhile,

Harls was wandering around dazed after copping a knock in a marking contest. He played the second half but is on record as recalling little of the game. For a couple of weeks after the game he struggled to recover.

As we left the rooms at half-time, we still felt like we would turn it on, even though it did not feel like we had the game in control by any stretch. A Gary Ablett goal restored our lead early in the quarter but an inspired patch of football by the Hawks, with Stuart Dew unstoppable, saw them kick six unanswered goals with only behinds coming from us. We went from four points down after Gary's goal to 30 points behind. I remember thinking that winning this was going to be hard, despite late goals from Darren Milburn and Stevie Johnson cutting the margin back to 17 points at the last break. The margin had opened so quickly, we became rushed as individuals, moving away from the basics that had been drilled into us. We still had the mindset we could win the game off our own boots. All along we thought we would click into gear; but Hawthorn did not let us.

A margin of 17 points was very gettable, but Bomber later said he had looked into our eyes at the break and saw we had stopped believing. We weren't used to being in that position. The final siren left me in a state of disbelief, which quickly became anger. I thought to myself I couldn't believe we had fucked it up. I was embarrassed and for the rest of my career I remembered that game much more than the Grand Finals we won.

Bomber did not say much post-game. No-one did. He just reminded us it was a wasted opportunity. We knew that. There was no deep and meaningful conversation. We just knew by looking at each other as we departed the MCG that we had no option but to win the premiership in 2009 if we were to gain any sense of redemption.

Everything remained unspoken. This was a normal response for us since the air had been cleared after our round five loss in 2007. There are generally very few real gains to be made in talking while emotional, even a perceived desire to never lose to Hawthorn again, a commitment that gained weight when Hawthorn president Jeff Kennett made his well-documented comment on ABC-TV's *Offsiders* soon after the Grand Final when he claimed Hawthorn had a mental superiority over us. It is worth repeating what he said: 'What they don't have, I think, is the quality of some of our players. They don't have the psychological drive we have. We've beaten Geelong when it matters.' His theory was, of course, laughable. It has often been said that the 'beat Hawthorn at all costs' pact was led by Paul Chapman. Truth is, there was no pact, but we did have a steely determination to beat the Hawks again and again. We certainly enjoyed winning the next 11 matches against them (nine by 10 points or less), a run of victories that led to the wonderfully titled 'Kennett's curse'. Who knows if his words were relevant to future results but if only a small percentage of what he said led to the games being as good as they became, I have to thank him. My sense is we were just two talented groups who were evenly matched – and that brought the best out of each of us.

I hated losing the Grand Final, but I managed to find a moment in the locker room after the game to fire off a congratulatory text to Xavier Ellis, who had been one of the Hawks' best, particularly in the first half. He knew me well but was rather shocked when he saw a message pop up on his phone as he sat on the bus heading to the Hawks' celebrations at Federation Square. I wrote: 'Congratulations brother, enjoy it. It is going to be one of the best moments of your life.' We are still mates. I have forgiven him for that day, but I don't think I will ever get over him stealing my Xavier Martinez T-shirt during one of our regular catch-ups when we were in year 11!

Inside the club, the shock Grand Final loss hurt but it did not divide us. That became a trait of Geelong when I was there. In those times when we were knocked out of contention, we would assess what had happened but there were rarely recriminations. Even when supporters called for it, neither Bomber, nor Chris Scott later, chose to engage in the blame game or find a scapegoat. We would hurt as individuals and as a group more than anyone outside could imagine but we never blamed anyone for any failures.

If anything, that shared pain in 2008 brought the group closer together as we had one simple focus: to make amends by winning in 2009.

Chapter 6

Redemption

A T THE BEGINNING of 2009, I was still six months from celebrating my 21st birthday and still short of 50 games when I was voted by the players to join our skipper Tom Harley, vice-captain Cameron Ling, Gary Ablett, Jimmy Bartel, Corey Enright and Joel Corey in the club's leadership group. I wasn't intimidated but I was respectful of my place, there to learn, as much as lead. Getting voted on the group was important but Harls also liked having diversity in the group and he believed I could be a valuable conduit to the younger players on our list. Harls and I had a strong connection and he knew from the day I arrived that my reason for having a spot on the list was to help the club win flags. After my first two seasons no-one was questioning my capacity to provide value to the leadership group. Somehow, I'd managed 19 votes in the Brownlow medal in 2008 but the quality of the Cats' midfield was on display in the best and fairest when Joel Corey beat out Gary Ablett, Jimmy Bartel and Cameron Ling to fill the top four placings. I was honoured and happy to finish fifth in a Group 1 field.

The extra responsibility didn't mean I couldn't still enjoy myself because the leaders were keen for me to still enjoy being a young man. I was comfortable enough around the club to team up with Hawk in terrorising the boys with pranks that made any player's car a target. We would cover someone's car with hamburgers, sausages and sauce or chocolate and leave on their locker a photo of us dressed as ghosts and words saying thanks for the barbecue. We thought we were being hilarious as whispers went around about who might be the culprits.

Eventually Hawk and I decided to out ourselves and we organised with security to be caught out on CCTV smothering someone's car before throwing on a white sheet and taking a photo. The footage exposing us was shown in a team meeting which then descended into chaos.

It was pretty basic stuff and a bit smarter than the failed prank by Billie Smedts and Josh Caddy who were apprehended by police in 2013 – and fair enough too – after they decided to scare Jackson Thurlow by lobbing into his house unannounced wearing balaclavas. Unfortunately, they had fronted up to the wrong address.

Despite our hijinx, Stevie Johnson and James Kelly were the masters of such shenanigans; they would go after anyone. We weren't spared because we were young. In fact, because they knew Hawk and I were such great mates we often felt their wrath. Having fun had become part of the culture and the introduction of a joke box that gave us something to laugh about after team meetings was critical, I am sure, to what had happened through 2007, and it set the tone for us to rebound in 2009.

The Joke Box committee – Corey Enright, Steven King, Dave Johnson, Sam Hunt and Henry Playfair – held an esteemed position within the team. Their concept was very simple. The joke box was placed in the middle of the locker room next to the box containing our trademark player votes. Anyone could put a joke in the box, and it would then be in the running to be told at the main training session later in the week. The jokes were read out by the committee and typically were about each other, all good fun. One particular subject of a number of jokes was our video man, Eugene Dickinson. Eugene sported a goatee back in the day so 'Eugene's Goatee' would be the answer to many a joke. For example, the answer to the question, 'Why is the earth round?' was Eugene's Goatee. Like so much of such humour, it made no sense to anyone outside the team.

In the week before the 2007 Grand Final, the committee believed that they needed to deliver a joke box session befitting the occasion. So, the same standard jokes were rolled out and just when Corey Enright was about to answer, 'Eugene's Goatee' a bloody goat ran into the changeroom fully decked out in our playing kit, socks and all. I'm not sure having a goat joining us for our final training session before the Grand Final was part of any strategic plan.

It has taken a while but the best football clubs in the professional era know there is a time to switch on and a time to switch off. Things like the joke sessions were great for bonding and to ease the tension that surrounds AFL, as long as there were also some cool heads to temper anything that might cause someone to be upset. The perspective the laughs provided helped us recover from the disappointment of 2008.

I had now moved out from the Jenners. After living with Jimmy Bartel and Ryan 'Vegas' Gamble and his pet snake, Floyd, for a while in Newtown, I was able to buy a house in Preston Street, Geelong West. My Bendigo mates Brock Bouch, who was working at Advance Finance, and John Leyden, who was studying exercise sports science at Deakin, moved in. Their presence and the activity around the house kept me in touch with reality. Hawk had also moved into a house in Newtown with Simon Hogan.

I was still managing my body religiously and the knee was now not an issue. Through the season I would often be found lying on the couch applying ice to sore spots – after getting my housemates to grab the ice packs from the fridge. I did own the house, after all, and their rent was just $50 a week! They might wander in at all hours of a night on weekends, and if I wasn't with them – which was most of the time – at least they kept me abreast of what was happening around town.

The plaudits came my way as we thrashed Collingwood to win the NAB Cup premiership and I was awarded the Michael Tuck Medal for best on ground. The *Herald Sun's* chief football writer, Mike Sheahan, was referring to me in April when he wrote: 'Occasionally a young man arrives in the AFL scene and looks as if he has been around for five or six years.'

The club's focus – and mine – through 2009 was simply to make amends for the loss in the 2008 Grand Final. That was going to be easier said than done because St Kilda had emerged as a genuine threat under Ross Lyon. As we had done, St Kilda had spent the first part of the decade building their list through the draft; both clubs had assembled gun teams.

The Saints were very good. Hawthorn coach Alastair Clarkson's 'cluster' was heralded as the reason for their flag victory, but we had still managed 62 inside 50s compared to Hawthorn's 43 on Grand Final day. But in 2009, Clarkson's innovation had been built upon and the Saints were a different proposition. They were very talented across the ground and had a superb defensive mindset. It seemed that no-one could score against them.

They challenged our skills and we were tested mentally. Scoring regularly meant the ball would go back to the centre often and we would start again. But against us, the Saints could hold on to the ball longer than any other team; consequently, the ball would be in play without scores for longer. That meant we had the ball less often as a team and as individuals. This hit our egos and made us impatient. We would then do things in games we would not normally do. The Saints were also genuinely tough. They had as many players as we did who had done six or seven pre-seasons and they, too, had bodies like concrete.

Collingwood were also hunting us, but they weren't yet there. The Western Bulldogs always threatened in that era, but they were a key forward short and we generally did just enough to beat them.

I gained some further positive coverage after round six when I ran back with the flight of the ball against Melbourne to mark a ball that had the Demons' Brad Miller's name written all over it. Harry Taylor was calling out to me to look out but I just kept my eyes on the ball and took the mark. Harry was aghast, as he was aware that Miller had been the opponent who had, without any malice, collided into Tom Lonergan three years earlier in an incident that nearly cost Tom his life.

I won the first of my four AFL Players' Association most courageous awards that year, but I developed reservations as to whether that award is judged for the right things. There was no way I was more courageous than Tom, who was playing AFL with one kidney. I saw his big, ugly scar every day. Over the journey, more and more examples have arisen of players showing genuine courage – returning after cancer battles as Jarryd Roughead, Sam Docherty and Ben Cunnington have done for instance – which had me thinking the award might need a rethink. Fighting back from adversity takes great courage.

Going back with the flight of the football was just playing the game to me as I never felt afraid, although, as I became older, I was smart enough to know it was okay to pick and choose occasionally when the risk of injury was too high. I look back now on some of the things I did in the early days and think I was probably a bit silly, but most people could say that about many events in their life, not just about what they did on a sporting field.

Hawthorn were suffering a premiership hangover – they were 6–5 at the halfway mark – but would only win three more, finishing ninth. Happily, we won both encounters against the Hawks, although both were tight contests.

The Saints were the danger. In the first 13 rounds that season they were undefeated and had only conceded two scores above 80 points. We had scored fewer than 80 points in one game since round 11, 2007 and were also undefeated in the first 13

LEFT: This photo was taken before heading off to primary school for footy colours day. My uncle convinced me to follow the Cats, but I did not dare dream I would end up playing with them.

BELOW: Arms folded in the classic footballer's pose (second from right), I was straight into the Geelong jumper at Auskick. We all had number 5 on our jumpers, the number worn by Geelong champion Gary Ablett Sr.

RIGHT: My brother Scott and I made sure we got a photo with Gary Ablett Sr when he came down to the rooms after the Victorian Schoolboys game my twin brothers Troy and Adam played in alongside Gary Ablett Jr.

BELOW LEFT: I was a happy, relaxed child who just loved playing sport.

BELOW RIGHT: Captain of the Victorian Schoolboys under-12 team at TIO Stadium in Darwin.

RIGHT: My draft age year playing with Bendigo Pioneers in 2006 was cut short due to knee issues but I made the All-Australian team as a bottom-aged player in 2005. BENDIGO ADVERTISER

BELOW: Brothers Troy, Adam, Scott and me. It's impossible not to smile when we get together, four brothers who love each other's company. We adored sport and competing and supporting each other in our pursuits. All of us appreciate that anything we have achieved in football would not have been possible without the other's input. When this Christmas rolled around in 2009 we were all on an AFL list.

Socks up and a clean jumper means it must have been at the start of the game in this February 2007 NAB Cup match very early in my career with Geelong. AFL PHOTOS

ABOVE: Tom Hawkins, myself and Travis Varcoe enjoying our first win as Cats in round two, 2007. AFL PHOTOS

LEFT: Winning the Rising Star in 2007 was a great honour with the star-studded teammates helping me be at my best throughout the year. AFL PHOTOS

TOP: What a year. The Cats break a 44-year premiership drought with a record breaking win over Port Adelaide in the 2007 Grand Final. AFL PHOTOS

RIGHT: Myself and Collingwood's Scott Pendlebury were the young additions to the Victorian State Team when the Big V played the Hall of Fame tribute match at the MCG in 2008. Mark Thompson was Victorian coach and Chris Scott was an assistant coach. AFL PHOTOS

LEFT: Gary Ablett holds the Most Valuable Player Award and I hold the Most Courageous Player Award at the AFL Players Association Awards in 2009. AFL PHOTOS

LEFT AND BELOW: I became All-Australian for the first time in 2009 playing alongside some of Geelong's greatest ever players with Gary Ablett Jr – the best of them all at that time. AFL PHOTOS

ABOVE: Max Rooke, Tom Hawkins, myself and Steve Johnson celebrate winning the 2009 AFL Grand Final between St Kilda and Geelong. AFL PHOTOS

I accepted my first official leadership position at the club when I entered the players leadership group in 2009. The next three seasons taught me many valuable lessons that held me in good stead when I was made captain in 2012. AFL PHOTOS

rounds. When we met at Docklands in round 14, we were both the undefeated heavyweights of the season.

Despite the build-up to the match, I had no nervous tension before that game, or any other for that matter; nerves did not happen for me. I did not need music or anything external to pump me up. I just needed a contest and I knew we would have that against the Saints. I remember preparing for that game in the usual manner, focusing on my opponents, not the occasion. It was also the first time I would line up against Jarryn Geary, who had earned a spot in that team through hard work and had become a regular for the Saints. As I entered the game my winning percentage after 59 games was 93.10. His, after 23 games, was 78.26. This was a far cry from our days at the Bendigo Pioneers.

The game lived up to the anticipation. In my opinion, this season was when the AFL game reached its apex. Expansion had not happened so each of the 16 teams was packed with good players. There were more than 54,000 under the roof at the Docklands, a capacity crowd. The Saints jumped us to kick the first five goals. After that sluggish start, we pegged them back, but they always seemed to kick a goal just as we were on the verge of levelling the score. We finally did that with just under five minutes remaining when Mat Stokes goaled. I was exhausted, having run down one of my footballing heroes Lenny Hayes before feeding out a handball to get that play started. In commentary Leigh Matthews said I was 'untackleable', which caught my ear the following week as I reviewed the game. Unfortunately, Michael Gardiner took a great mark on the siren to kick the match-winning goal for St Kilda.

It was a tough game to review because of the speed in which it had been played. The ball was always in motion with very few stoppages or slow plays for the coaches to assess. The clash had been a players' game played mainly on instinct.

Although we had dropped the game, we knew we could match the Saints; but we also knew they could match us.

* * *

The toll on our team was huge. We had to make seven changes for the next match, against Brisbane at the Gabba, after Andrew Mackie hurt his quad on our morning walk when kicking a soccer ball around. Jeremy Laidler and Tom Gillies made their debut. Nathan Djerrkura and Simon Hogan were both playing their third games after three seasons at the club. They had both been selected in my draft.

Brisbane, in their first season with Michael Voss as coach, were competitive, having won eight of their first 14, but even with all the changes we still expected to win given we had lost just four games since round five, 2007. Bomber wasn't happy when we found ourselves 26 points down at half-time but I was still shocked by what happened as we walked to the rooms for the break. Bomber raced down from the coach's box and began targeting me. As he walked across the ground he was talking aggressively in my ear: 'What the fuck you doing out there? You've fucking got to start leading this side you fuckin' useless little prick.' Even now, at the end of my career, I can remember every word, and the anger in his voice.

I had not copped such a barrage before and didn't know

what to make of it. During the third quarter I copped the same treatment as I reached the bench, this time on the phone. I was confused more than anything. What had I done to deserve such abuse? I knew I was in the leadership group but I didn't think I was playing badly. Certainly, I didn't believe I was the reason we lost the match by 43 points.

The next month was brutal. It seemed like I could do nothing right in Bomber's eyes and I was thinking that we had to sort this out, but I didn't want to talk to him when he was in that mood. I was still only 21. I began to think the coach had gone mad. The popular perception is that most of them *do* go mad in the end.

Tom Harley was in earshot when most of the exchanges happened, which was fortunate because he made a point of continually checking in on me. It became obvious it was a phase Bomber went through with most players to ensure they did not get ahead of themselves. I didn't believe I had been thinking that way but he must have noticed something. Bomber could be particularly hard on the captain and I remember overhearing a fierce spray to Harls during the 2009 Grand Final after Lenny Hayes had evaded him too easily. Harls reassured me Bomber's stern words towards me were because he thought I could cope, and he wanted to use me to make a statement to the rest of the team and that Bomber actually loved me. However, I did not enjoy the experience which I now ruefully describe as my 'growing up' period.

That was the way it was in footy back then. Harls was an outstanding captain; he knew there was more happening inside players' minds than they might show to the world and anyone – regardless of their toughness – could be affected by the tactics Bomber was employing. Harls and I had enormous respect for each other; he would know when to harness my more aggressive on-field tendencies. I did not mind pushing the issue on the field but I did not get reported until 2011; part of that was due to his influence.

Not only was he a great captain, he was an outstanding player, but he never saw himself as a great player, more a binding influence on the team. He was down back with uncompromising characters in Matthew Scarlett and Darren 'Dasher' Milburn and the quiet assassin Corey Enright. But he also found a way to support the more cerebral characters down there such as Andrew Mackie, who walked with a Tom Cruise swagger, and my mate Harry Taylor, who took down notes on every player and was deep into military history. Dasher Milburn was one of Bomber's favourites, but the coach could also turn on him as he knew he could cop it.

* * *

Tom Harley's influence on me when I later became captain was profound. He gave me confidence that I could handle the role, particularly in the areas of the job that required a mature outlook. He knew the foundations the club had in place that had helped both him and Lingy manage the role and as a result he made it clear I should not be daunted by the responsibility, even at my relatively young age.

The midfield was tough on each other at training while the forwards were hilarious but there were a few egos down there, with Cameron Mooney, Stevie Johnson, Paul Chapman and Mat

Stokes all wanting to be *the man*. Ken Hinkley managed to pull it all together.

I was blessed to be surrounded by genuinely great midfielders in Cameron Ling, Jimmy Bartel, Joel Corey, Gary Ablett and James Kelly. We had an attention to detail that meant each person prioritised the midfield group's total performance over anything individual. Their lessons stuck with me for the rest of my career. As individuals they had great attributes and they complemented each other.

Lingy was just a raging bull who demanded high expectations. His training standards were elite, and he set the culture. He was all about having a beer with teammates when the time was right. He had gears when it came to socialising but he set boundaries that demonstrated the extra responsibilities you carried as an AFL player. I became used to Lingy opening midfield meetings with the same sentence: 'We will win the contested ball this week.' Jimmy Bartel could play anywhere and became the glue in many parts of the ground. Joel Corey's spread was elite as he had a high cruising speed. He was the forerunner of the tall mid that every team wants. We could have used him as a power athlete because he was so big and strong.

My approach to leadership was to play as well as I could and when I spoke it was more to the group rather than giving it to individuals between the eyes. I was still learning and Harls and Lingy were such good teachers but I also had my own sense of the dynamics within the group, aware that not everyone had to be best mates. One of our values was to be ruthless but I understood that such a word can be used as an excuse for being thoughtless unless the leadership is on the ball.

'Ruthless' was appropriate as a value at that time but around 2012, as the playing group transitioned, it was not so important. By then, we needed to do things differently, to play to the strengths of a new crop of players, to establish a framework but to let players be themselves within that framework. Surely in a high-performance sport being both ruthless and caring can co-exist. Perhaps it should be about being relentless in the pursuit of improvement rather than being ruthless.

* * *

Bomber's mood through these weeks showed the tension he was carrying. We won five of the last nine matches and three of those wins were by less than a goal. We were not performing to the level we all expected. Many players were sore and a few, such as Max Rooke and Paul Chapman, were battling soft tissue injuries. Brad Ottens had missed most of the season with a knee injury Neil Balme had famously listed as a 'two-week injury' for 20 weeks and played his first game since round two in round 22. Mat Stokes was injured in the qualifying final when we just held off the Bulldogs winning by 14 points after they had outscored us in the last quarter after we had taken a 29-point lead. But unlike throughout 2008 we were never at a stage where we knew we would win. We even renamed our weekly Spirit award, the 'Scrapper Spirit award'. It fitted our ethos. The coach kept at us to believe in what we were doing; that created an edge we needed.

Collingwood battled hard in the preliminary final but we took the game away in the third quarter, kicking the first four goals after half-time. As we swept the ball out of the centre time after time, Mick Malthouse, the Collingwood coach, was impressed. 'Shit, they're good,' he said aloud in the coach's box. We ended up winning by 73 points.

On the Monday, Gary Ablett was a red-hot favourite to win the Brownlow medal and he did just that, polling 30 votes, a lazy eight votes ahead of the runner-up Chris Judd. After polling 19 votes in 2008, I managed 16 votes and jumped a place in our best and fairest, finishing fourth behind the joint winners, Corey Enright and Gary Ablett.

St Kilda just got over the line in the preliminary final against the Western Bulldogs, tightening up a little as we had in 2007 to win by just seven points. But the match-up, as projected after that round 14 epic, was right – we were the two best teams. Brad Ottens and Stevie Johnson had replaced Shane Mumford and Simon Hogan from the round 14 clash while for the Saints, Steven King and Sean Dempster replaced Ben McEvoy and Jarryn Geary.

I was ready to be more than a handy contributor. I had been named All-Australian for the first time, alongside four teammates – Corey Enright, Matthew Scarlett, Paul Chapman and Gary Ablett, with Bomber named as coach – while five Saints had earned the honour, meaning 10 of the 22 All-Australians were playing in the Grand Final.

During the media conference before the game, Bomber summed it up: 'This is the moment, isn't it? Two hours of footy to determine the premier.' He could have been speaking of any Grand Final but given the way we had gone at each other in round 14, he was surely right this time. Ross Lyon was on the same wavelength when he told his team: 'This is the ultimate test of what we actually stand for.'

Harry Taylor had the task of playing on St Kilda champion Nick Riewoldt. I kept telling Harry during the week how suited he was to that role, his aerial strength and his supreme fitness would allow him to keep up with Nick, who was one of the great runners in the game – he never stopped moving. Hawk had finally cemented a spot in the team and looked set to battle Zac Dawson after the Saints decided to leave the veteran Max Hudghton out of their line-up.

Bomber's instructions were to employ constant ball movement that would hurt them: 'kamikaze, off-line ball use, reverse lateral.' He just wanted us to keep the ball moving at all costs, switching angles if necessary.

Lyon indicated in his address the way in which the game would be played: 'When the ball is bounced, bodies are flying, they will try to stamp us early. We have got to stand our ground, no undisciplined acts, play the ball, play the ball, but you have got to take them to ground. Tackle and dump, tackle and dump. Are you clear?'

The day was wet so I knew the ball would be on the ground which meant the role of our midfield would be critical. We were a solid unit and we had each other's backs. I had been tagged that season for the first time as they decided Gary Ablett was impossible to stop and Jimmy Bartel was too versatile. It did not worry me much, although my mind had to keep buzzing to ensure I was working with my teammates to beat the opposition. Jimmy and I could switch and swap on the wing or we could drift forward and Stevie Johnson could move up for a bit. James Kelly had moved down back, as Josh Hunt missed the season after he did his ACL in the NAB Cup, and was to play on the Saints' Stephen Milne. We also supported whoever was tagged to help him break free. If one of us was double-teamed that would give us an extra.

The opening was blistering, as we expected. I was in my element and kicked a goal in the first quarter when I burst clear from a stoppage, knocked over an off-balance Clint Jones and kicked truly. But the Saints were good, and Lenny Hayes was dominating with 10 touches. Bomber raced down at quarter-time and rather than switch Lingy, who was tagging Nick Dal Santo, on to Lenny, he told Jimmy Bartel that Lenny was to be his man from that point on.

Eventually we settled down to battle it out. The biggest margin had been no greater than 12 points from late in the second quarter. The Saints had 22 more inside 50s than us at half-time but had kicked inaccurately – 7.7 to our 7.1 – and we had some good fortune when Hawk was awarded a goal despite his shot hitting the post after smothering a kick out, gathering the ball and snapping – well, truly. It took until 2012 – and another controversy in the 2011 Grand Final when Collingwood's Sharrod Wellingham had a goal awarded against us after the ball he kicked hit the post – before the AFL invested in the technology to assist with goal-umpiring decisions.

People were amazed when they saw footage of me addressing the group in a huddle at half-time. Looking back, I can see why, as I was only 21 but, to me, it felt natural. I didn't care whether it was my turn to talk or not. I just did it and the boys were happy to listen as I emphasised the basics such as tackling effectively.

I also reminded them we had set ourselves to win the flag and the time had arrived for us to complete the job. Those few words did reflect my sense of ownership over what happened, whether that could be justified or not.

Even though he knew we were putting everything on the line, Brendan McCartney had given it to the midfield at the final break, exhorting us to do more to overcome the seven-point deficit. I loved being in that moment in that game. The need to win was real but I did not give any thought to any ramifications of losing. I just went out and played footy. So did Shannon Byrnes, who was brilliant in the most important game of his career after copping it from supporters while playing one of the hardest positions on the ground at times during his previous 75 games. He won game-changing contests consistently in the second half.

Hawk goaled within the first couple of minutes of the last quarter, but from then it was a classic wrestling match, with a series of behinds from both sides. I had a chance to put us in front from about 45 metres out with about 10 minutes left but pulled the shot and could only level the scores. With the scores locked together, Stevie Johnson went inboard to Gary Ablett, who had found space in the centre square. Stevie only had the ball because Harry Taylor had backed his judgement and had left Riewoldt to take an intercept mark. He then kicked short to Corey Enright who passed to Stevie. I was standing on the wing near Brendan Goddard, who had his head wrapped in a bandage, a la Hannibal Lecter; I pointed to the middle where Gary was in space. Zac Dawson saw him too. Stevie's kick was a little high and Dawson was able to spoil. With the ball loose, it looked like the Saints would clear and go forward but Dawson and Justin Koschitzke collided, which gave rise to Matthew Scarlett's famous toe poke to Gary, who kicked long to the square. Travis Varcoe grabbed the spill and handballed to Paul Chapman, who kicked what turned out to be the match-winning goal.

The next three minutes was just tough, contested, desperate football, with behinds to Max Rooke and a desperate rushed behind to the Saints courtesy of Scarlett's fanatical contest with Adam Schneider. With the margin just six points, the kick-in from Darren Milburn was critical. We had to retain possession. In stepped Harry Taylor to take a superb mark. That too could have been a match-saver/match-winner and we were able to hang on after rushing the ball down the members' wing. The siren sounded as Max Rooke marked inside 50. His goal after the siren was an anticlimax, as the Saints did not offer any defence, and the shot dribbled through to make the margin 12 points.

We had won a great match, becoming the first team since Essendon in 1984 to come from behind at three-quarter-time in a Grand Final and win. Paul Chapman won the Norm Smith Medal. We could not have given anymore. That night was slow as we were completely exhausted.

I still think the footy in 2009 was the best standard I experienced. The Saints, who had won the first 19 matches that season, were the best team I played – by a long way – but still could not win a flag.

Of course football, like life, doesn't always reward you with what you deserve. I never forget that cards don't always fall for people in the way they hope or imagine.

Chapter 7

Movement at the station

GOLD COAST WERE to enter the competition in 2011. We knew our best players would be targeted. But few imagined the Suns could land Gary Ablett.

In an interview on 3AW during the September finals series, Frank Costa, who would depart as president at the end of 2010, to be replaced by Colin Carter, said he was confident our best players would stay with the Cats due to the promise of continued success and the desire to play in one jumper. He also said what many people had been saying during the year: 'Selwood has got captaincy written all over him.' With Harls retiring, the job was available and, despite Frank's words, Cameron Ling was the natural successor and although some thought I would have been capable, it was great for me to have another couple of seasons as – we would joke – an 'under-Ling'.

I was blissfully unaware of most of the details being reported but I was conscious articles were being written suggesting the

Gold Coast were targeting me and Gary as we would both be out of contract at the end of 2010. I had no intention of leaving – the idea did not really enter my head. I loved being a Geelong player. I had just bought a house and I spent very little time thinking about money, although I was aware that a move to the Gold Coast would likely mean a large increase in any contract.

We were all aware the landscape was changing, with expansion clubs and free agency on the horizon. Geelong did not want to take anything for granted so a meeting was arranged with chief executive, Brian Cook, football manager, Neil Balme, recruiting manager, Stephen Wells, assistant football manager, Steve Hocking, my manager, Tom Petroro, and me.

The Cats wanted to reassure me about the direction of the club and where I might fit in. I was a bit naive and was just thinking it was pretty exciting to be sitting down with such an important bunch of people. I trusted Tom and his approach to protect his clients and to maximise their earning potential but to do so with the big picture in mind – meaning on-field success, valuing integrity, staying true to your values and maintaining positive relationships with key decision-makers was important. He knew me well and what the club meant to me. I think the longest contract negotiation in my career lasted about a month. The club wanted me to extend my contract for another three years but Tom suggested a two-year deal, given free agency was likely in the near future. He was reading the future well – free agency came into play at the end of the 2012 season.

I did not meet or speak with Gold Coast, but I assumed Tom did although he never told me or whether any numbers were suggested. He later told me Gold Coast had discussed my future, but Tom always believed their focus was Gary Ablett. He knew me well enough to not tell me anything for the sake of telling me. I just focused on whether what the Cats were offering was fair and reasonable, and it always was. There was nothing particularly scientific that went into my decision. Simply, I was happy living in Geelong and playing for Geelong. Why would I leave?

The leadership group was also faced with a very public test of managing the fallout from our 2007 premiership teammate Mat Stokes being charged with cocaine possession and trafficking early in 2010. We had something of a template to follow with Stevie Johnson's penalty in 2007, but every person and situation is different and so it was with the way we considered Mat's situation.

It was a classic case of 'support the person, condemn the action' but it wasn't just about mouthing those words. We had to care for Mat. We knew he was a good person and it was important we talk *with* him rather than *at* him so he could eventually own the mistake, and to accept that he must work outside the club for a period. He also had to win back the group's trust. He accepted responsibility, worked his butt off and returned in round eight after escaping a conviction. He did not miss a game for the rest of the season.

Gary Ablett's future was a constant in the media throughout the pre-season. Bomber did not hide his feelings when it came to the prospect of losing Gary. At the 2010 season launch he emotionally called on Gary to stay and then, after I signed for two more seasons in May, he compared my decision with what Gary was considering. When asked whether Gary would be torn about the decision he faced, Bomber said, 'I love Joel

Selwood and what he's been able to do. It's just all class and just integrity … '.

It just added fuel to the growing frustration between Bomber and Gary during 2010 but I didn't get involved nor was I affected. I did not spend any time reading about myself unless it could help me play better. I respected the difficulty of Gary's decision and knew that his was much bigger than mine. His was a life-changer as not only did the Suns want him to be their leader, the AFL wanted him to be the face of its new club on the Gold Coast. He was 26 and in his ninth season, was a Brownlow Medallist and a two-time Geelong best and fairest. I was 21 and had played only three seasons. There was no comparison in my mind. But it signalled a shift in the way player contracts were covered with the 'will he or won't he stay' discussions around individuals now fodder for the media.

Occasionally Gary would express how he was feeling to the leadership group but we had no issue with him. He was still our best player and was still playing at his best, despite what he must have been thinking. And although it was a big issue for others, the media didn't really ask me about it much. I could avoid the media scrutiny a bit, hidden down in Geelong.

Throughout that season Gary showed that players can be prepared to move but still finish their final year at a club contributing wholeheartedly and professionally to the team. Countless others before and since have shown what is possible if the club and player act professionally. I eventually made it a point as my career progressed to not bag or sledge players on the field who had chosen to depart the Cats. It didn't make sense to me. Once a Geelong man, always a Geelong man.

We had already lost Shane Mumford as he sought more opportunities with Sydney after missing out on our premiership, but we were still finding players with Daniel Menzel and Mitch Duncan being drafted and James Podsiadly added to the rookie list despite his age after impressing at training. Mitch's talent was obvious from the beginning and he worked his way into the defending premier's team in round one while Podsiadly, at the age of 28, created headlines when he made his debut in round three. Tom Lonergan was given a chance to prove himself as a defender having lost his spot up forward.

We were still excellent but Collingwood had matched St Kilda's defensive system and were formidable as they added the Saints' Luke Ball – who had sat on the bench for most of the second half of the 2009 Grand Final – and Sydney ruckman Darren Jolly. We still wanted to move the ball quickly and to play a high possession game but opponents were squeezing the ground even further, putting pressure on our skills.

My form remained strong and the umpires obviously liked the way I was playing, as I polled Brownlow votes in eight consecutive games between rounds 14 and 21 but from round 16, we conceded top spot to Collingwood and eventually finished second with 17 wins, one fewer than in 2009. The top four teams were the same as in 2009.

We copped St Kilda in the qualifying final and, as in the 2008 Grand Final against Hawthorn, we let our guard down in one quarter and the Saints jumped us. Stephen Milne kicked three goals in six minutes in the second quarter, and we then found ourselves 33 points down early in the second half. We responded, as we always did, and hit the front with less than a minute remaining when Cameron Ling kicked a goal that was disallowed after a free kick was paid against Cameron Mooney for pushing St Kilda's James Gwilt in the back. Moons kept saying to umpire Matt Stevic: 'You cost us the game' but in reality, it was our first half that had done that. It was our second loss to the Saints for the season, some (minor) consolation for their Grand Final loss.

Adam McPhee tagged me in our easy semi-final win over Fremantle. He was seven centimetres taller and eight kilograms heavier than me. At that time teams were trying players of all shapes and sizes as taggers. St Kilda's Clint Jones would normally go to Gary Ablett and Hawthorn would try two-way runners such as Chance Bateman on the opposition's most influential midfielder. As we had been near the top for four seasons, it was inevitable we would be picked apart, player by player.

Our game style during the four seasons I'd played suited a team that was so skilful, we would try what others might believe impossible. It was great for me as I soon worked out that if I was within 60 metres of the ball, I had a chance to receive it. There wasn't too much playing the percentages. We had dragged the game from the stodgy period when West Coast and Sydney dominated, although that was a rivalry I really enjoyed watching.

In the preliminary final, nothing worked, with Collingwood thrashing us from start to finish. In what was his last game for Geelong until his return in 2018, Gary Ablett had 40 touches to be our best by miles. Such was the nature of the defeat that we were quickly rated as being too old and too slow. It would become a familiar refrain. The reality was we were tired, having played 100 games in four seasons. Perhaps if we had beaten the

Saints in the qualifying final, we may have been able to regroup and be refreshed but it was not to be. I had been on the winning team in 79 of my 94 games to that point, so I could not complain.

Gary polled 26 Brownlow votes finishing second to Carlton's Chris Judd (30), who won his second Brownlow. I got 21 votes, but in four of the five games where we both polled votes, he was awarded more than me so I could not be accused of stealing votes from Gary. The other three players in the top five were Judd and Collingwood pair Dane Swan and Scott Pendlebury, good company. Although our season was disappointing in the end, I did win my first club best and fairest (Gary finished second) and was selected All-Australian again. Winning individual awards didn't motivate me but I did know that winning the best and fairest meant my name went up on the honour board in the locker room. I was genuinely proud to sit alongside the names of our best and fairest winners. Of course, nothing compares to winning a flag.

I immediately headed to Mount Buller with my brothers to be away from everything when the Grand Final was played. They still laugh at the memory of me looking out the window as we drove up the mountain and saying: 'Look, baby bears' before it dawned on them that I was talking about wombats. I was no David Attenborough at that stage!

Bomber and Gary weren't really talking by season's end and no-one was surprised when Gary announced soon after our last match he was leaving for the Suns. Both men respected each other and understood how important they were to their respective careers but the constant questions on the same topic had left them exhausted. I didn't realise it then, but Gary's departure probably allowed the Cats to keep four of our best players who might have otherwise been forced to leave, given salary cap issues.

What quickly became bigger news was Bomber's shock decision to step down as coach with a year remaining on his contract. The leadership group had not been told of it beforehand. He had coached the Cats since 2000 and left with a 63 per cent winning record and two flags. He said he was exhausted when announcing his decision. Just as surprising as his departure was his later decision to become James Hird's assistant at Essendon.

I wasn't overly close to Bomber, as he tended to make sure the senior players were aware of what was needed and then the message would flow down. But it was still a shock to me when he took up the job with his former club. At the time I was asking myself: 'Why would he do that?' but looking back I think: 'What else was he going to do?' He was a career coach and he was tired of being the main man. He could have moved into the assistant's chair at the Cats but I can understand why he didn't; it would not have worked. I also suspect he did not want to be the one telling his favourites that it was time for them to move on in the years that lay ahead.

There was later controversy when phone records showed he had been in touch with the Bombers midway through the year. I was not fussed to hear that. All I knew was that while I was overseas on holidays, it sank in that our coach and our best player were gone.

Chapter 8

New coach, new direction

NEIL BALME, STEVE Hocking and Brian Cook had the job of finding a replacement for Bomber and we all had faith they would make the right call. Our assistant coaches, Ken Hinkley and Brenton Sanderson, were candidates as was Chris Scott, who had been an assistant coach at Fremantle since 2008, after 215 games in his 14 seasons playing with the Brisbane Lions.

I had played in Chris's farewell game for Brisbane, against the Cats at the Gabba, as his playing career finished at the age of 31. It was just his second game in two seasons as he fought injury to his midriff. I knew of him, as my brother Troy also played in that game, and Chris's best mate from football, Nigel Lappin, had worked at the Cats as an assistant since 2009. Chris had a great career, finishing with the 1994 Rising Star Award in his first season, Brisbane's 1998 best and fairest, two premierships and a reputation as a tough, uncompromising player. But I didn't know him personally.

He had been approached to apply for the Geelong job after just missing out on the job at Port Adelaide, after Mark Williams had been sacked, but Ken or Brenton was favoured to win the gig. The players didn't make the decision, but their input was sought, and we were kept abreast of the process. That led to a memorable phone hook-up between the leadership group and Hocking and Balme when we were on our end of season trips. I was in Austin, Texas with the rest of the crew spread around the world.

I listened more than spoke during the 70-minute call but discovered later it had been an expensive exercise when a phone bill for $2800 appeared in the mail. I was earning okay money at the time but I was not sure I wanted to pay that much to stay informed! I did not want to cost the club money but approached my manager to see whether I was liable or not. Eventually Tom Petroro organised that I paid half and the club paid half, which I was happy to do even if $1400 was a fair whack for a meeting that had merely emphasised the club would get us a good coach to have another crack at a flag.

Chris was just 34 when his surprising and brave appointment was announced on 18 October but I recall him saying it was his responsibility to get with the program rather than the other way around. Brian Cook explained the appointment at the subsequent media conference: 'He brings to this club an immense amount of leadership quality, we believe great management potential, has a great understanding of the sports science world and the IT world, is a person we think is a future-type of coach if that's the right way of putting it – a coach-manager, that's the way we're heading.'

I felt for Ken and Brenton but the veteran players probably felt it more. To their credit they backed in the club's decision. Ken took up the chance to join Gary Ablett on the Gold Coast as an assistant to Guy McKenna while Brenton remained as defensive coach. It was inevitable that both would become senior coaches.

Chris rang me to introduce himself and that was about it. A new era had started. When he took over, our new coach was less than a year older than the oldest player on our list, Darren Milburn. He was the same age, give or take a few months, as his mentor Leigh Matthews – who coached Chris at the Lions – was when he took over from Bob Rose as Collingwood's coach after three rounds in 1986.

It was a unique appointment as his twin brother, Brad, had been appointed coach of the lowly North Melbourne a year earlier. North had finished 2009 in the bottom four. Chris's task was rather different. He was taking over a top-four team that had played in three of the previous four Grand Finals, winning two.

Many observers wondered about the challenge Chris faced, when taking over a contender. It was a genuine query. The view was that it would be easier to make a mess of things than get it right. Internally, the change of coach enthused most of us, with Chris certain to bring a fresh perspective, but there was some concern as to how those who loved Bomber would react to the appointment. Only Matt Scarlett, Darren Milburn, David Wojcinksi – and those who had come from other clubs, Cam Mooney, Brad Ottens and Marcus Drum – had known another senior coach.

Chris quickly showed he knew as much about the art of coaching as the technical aspects of the game when he reassured the group that we were doing a lot right. What was needed, he said, was a fine-tuning of the defensive aspects of the game. That was an interesting perspective, given he had been an assistant at Fremantle for three seasons, and had been in the box when we beat Freo by 69 points a few weeks earlier in the semi-final. Instead of defending one-on-one, all lines need to embrace team defence. The back six were already well versed on team defence but the other lines needed to embrace that approach too, adhering to a defensive structure up the field by handing off opponents for teammates to cover, and also being prepared to cover the most dangerous player. Once the new style was ingrained in us, it allowed us to conserve energy as we defended more efficiently, allowing us to add that extra energy to apply to our attacking strength. That made us better. The senior players responded to Chris's message with maturity, professionalism and enough skill to adapt, backing the coach and his view on what was required to bounce back from our disappointing preliminary final exit, a game we had not reviewed as a group. He made another key point too, saying he would do everything he could to stop the club falling off the cliff as the Lions had soon after they had played in four straight Grand Finals, winning three flags. Astute list management would be vital.

He also needed to manage the arrival of new faces in the football department, with assistant Brendan McCartney and high-performance manager Dean Robinson moving to Essendon with Bomber, and Ken Hinkley and Paul Haines, the conditioning manager, moved to the Gold Coast.

Kris Hinck and Chris Spinks led a new fitness regime but the other pillars, Brian Cook as chief executive, Neil Balme as general manager of football and Cameron Ling as skipper remained and continued to be strong and authoritative. Our base was strong – our list included 11 players with 150-plus games, and 20 premiership players.

We all got on well and my competitiveness was on display at David Johnson's buck's turn at the end of the year. His best man, James Podsiadly, had organised events as we relaxed over a few beers at a property in Teesdale near Geelong, splitting us into two teams – Pods's team and Dave's team. One activity required me to hold a golf club above my head, look up and spin around 10 times before kicking a soccer ball into a net. I made a bit of a spectacle of myself as I lost my legs straight away and went hurtling towards a barbed wire fence before hitting the ground. There was some blood coming from my head but I refused to give up and stuck at the task, once, twice, three, four times with everyone losing count as I kept going until that soccer ball hit the back of the net.

* * *

It was obvious early on that Chris's appointment had been a good call. He is a very smart person, had come to the role with good experience as an assistant, and quickly formed an empathy with the playing group. Combine that with a competitiveness obvious from his playing days, and he was clearly well suited to the senior role. He was also a good listener.

Off the field he is more cerebral than most, similar to Balmey in that he never saw the value of ranting and raving. He was more interested in finding an edge over the opposition than creating some grand emotional narrative to inspire a win. Sometimes I would genuinely sit in awe, or at least in wonder, at some of the ideas he would come up with. Occasionally his theories would float above me such as the day he showed us how small Australia was compared to the rest of the world when explaining the importance of space in football. The smart blokes in the group got it instantly but I was with the other group, scratching our heads. Chris was always prepared to laugh at himself and was exceptional at changing tack if he needed to, so that everyone would get his message. Doing that to an audience as diverse in age and interests as in a football team over a long period is a great skill. Not all his ideas worked or were ticked off but plenty did, and he appeared to relish working at a fast pace to solve the inevitable problems that continually arise in the chaotic footballing environment. On game day that strength was most useful as he proved superb at reading what was needed and when to intervene.

My attitude had not changed. I just needed to get better. The change of coach gave me someone new who I needed to impress, and that kept me motivated to train at a high level. I was now entering my fifth season and was within sight of 100 games, and with Gary Ablett gone, I believed I could have an even greater influence on games than I had previously. We did not mull over how to cover Gary's departure. Our attitude was merely 'next man up' and that we had enough talent on the flanks to fill the void.

I kept doing touch sessions with the bag of balls three or four times a week, often working with a teammate rather than an assistant. I understood my game. I tried to get to stoppages early to assess the cues so I could take the best position on my opponent. I also worked on the timing of my movement once the umpire restarted play. My preference was to move as late as possible. This meant I would often have to pick up the loose ball from the deck. That was okay, as flying through and hoping to take the ball on the full while moving at pace was to take a punt on gaining a miracle clearance rather than playing the percentages. That's why my touch was so critical. When I was below my best, I was moving too early and going past the ball, which would waste energy and affect my capacity to follow up and stay in the contest. Also crucial was to work on my first five metres away from the contest. I trained for this, so my initial burst became a habit. That allowed me to either break into space with the ball or at worst be at the next contest to lend support. Touch sessions included picking up the ball between my feet, so I was in a strong position and was well-balanced. Training for these game day issues meant my reaction to looming pressure was to speed up rather than slow down, which raised my chances of exploding through a tackle. Having a low centre of gravity helped but the habits I had built through regular training made my approach at stoppages instinctive.

As fate would have it, I was, as vice-captain, made captain in Chris's first game as Lingy was missing with a hamstring injury when we opened our season with a Friday-night clash against St Kilda at the MCG. In more ways than one, it was not a memorable occasion, at least for me. With four minutes remaining in the first quarter a kick-in from Harry Taylor went over my head and I charged back to win the loose ball. My head collided with the hip of the Saints' Farren Ray as we reached the football at the same time. I was out cold, stiff as a board, on my back with blood running down my cheek. On the TV it looked terrible as the blood appeared to be running from my mouth, but the contact had cut my lip. The doctors put an oxygen mask on me as they prepared the stretcher which made the situation look even worse. Poor Mum needed to be strong again in the aftermath as she headed from the grandstand to the rooms. Only two years earlier Troy had had an even nastier collision with Richmond's Alex Rance when they clashed heads chasing a loose ball on the MCG wing; he was also knocked out cold. Mum was on the spot then too.

I had done everything Brendan McCartney had taught me not to do, sliding front on to a loose ball without protecting myself. Ray's positioning was perfect, low and side on, but he was reported; the Match Review Panel cleared him of any intent. He would probably get suspended nowadays for a similar incident.

I came to in the rooms with medical staff looking over me with our welfare manager, Ron Watt, at my side. The doctors were worried about my jaw and sent me to the Epworth hospital in Richmond for scans, with Mum and Ron joining me there. Being clearly concussed meant I was ruled out of the game.

Unbeknown to me, Tom Petroro had been at Stride chairman Ian Foote's 60th birthday party when they were alerted to the knock I had copped. Concerned when he saw the vision, he grabbed Kathryn Cotsopoulos to visit me in the hospital. I didn't appreciate their concern or their effort to get to the hospital. 'What the fuck are you doing here?' I asked. 'I'm fucking fine. Isn't it Friday night?' Tom grinned and left. I rang him the next morning to apologise. He said I didn't have to but he now reckons it's the only time I have been genuinely rude to him. I doubt that but the memory makes him laugh.

My jaw was fine, not so my lip, which needed 15 stitches, but I was able to return to the MCG to sing the song with the boys. I doubt the stitches helped the melody! Darren Milburn, the sub who replaced me, had kicked the winning goal to give us a one-point win over the Saints in a game so dour, the scores were 48 to 47.

Ron Watt drove my car home while our club doctor, Geoff Allen, drove me to his beautiful hobby farm in Point Lonsdale so he could check on my condition through the night. I stayed in the spare room and cooked bacon and eggs in the morning while looking over Lake Victoria. Such a level of care was standard, but it still blows my mind what football staff do for players.

It was the first time I had been concussed but I passed all the tests and had no after-effects. I had no headaches or dizziness, which was the same in the only other two times I was concussed in my career. Michael Makdissi, an expert in concussion, then Hawthorn's medical officer, (and eventually the AFL's chief medical officer) conducted brain scans in Bundoora, the first of about half a dozen MRIs I had during my career.

I take the issue of head knocks and concussion seriously, so I do feel a little uncomfortable noting that I have not had any after-effects from my hits, because I know that is not everyone's experience. Whenever rules changed or training was modified to minimise the risk of head knocks, I supported the changes.

Despite the heavy hit against St Kilda I felt I could and should play the next week but the club, and those around me, were not about to let that happen. Tom Petroro even made a slightly nervous phone call to Balmey to ensure there was no thought of me playing. The club did keep the question of me playing open as they did not want to reveal the team to Fremantle, who we were playing in Perth. But no-one told me a decision had been made so I just assumed I was playing while they had assumed I knew I wouldn't be there.

That led to the farcical situation, where I drove to Tullamarine to jump on the plane with the team only to be told at the airport I wasn't playing. If there was a Cats game being played, I wanted to be playing in it. I suppose it showed that I had progressed from watching *The Footy Show* in 2007 to see whether I was in the team to assuming I was an automatic selection.

Unfortunately, I became something of a poster boy for head knocks, with Alastair Clarkson claiming erroneously in 2018 that I had had '10 concussions or thereabouts' during my career. Chris was quick to slam that claim as 'alternative facts'. Although I didn't doubt Clarko's intent was good, I was a bit annoyed as I still had plenty of life to live within football and beyond at jobs that would require my brain to function effectively!

Happily, I can say that I have finished my career with just three confirmed concussions and with a brain that is functioning well. One was in 2012, in a game in which Brisbane's tagger, Andrew Raines, was reported for striking me – he got a week – after we had a minor altercation where I threw a hand at him and he retaliated. I had the staggers but I do remember Jonathan Brown's booming voice advising me to get off the ground. The other hit was in round 14, 2017 against Fremantle at Kardinia Park. I lasted barely a minute before colliding with Hayden Ballantyne. It was a clean KO. Mum and Brit were worried as it was the first time I had been told to remain still on the ground while I was being assessed. I did end up running from the field and waved, reassuring them. I spent the rest of the game on the bench, in my tracksuit. Although, again, I felt fine, but no matter how I felt, the club made me miss the following week each time I was concussed.

* * *

After that one-point, last-gasp win over the Saints, Geelong won the next 12 matches which meant that Chris Scott had set a new record for most wins (13) before a loss by a first-year coach.

My form was good but my season was rudely interrupted after round 12 when the match review panel suspended me for four weeks for striking Hawthorn's Brent Guerra in the last quarter. If I pleaded guilty, the fixed suspension would have been reduced to three. The footage from behind the Punt Road goals was fuzzy and from long range. I had swung my arm around to get past Guerra as he blocked my space, a regular action, but connected with the side of his head. He left the ground with a perforated eardrum and did not return. It was my first suspension after 104 games, although there would be 13 more penalties to follow, including two for careless contact with the umpire. I finished my career with fines of $13,950 which, when added up, is no small amount of money wasted doing stupid things on the field. Each time one arrived, it gave Steve Hocking a good opportunity to tell me I should change my behaviour.

It was the fifth time in eight matches against the Hawks I had been involved in some sort of incident that led to an investigation or suspension. On three occasions I had been on the receiving end – a knee from Simon Taylor (he was suspended for two matches), front-on contact from Michael Osborne (one match suspension) and Jordan Lewis was investigated and cleared for striking me. I was clearly not that popular at the Hawks. The only other time I found trouble against the Hawks was in 2010 when I was investigated for striking my mate Xavier Ellis. I was cleared apparently due to the 'inconclusive nature of the video evidence' which was a bit harsh.

With the hit against Guerra I had nowhere to go and I would have been content to accept a three-week holiday. Neil Balme, however, never thought I had done enough to warrant a suspension. We went to the tribunal and tried to get the charge downgraded from intentional to reckless which would mean a two-week penalty. The plea failed and I missed the four games. My statement to the tribunal indicated my on-field mindset, however it's unlikely it helped my argument: 'You have to take into account what time of the game it is. Two minutes to go, game in the balance. You do anything to help your side win. That's the way I play. That's the way I always will play.'

It was the first time I had been reported or suspended since I began playing at the age of eight but I felt guilty when I rocked up to training that week as I felt, as vice-captain, I had let the side down by being unavailable. I was also shattered not to be playing. My form was good, the team was unbeaten, I was fit, fresh and about to enter my prime and was to miss a month of footy. Happily, there would only be one more suspension, in round 15, 2015, for rough conduct when controversy raged about a so-called chicken-wing tackle on North Melbourne's

Sam Wright. That incident did not look good but there was no intent and Wright accepted that I was not deliberately trying to hurt him.

The club wanted to turn the negative into a positive, so they sent me to Western Australia to trial a heat room at Curtin University they had their eyes on. Trav Varcoe's form was flat so he missed the round 15 loss to Essendon to join these sessions, with David Johnson and sports scientist Dr Simon Sostaric accompanying us. The idea was for us to train hard and reload for the second phase of the season. Collingwood – then favourites for the flag – already had a heat chamber in their facility on the Yarra.

We would enter the chamber and cycle furiously for anywhere between 70 and 100 minutes before training with South Fremantle in the afternoon. Trav and I were exhausted but it not only kept me occupied for 10 days, I was able to stay with Adam and spend time with Scott, as both were enjoying being part of the West Coast resurgence. The Eagles were on the way to a top-four finish and handed us our second successive defeat in round 16. It was the fourth week of my suspension and I could only watch from the sidelines while my brothers were playing. Our two straight losses saw Collingwood claim top spot for the first time since we had beaten them in round eight.

Whether it was the enforced break or the heat chamber work, I returned with a freshness that sustained me to the end of the season. Chris was remarkably calm during that period, just reinforcing our need to improve. Winning 13 consecutive games to start the season had given us strong belief in the system so two losses, each by less than 10 points, was seen as a minor blip. Chris was also resting players, keeping us fresh. None of us played every game that season. The match committee also made hard decisions on whether premiership-winning veterans Dasher Milburn and Cam Mooney would be in our best 22 at the end of the season, as both had been in and out of the side. Cam played only five of our first 17 games but returned to play against Melbourne in round 19 and kicked five goals in the famous 186-point victory.

It was an incredible win for us, the biggest winning margin in the club's history, but that weekend had not been easy for me. The night before the match, a person in the club who I was very close to had an accident. It was clearly a cry for help. I went to visit him, and we sat talking all night. We were both in tears for much of the time as I attempted to help him gain perspective on his situation. I was feeling his pain when I finally called it a night just before dawn and was able to grab only a couple of hours of broken sleep. I told Nigel Lappin the situation, so he had an eye out for me. I felt wrecked as I put on the jumper. I did not consider missing the game but my mind was anywhere but on the footy. In such moments my muscle memory kicks in and so does my competitiveness. I figured someone has been preparing to play on me all week and now they are going to get me after I had so little sleep. That was just the challenge I needed. How would I perform under such adversity? I also knew that I couldn't let the team down.

It's no surprise, given the score line, that everything went right for us. It was like we had the ball on remote control, and it had to be in a Geelong player's hands. We were ruthless. When I went to the bench with about four minutes to go, I had racked up

39 disposals. Nigel heard the stat via the headphones connecting the bench to the coach's box. He told me to get back out there and try to make it 40. In one passage of play I managed four disposals and left the ground with 43. It had been one hell of a 24 hours. The experience would help me during my captaincy as I learnt that I could compartmentalise my life and keep doing the job I needed to do as a player.

In the leadership group you are often made aware of things happening away from the field that could affect our performance if we let it. I didn't steel myself to 'just get through it' in the future as I had that weekend. That would be leaving too much to chance and would not be healthy either. I eventually learnt that when issues affecting me and others needed to be resolved, it was best to rely on experts rather than thinking it was my job to resolve everything. That took time and was not without mistakes as I did not always adhere to that philosophy, but it eventually did sink in.

The game also taught me that rigid preparation was not always possible. What *was* possible was that I could switch on as soon as I dragged the jumper over my head. Eventually the assistants would refer to me as Sir William Wallace, the hero of the Mel Gibson film *Braveheart*, when they saw me put on the jumper and joke whether I would be able to go over the hill one more time. They knew that was my cue to put all aside and concentrate on the game. It became a habit for me. They thought that trait was remarkable.

* * *

Cam Mooney made a tough decision on his future easier when he was suspended in round 21 for front-on contact with Adelaide's Graham Johncock. A week later he announced his intention to retire at the end of the season. The Crows' contest proved to be the last of his 221 games and Hawk and James Podsiadly became our twin towers in attack. Moons always looked out for me after I arrived at the club, and he always spoke his mind. He did cop some backlash – externally – through his career for the odd mistake, but the group learnt as much as he did from those errors. He was a focal point in two flags and stood tall. Dasher Milburn had battled an Achilles all season but came in for the final round, a dead rubber against Collingwood that would eventually prove significant. It was to be the last of his 292 games – then the third highest games tally at the Cats. After being named an emergency in the Grand Final, he too announced his retirement.

We headed into the Collingwood game after our 29-game winning streak at Kardinia Park came to an end with a loss to Sydney. It was only my second loss at the venue and my first there since the club's turning point loss to North Melbourne in round five 2007. I would eventually end my career with 97 wins in 111 games at Kardinia Park at the ridiculous winning record of 87 per cent.

There was no uncertainty in our mind heading into that last round about how to approach the match. We had been searching for constant improvement all year whereas Collingwood had been waiting for the finals. They appeared concerned about preservation as we played the near-perfect game to win by 96 points. We knew we were in good form whereas the Magpies had some injury worries and were looking at each other, wondering what to make of us, a team they must have thought they had buried once and for all a year earlier in that preliminary final thrashing.

We lost Dan Menzel to an unfortunate knee injury in the qualifying final against Hawthorn – a rare five-goal margin over the Hawks – and then defeated West Coast easily at the MCG in the preliminary final. I carried a broken knuckle into that game after suffering what I thought was a bruised hand or burst blood vessel when laying a tackle in the qualifying final. There was no thought I wouldn't play but it did make cooling down after the two finals slightly uncomfortable.

The preliminary final was my first final against my brothers Adam and Scott. It didn't seem different until I found myself matched up against Adam inside our forward-50 late in the game. I told him I'd love the ball to come down with the forward 50 vacant apart from the two of us so I could show him a clean pair of heels. I'm not sure he appreciated the comment, but I reckon he was happy the ball didn't come near us.

Scott had tagged me and although he suspected I had a break in my hand he decided to try to beat me in a way he would describe as being ethical. I asked him later why he had not tried to punch my hand and he said he wanted to beat me fair and square. He was also conscious of the fallout from a battle between St Kilda's Steven Baker and Stevie Johnson a year earlier when Baker targeted Stevie's hand and copped a nine-match suspension, the accumulation of three charges of striking Stevie and one of 'unnecessary contact with an injured player'. I told him if I'd been him, I'd have smashed into the hand at every chance I got. He was a little shocked at the lengths I would go to win.

Stevie also hurt his knee after trying to gather a loose handball from me (I blame the busted hand!). He declared himself fit to play against Collingwood in the Grand Final after the Magpies had beaten the Hawks in the preliminary final. We only found out later the lengths he went to to convince the coach he was right. The leadership group did not need to emphasise to him what was at stake – we knew he understood that it wasn't just a case of him being out there, he needed to perform.

I'm not sure whether I am wired differently or whether I was used to big games by then, but I had no nerves going into the match. I drove Mitch Duncan and Allen Christensen – both three years younger than me – to the game and we kept the mood light-hearted, although Meatloaf's pre-game performance ensured laughs weren't hard to find.

Chris's message to the players was simple. He said the result would hinge on our ability to win contests, which suited me. Two Grand Final wins out of three had not been bad but three out of four would be much better.

At the opening bounce Brad Ottens, who had been caught snoozing through the midfield meeting the day before, shovelled the ball to me and I handballed to Trav Varcoe, who kicked the first goal of the Grand Final after just 15 seconds, and he followed with another three minutes later. After four minutes, we had had four shots on goal, with behinds by Stevie Johnson and James Podsiadly. Collingwood responded quickly, and it was four goals apiece at quarter-time. Jimmy Bartel and I kicked crucial goals just before half-time, my second for the half. We were hanging in against a formidable opponent.

Collingwood led narrowly at half-time before Hawk put in a match-turning quarter with three goals, while Tom Lonergan was able to quell Travis Cloke after the big Magpie had kicked three goals in the first half. He was on top of Harry Taylor after Harry had copped a knock to the head. Hawk's goal late in the third quarter gave us a seven-point lead into the last break, and we soon broke the shackles, with five unanswered goals. Trav's third, giving us a 21-point lead, was the final straw for the Magpies. I have no doubt our stint in Perth helped the two of us perform well. We were both running on top of the ground. Cameron Ling kicked the last goal of the match in what would be the last of his 246 games. Brad Ottens would also end his great career after 245 games.

Hawk and I had played in a premiership in 2009 and he had kicked a big goal in the last quarter of that win, but this flag was different. He wanted to be the man at that point and although we did not know it then, he would prove to be a big-game performer. His contested marks and goals made a big statement. I saw his performance as an 'up yours' to the doubters more than he did. He had done it hard during the early phase of his career and although I was never defensive of him publicly, I supported him in any way I could, even if it was just keeping him busy.

The club had been encouraging throughout, but there were times Hawk had to sit through some tough peer assessments via Leading Teams when other young players were spared. The sessions were supportive with his teammates telling him they believed in him, but he would need to change a few things to make the grade. That just meant becoming a little more professional in his habits, moving from being a schoolboy footballer to an elite

AFL player. We wanted him to get there quickly because we saw how he could make us better on and off the field. His character was exceptional but a harder edge was needed.

I was happy to finish runner-up to Jimmy Bartel in the Norm Smith Medal voting with nine votes but even more excited to have a third premiership medallion. I had now played in four Grand Finals for three flags in my first 114 games. Fifteen of those games had been finals and I had won a best and fairest and been All-Australian three times. For all that, I just felt fortunate to be part of such a great club. The win was also confirmation that the choice of Chris as coach was inspired. The club had certainly chosen the right man to lead us into another era.

Chapter 9

Tackling tacklers

FOR AT LEAST two weeks of every season from 2009, my ability to earn free kicks – or, more specifically, free kicks for head-high contact – made my playing style the subject of intense debate. These annual conversations just became part of my year. It didn't worry me nor deter me from playing the way I did.

I entered the discussion only once, in 2012. I saw no value in trying to convince opposition supporters that I thought it was unreasonable to dislike me because of the head-high free kicks I received. I wasn't deliberately trying to annoy them, and the fans were entitled to their opinion.

And I *had* thought about it. I wasn't just being stubborn. As a junior I could generally break tackles as my legs were strong and my body was often harder than my opponent's.

In the AFL my ability to win head-high free kicks was more obvious as I wouldn't always burst through the tackle, instead I would need to manoeuvre my body to break the tackle, and that was always my first intent. That movement would often lead to the opponent catching me high and the free kick would be mine. I was also tackled more than most as I was in congestion more often, trying to win the ball and to find space.

I did note what was being said and who was saying it because I have always believed there might be something to learn from the commentary about the game. It was also reassuring to hear some of the game's best former players – Leigh Matthews, Michael Voss, Wayne Carey – assess what I was doing in a way that was consistent with my thoughts on the issue. It was also satisfying to hear respected former opponents such as Nick Riewoldt, Leigh Montagna and Jordan Lewis support my style after they left the game for careers in the media. In 2021 Montagna said on Triple M: 'I have a strong view on it. I think Joel Selwood shrugs,' he said. 'He shrugs to legitimately break a tackle.'

It didn't take me long to recognise I could gain an advantage over my opposition by exploiting the difficult skill of tackling. And, in my opinion, tackling is the worst executed skill in football. That isn't because players aren't good at tackling. It's just difficult to run 12 or 15 kilometres in a game and also execute such a technical skill when an opponent, with the whole ground to work with, is carrying the ball and running quickly at you or away from you. I identified this as a real weakness in our game and took advantage of that. I prided myself on knowing the rule book better than most and I knew exactly what the umpires were expected to adjudicate when it came to head-high contact. As a competitive professional, knowing every angle mattered.

As a midfielder I was getting first look at the ball at most stoppages. This would put opponents on the back foot if I kept moving. As I kept running with the intent of dishing off the ball or finding space, I could also lower my centre of gravity and draw opponents to me. If they got hold of me, we would be in a test of strength as I wriggled my strong core and arms, giving me an advantage.

I would be stronger than most tacklers and could use my body to make them stand up in a tackle. Paddy Dangerfield would tell our group consistently that we needed to be stronger than the tackler after Chris Scott would throw him a Dorothy Dixer every now and again asking him what's your theory on tackling again? Paddy's responses only reinforced my belief.

Sydney midfielder Brett Kirk – a prolific tackler and superior tagger – was the only opponent who never seemed to get me high because he was wearing me so tight at the start. He was also so strong you couldn't wriggle to put him in a position of vulnerability.

My technique was similar to West Coast's champion midfielder Daniel Kerr. As a teenager I often watched Daniel play but I did not set out to replicate his style. We had a similar nuggety build – and it was clear to see how he would roll out of a tackle and move on to the next play. That was just what I was trying to do unless the game needed to be slowed down and that was rare as our game was based on moving the ball quickly. In simple terms I put the onus on the tackler, who would often get 95 per cent right but then muck up the last five per cent – to my advantage.

Occasionally a tackle would finish with a head lock that would linger if I had received a free kick. I could only manage a wry smile as I thought I had an edge on an opponent if I saw him getting angry. I know I performed less effectively when angry. I was better off carrying a steely resolve and focusing only on the next context.

Not everyone believed my approach was fair but those commentators who were critical of the tactic didn't seem to know the rules as well as I did despite being educated on them each season. They chose opinion over the Laws of the Game. I kept on top of any changes and modified my game accordingly. Such commentary bugged me occasionally but what annoyed me most was that the umpires adjudicated to the letter of the law until controversy erupted. Then, for a period, it seemed they would move away from the rule book, apparently to satisfy the loudest voices.

We were never coached to lead with the head or seek a free kick; we players were taught to evade tackles. Clubs would also complain to the AFL about my free-kick count and I could understand that because sometimes their players did not seem to receive the same treatment as me. Champion Data statistics showed the discrepancy, as I was awarded 459 head-high free kicks between 2007-2022. The next best during that period was West Coast's Luke Shuey (177), then Richmond's Trent Cotchin (154), Carlton's Marc Murphy (148) and my brother Adam (145). But none of that was my fault.

My attitude was that the opposition needed to shift their approach more than me. The more successful clubs did. In recent years they have concentrated more on applying pressure than laying a perfect tackle. Richmond players, for instance, would be on top of you so quickly with their pressure game, you would feel the need to dispose of the ball quickly. That was exactly what they wanted because when they did tackle, they often conceded a free kick.

In recent seasons, a new generation of players have started to gain a high number of head-highfree kicks by falling diagonally under their opponent's arms. I was as worried about that style creeping into our game as much as everyone else, but I did not see my style as the same. I saw mine as a roll whereas those who grabbed the ball and fell into the tackle could only achieve two things: win a free kick or a ball-up. Continuous play was not their style. But I became the poster boy for those receiving high numbers of head-high free kicks even though the way they were being earned was different. Unfortunately, few could see the difference.

I was not perfect. I am sure there will be footage of me falling into a tackle in the same manner as that 'modern' generation, but it was not a regular feature of my method when tackled. At one stage I got into a bad habit of reaching my arm skywards to push the opponent's arm to my neck and make it obvious to everyone what had happened. But I tried to remove that from my game as I wasn't proud of it and I think I did that successfully by modifying my technique. Chris Scott believed in my style of play. He and others I trusted would have advised me if they thought what I was doing was bad for the game.

I am all for the AFL's initiatives to protect the head but as each new iteration of the rules was released, I studied them closely to understand what they meant and how to play within them. Perhaps younger players thought they could replicate what I was doing to get a free kick and came up with a different version. I did not want any new version of slipping a tackle to be dangerous.

Now that I have retired it will be interesting to watch whether the Laws relating to head-high tackles continue to evolve, and whether commentators will do more to understand how the players work on their methods when tackled. It will also be interesting to see whether my analysis, as an observer, will differ when no longer at the heart of the action!

Chapter 10

New deal, new job

AFTER THE 2011 flag, the club locked me into a five-year deal. The local press reported I was the first player at the club to gain a deal of that length since Gary Ablett Senior in 1987. The negotiations were complicated but essentially cooperative. Tom Petroro and our football manager, Neil Balme, had a bit of a puzzle to solve: how to lock in a long-term deal without knowing what the salary cap would be beyond 2011 as a new CBA was being negotiated. They arrived at a fair figure for the 2011 season and agreed that I should remain in the upper level of total player payments during the next phase of my career. To achieve that goal, they needed to be innovative. As a consequence, I became one of the few players in the League who had their salary tied to a percentage of the club's total player payments. Tom workshopped the idea and Balmey ended up applying the formula to other players after he left the Cats at the end of the 2014 season.

Other parts of my contract weren't without controversy as the AFL began to get twitchy about third-party deals and had just halted a deal between Carlton's Chris Judd and Visy. I had an approved third-party deal with the Costa Property Group which saw my image appear on billboards promoting the company. I also met occasionally with the company's founder and chair, Frank Costa, discussing leadership. He and I would share our understanding of leadership. Frank was one of the Geelong footy club's most significant figures, leading the place from 1999 until he handed over to Colin Carter at the end of 2010. The Costa deal was similar to others across the AFL but they were now making headlines. I was a little upset that my integrity was being questioned because this arrangement had been approved by the AFL, and I also thought the League was missing an important issue in their crackdown. In my view they should have been encouraging companies to use players in promotions as long as any deals were transparent and policed appropriately. Even though the amount of the Costa deal was insignificant relative to the rest of my contract, such a deal did put money in players' pockets while also broadening the game's branding. In the end, we had to abide by the League's ruling: that such a deal impacted the integrity of the salary cap and could not happen.

There were other matters in which Tom Pretroro had to stand up for me after the AFL backflipped on rules they had set in ways that affected my contract. Geelong's huge apparel company Cotton On was about to fund a community program which I would be paid to work in and to promote as well. Tom asked the AFL for advice and was told to implement what they called an 'employment arrangement'. Based on that advice we went ahead with the arrangement with Cotton On but again the AFL became nervous about it and said it could not continue. Away from the spotlight Tom, and Stride, battled the AFL on this issue for years as a matter of principle. In the end rather than going to a grievance procedure, an independent QC was appointed to adjudicate on the matter, receiving submissions from us and the AFL. The file read 'Joel Arbitration'. The QC decided our deal was within the rules and had also been constructed after AFL advice. We had a win.

* * *

Just before the players were set to vote on who should replace Cameron Ling as captain, Chris Scott grabbed me in the corridor. He didn't waste words. 'You're going to be captain. I just want you to know that.' There was always a vote but that was as much for the coaching staff to get a feel for the group and who was influential as it was to determine our captain. The club's leaders always made the final call with a recommendation from the executive to the board. It was a whirlwind from there. I managed just a few words to the group saying how humbled I was before I found myself facing a hastily convened media conference.

I had learnt plenty from being in the leadership group since 2009 and had been mentioned as a future captain for some time but actually becoming captain presented a new challenge. Tom Petroro knew that too. In his meetings with the club, he had stressed that they couldn't throw me to the wolves, particularly with such decorated players as teammates. The football club and the coach were aware of that too and were also conscious of my age. I had just turned 23 and they knew I was rawer than I felt.

Chris Scott had a sense of what lay ahead for me, having been a teammate of the great Michael Voss when he became a co-captain alongside Alastair Lynch at the Brisbane Lions in 1997 at just 21. Vossy made the leap after just 79 games and five seasons; I had played 114 games in five seasons. Chris had only been my coach for one year and he needed to be certain too that the captaincy would not weigh down my performance nor that I would be negatively caught up in club politics when hard decisions were being made, particularly with the likely transition of the list. He needed to be confident that these issues would not fall on my shoulders.

Part of my preparation for the role had included a long chat over coffee in Sydney in 2010 with Tom Harley, who had moved north to take up the role as general manager of AFL NSW/ACT. He told me I was ready, and he reminded me to be myself. His words carried weight as although I had been touted as the next captain after Lingy, it was a relief to hear he believed in me. I was also keen to pick his brains about the role and what actually came with it. I peppered him with all sorts of questions, ranging from dealing with the board to dealing with supporters. I also knew that most of my authority would stem from my on-field performance. A high level had to be maintained as I knew I would be more a players' captain than an all-encompassing club captain at that stage.

The other question the club needed to resolve was not whether I would be an effective skipper but whether my senior teammates would support me unconditionally as any captain relies heavily on such support to be successful. I had not spoken to Jimmy Bartel, who was named vice-captain, Matt Scarlett, 'Boris' Enright, James Kelly or Joel Corey to get their thoughts but I suspected Neil Balme or Steve Hocking had. I later learnt that they had and were confident my teammates were happy for me to gain the title. As well as Jimmy, the new leadership group was Kelly, Corey, Boris, Harry Taylor and Stevie Johnson. I always felt those teammates had my back.

Playing in three premierships carried weight, but these guys' approach showed the club-first mentality they carried was strong. I said little to the players or the media when the appointment was announced, keeping things short and sweet. It was January and I wanted to train rather than talk too much. My predecessors had laid a solid foundation, and now I needed to follow their lead.

That was easier said than done, as I found out just one match into the new season. Matt Scarlett – nine seasons and 154 games more experienced than me – had punched Fremantle's Hayden Ballantyne after the cheeky forward sledged him for being run down in a tackle. Scarlo landed an old-fashioned left jab to the jaw that felled the cheeky Docker. Despite the provocation, it was an undisciplined act and cost him – and us – three weeks.

After his suspension I thought to myself, 'I'm going to have to chat to him about that.' Such an act sat outside our trademark culture. Early the next week I found myself in the computer room reviewing a game. Scarlo was nearby doing his game edits alone. I thought, 'This is my moment' and approached him.

'Hi mate, is everything okay?' I said. 'Yeah, what do you mean?' he replied. I thought: 'You know exactly what I mean' but I said: 'You know, on the weekend'. He was short with me again. I left it at that and thought ruefully: 'Okay, Balmey or Hock can deal with this.'

He wasn't being disrespectful, although some might interpret his reaction as such. It was just his way. He knew he had done the wrong thing and was smart enough and experienced enough to work that out himself. He knew the side needed him as we had lost narrowly to Fremantle and had a tough run ahead with Hawthorn, North Melbourne and Richmond to come.

His response, or lack of it, reminded me the title of captain is not everything, but it did not make the exchange any easier. I had hoped to gain some confidence in my captaincy by dealing successfully with Scarlo on such an important matter, but I had failed. I gained zero. I moved on quickly, as I reminded myself of something that I had learnt early in my career: if a player does something wrong, he has let the club down (and probably himself) rather than it being anything personal against the captain or a teammate. Most of the time the guilty party knows it too.

That realisation stopped me from feeling any bitterness towards a teammate if they messed up, although I was capable of telling them what I thought. It just limited my involvement to what was needed from me, nothing more, nothing less. Most of the time I left it to experts to deal with tricky matters even if my natural inclination early on was for me to think I could fix any issue that arose.

That philosophy meant eventually I would only lay awake at night worrying about an upcoming game. Rarely did a situation that had arisen which might have caused the club some embarrassment, or even cost us, sit in my mind for too long. My main responsibility was to be a good teammate.

Again, that theory was good, but I wasn't always right in my judgement nor did I stick with my philosophy every time. I had to mature quickly – only six players in our opener against Fremantle were younger than me; I knew I was nowhere near the finished product. At times it stuck in my craw if a person did not act in a way that I thought was appropriate and sometimes I made that known.

I was far from perfect myself. Chris said publicly I was lucky to escape without penalty after I tangled with the Brisbane Lions' tagger Andrew Raines in round five, just a month after thinking I needed to speak to Scarlo about his on-field indiscretion.

* * *

My temper on the field was also being discussed in the media, and Chris admitted the way I responded to defensive tactics was something I needed to address. Behind closed doors his approach was more subtle but effective. He would say to me in an offhand manner: 'If you want to be a wrestler, go be a wrestler'. It was clear which one held more promise as a career.' Stone Cold Steve Austin, the pro wrestler, I was not. Occasionally Chris would ask me directly why I was engaging in off-the-ball battles as this was playing into the opposition's hands. Chris had played the game hard during his time with the Lions and he knew about temper. He also knew how important it was to the team for tempers to be controlled. My on-field actions were hurting the team and I had to temper my behaviour. Understanding the bigger picture became something I had to consider and develop in order to lead effectively.

In such discussions I was generally good at hiding any initial, sometimes emotional, reaction if I did not agree with a decision or if a comment riled me. Pausing allowed me to reflect on my response and then provide one from a measured perspective.

If I needed to talk over an issue with someone I trusted I would do so; if I then needed to talk it through with those responsible for the decision, I would do that too, regardless of whether or not they had a title or a leadership position. Chris was also very good at never becoming adversarial in his dealings with me. Our conversations could be robust but never disrespectful.

Chapter 11

Leading and learning

STEVIE JOHNSON NOT only joined me in the midfield for 2012, he also joined the leadership group for the first time. Like me, he had a killer instinct, wanting to win everything.

That's why I had laughed so hard when I polled the three Brownlow votes for my 43 touches in our round 19 thrashing of Melbourne in 2011. Stevie had picked up 34 disposals, kicked seven goals, had 10 goal-assists and 21 scoring involvements. As the round's votes were about to be called out, he sat back, rubbed his hands and announced he had a certain three votes coming up. 'Money in the bank,' he said. When Andrew Demetriou called: 'Geelong, S. Johnson, two votes.' I could not stop laughing when Demetriou then read out: 'Geelong, J. Selwood, three votes.'

Although he was not from the same mould as me, Stevie was a great teammate because he made you think differently about the way the game was played. That didn't mean he couldn't also be a pain when he wanted to play on his terms. I eventually came to realise it was simply because his mind ran quicker than anyone else's. Sometimes I would take matters up with him but he was not only a 'bush physio' when it came to fitness issues, he was a 'bush lawyer' too and he would passionately defend what he had done. I grew to love the way he could argue his way out of anything because he would present his case in a manner that made me smile. Any frustration I might have would melt under his charm. Watching and hearing him backing himself to the hilt made him fun to engage with and also led to him convincing others that his round-the-corner kick was a safer bet in front of goal. He was a genuine X-factor who energised me and the group.

I had a habit of asking him, just as we were about to run onto the field, what I should say to the boys in the pre-game huddle. He would always respond as though I had caught him on the hop and his first two words were inevitably: 'Fuck, fuck.' It was a good pre-game routine for me.

Fact was, I didn't need to say much. We weren't a ranting and raving group. Our focus was to rock up and kill the game early. But by 2012 there were signs that routine was going to become harder. We just weren't as talented or as strong as we had been. Brad Ottens, Cameron Ling, Cameron Mooney and Darren Milburn retired at the end of 2011. Daniel Menzel had done his knee. David Wojcinski would play only four games due to injury and suspension. Gary Ablett was at the Gold Coast.

We needed to find a way to defy gravity under the AFL's competitive balance rules and transform the list on the run. Chris Scott saw trading players and taking advantage of free agency as the best way to do that. He had seen what occurred after the Lions' golden era and was acutely aware of how hard it would be for me to play through the final years of my career without the chance of success. List management became a key part of the strategy.

For the first time in my career I became involved in speaking to players about potentially joining Geelong as free agency had changed the paradigm. It turned out to be an embarrassing failure at the first hurdle, when we decided to make a play for Port Adelaide's star midfielder, Travis Boak. I had known Travis all my career. He was a Torquay boy who had toured Ireland with me as a junior. We had been drafted in the same year, me at seven, Travis at five, and we both played in a Grand Final in our first season. Trav's mum and my mum had become friends. Tom Petroro was also his manager. At 23, with 90 games under his belt and clear leadership skills, he was exactly the type of player we could do with at Geelong.

We thought he would be worth a visit in July, after Port Adelaide had been well beaten by Essendon at Docklands and we had lost to Collingwood at the MCG. The aim was to convince him to return 'home'. The task fell to me, Chris, Stephen Wells and Jimmy Bartel. I was wearing a tracksuit bottom on the early flight to Adelaide because I was recovering from a corkie as we headed to meet Travis *in secret*, realising when we were door-stopped before we had left Adelaide airport that we had created a media storm through pure naivety. Tom Petroro was having a quiet Sunday in the garden when his phone began ringing off the hook.

We met Trav in his apartment, and we sensed within five minutes of talking, he was not about to move.

* * *

Our year had become a battle as we sat sixth, a game and percentage inside the top eight. Hawthorn were second, a game behind Sydney, as we faced them in round 19, another Friday night blockbuster at the MCG. We kicked our ninth highest first quarter score ever as we jumped the Hawks with 9.3 to 2.0 in the first quarter. We looked certain to stretch our eight-match winning streak against the Hawks.

But the reason we respected the Hawks so much during that era was because not only were they talented, they never gave up. They dropped to 51 points down early in the second quarter before the momentum shifted, slowly but steadily, with Sam Mitchell the architect of the change. They were still 19 points behind at the last change but Brad Sewell put them in front with less than five minutes remaining. They looked to have won the game when they led by eight points. Tom Hawkins then snapped a goal to cut the margin to two points and the game was again up for grabs, with about four minutes to play.

In such moments, my game sense peaked and I took any opportunity on offer. One arose when I noticed Mitchell had blood on his face as a result of a clash between us that had led to a stoppage in their forward 50 with less than a minute remaining. I wanted him off, so pointed at Mitchell and yelled, 'Blood, blood' to the umpire. He blew the whistle and a reluctant Mitchell dawdled to the bench to be off for the key play. They still won the clearance and we were lucky not to be penalised for holding the ball but when Paul Puopolo made a mistake deep in their forward line – Clarkson would admonish him post-game for his attempt to kick the ball in mid-air – we regained possession. The always cool Andrew Mackie scrubbed a kick to Mitch Duncan who found Stevie Johnson. We knew there was not much time left. My running pattern in such situations was through the middle and I knew Stevie was always going to the corridor so was ready as he swung on to his left foot and found me. Hawk also knew I would play on, so he charged forward on the lead. The only calculation he needed to make was whether he would be in range when he marked, which he did with 23 seconds remaining.

Hawk and I ended up playing 305 games together, but our on-field connection was already entrenched, in this our sixth season. I always looked out for him. At times I probably did it too much but it worked most times, so why wouldn't I? Richmond's David Astbury once told Hawk he could not believe the amount of times Mitch Duncan or myself would hit up Hawk on the lead because there were so many times when the defender appeared to have him covered. But we would find a way. According to Champion Data, Hawk marked 90 of my kicks inside 50 in 2007–2022, second behind Richmond pair Dustin Martin and Jack Riewoldt, who found each other 95 times. Mitch Duncan sought out Hawk 81 times inside 50 ranking that duo third in the game during my career. I also had 49 goal-assists to Hawk in our 305 games together, seven behind the Martin–Riewoldt combination (56) and three ahead of the Duncan–Hawkins duo (46).

I was confident in my skill to deliver a kick to the right place and the right time for Hawk to mark. One of my strengths was staying balanced and getting the ball to boot quickly, and I could usually find him regardless of what was going on around me. My kicking technique was also sound. I kept myself compact and although I could not kick long distances, I prided myself on hitting targets and kicking to a teammate's advantage.

Hawk kicked the winning goal after the siren with a magnificent kick from well outside 50. That passage of play remains one of my favourite football memories. The winning streak over the Hawks had now stretched to nine and we knew Kennett's curse must have felt a little too real for our opponents.

The headlines kept following me however and I also upset Mum the next week when I pushed my brother Adam into the ground after he came off second-best when he tried to bump me into the fifth row at Subiaco as I kicked the ball from just inside the boundary. I bounced back from the clash of heads, while Adam was on all fours, trying to get his breath. I pushed him off-balance and just kept running. I was already angry at the world after watching Hawk get carried off on a stretcher earlier when his head hit the ground after he flew for a mark, but it was like Adam and I were back on our backyard tennis court although Adam would have been doing the pushing then.

Adam's role had been to limit our impact if we were able to run out the front of a stoppage. He said he had imagined the potential thrill of running down or running through either myself or Troy in front of his home crowd so did not hesitate in trying to stop me. Unfortunately, in 20 seconds that dream had been dashed. He tried to argue he would have the upper hand if the same incident occurred another 99 times but eventually, he had to concede I had won the mini battle that time.

We ended up losing the match by five points. There were plenty of suggestions bouncing around that I should be suspended for the push. When I sat down for breakfast the next day with Adam and Scott, who had tagged me in the match, the egg on my forehead as a result of the head clash was the only sore point between us.

Scott admitted I had outpointed him at the stoppage and out of the corner of his eye he had seen Adam and I clash as Adam tried to halt my progress. Scott conceded that his first thought when he saw a body on the deck was: 'I hope that's Joel.' Scott had then ribbed Adam at half-time telling him he was twice my size and therefore should be less affected by the bump. All Adam could respond with at the time was that it was a pretty big hit.

I was eventually reprimanded after taking the pragmatic course and pleading guilty to the charge of making 'unnecessary or unreasonable contact with an injured player' so I would not miss a match. I made light of the situation on social media, posting my headshot with the caption: 'Egg on head but I'll live. Nothing's changed, Adam is soft! :) #getupquickernexttime'.

Unfortunately, the loss would prove costly as it meant we missed out on finishing top-four, finishing sixth, even though we won our last four games, including a win over eventual premier Sydney in the last round when we lost Stevie Johnson to a week's suspension, for rough conduct against Dan Hannebery. We were now in the first elimination final of my career, against Fremantle at the MCG.

We started favourites but the Dockers jumped us to lead by 38 points early in the second quarter after they had 15 scoring shots to our one – a behind! It began an unfortunate pattern for us of starting slowly in finals but also signalled the arrival of Fremantle under Ross Lyon. They were too good. So, in my first season as skipper, we were out after week one, our lowest finish in six seasons.

Chapter 12

A near miss

MY WILLINGNESS TO run at the ball without deviating saw me being categorised as a player whose game was based on will and courage. At the end of 2012 I was named the AFL's Most Courageous Player at the AFL Players Association awards for a second time. Images of me with blood dripping down my face entrenched my reputation but the fact was my crepe-paper skin tore easily. I was forced from the ground due to the blood rule 14 times in my first three seasons as skipper. The bandages swathed around my head made me look fearless.

I fuelled the perception that my game was built on brawn, when I told the *Herald Sun* in 2011: 'I am not a pretty footballer. I am slow. I don't kick it as well as the good kicks. I am what you would say an olden-day footballer in so many ways.' In reality it indicated my thinking that I needed to work harder than most for my talent to be realised.

I was embarrassed that I was considered more courageous than my peers, but I believed I could be the best player in the game. Despite what I told the *Herald Sun*, I knew my skills were better than most and I would continue to work on the basics four times a week. I trained with an intensity and consistency few matched as I loved that part of being a footballer. I was not lightning quick, but I was hard to knock over which was part of the reason I could hunt the ball with such ferocity.

My biggest strength was an ability to take clean possession of ground balls at pace and remain balanced enough no matter the attention around me and then offload a clean disposal. I had done so many touch sessions to become quick by hand and foot while remaining compact, and that skill made me hard to tackle. My coaches also rated my decision-making ability, an intangible to many spectators but something AFL players emphasise as separating the best from the very best. I understood the game well but I never saw myself as having the same football nous as someone like Collingwood's Scott Pendlebury. I rated Scott, Sam Mitchell and Jimmy Bartel as the best decision-makers in my time. They knew where to put themselves to impact games and did it over their whole career. I evaluated a player's ability to control the tempo of a game when they had the ball as a strong indicator of their decision-making capacity, even more than whether they made the right call on where to pass or kick the ball. Watching Pendlebury take a kick-in is a great example. Most would want him up the ground to receive but he can set up a passage of play with that first action, as he did when Collingwood ran the ball from end to end to beat Essendon after the siren in round 19, 2022.

During my teen years, athletics helped build my reflexes, springing from the blocks and uncoiling over hurdles. My awareness of my opponents and capacity to react quickly to in-game situations helped too as it allowed me to be that little bit ahead of an opponent as they looked to make contact. That helped me appear harder at the ball than anything else.

I was by no means arrogant about such talents because I understood that many people in the community were highly skilled in their chosen field. I was supremely confident in my football ability. I had also carried a monomaniacal approach to improvement from the moment I set myself to play AFL. As I entered the 2013 season, aged 24 with 135 games' experience, I was also relishing the responsibility I felt as skipper to stand up when the game got tough.

The early exit from 2012 had given us a chance to freshen up and we bounced back hard, winning 10 of the first 11 with the only loss coming in round eight against Collingwood. I began the year in good form, performing well in two comeback wins against Hawthorn (that winning streak had now reached double figures) and North Melbourne.

I could feel my game was blossoming, and I sometimes experienced a feeling within games that is hard to describe. I felt as though I could do anything I wanted to have an impact on the game – an invincibility combined with instinct. I could also stay relaxed while in the moment. I never got tired. I was hardened and 30 minutes of football would fly by. Having taggers attracted to Stevie Johnson more often than to me also gave me the freedom to run and play the game on my terms. I began kicking goals too, finishing the home-and-away season with 30, and I was equal third in the AFL for score-assists. It wasn't hard to be infected with the score-assists bug that had started under Bomber Thompson.

We eventually finished the season in second place, behind Hawthorn after we had fallen in against the Brisbane Lions in the final round, winning by a point after we had led by 20 points at three-quarter-time. The Lions had given us some trouble that season, clawing back a 52-point deficit late in the third quarter in round 13 to win, after an Ashley McGrath goal after the siren. It was the sort of unfathomable loss we began to experience for the first time since 2006.

After many years agitating for a home final, the AFL relented and forced the third-placed Dockers to play the qualifying final at Kardinia Park. We had beaten Fremantle by 41 points – at Kardinia Park – in our only clash for the year, and we thought we could not lose even after Hawk missed due to a back complaint on game day and the disappointment Paul Chapman struggled to hide when he was made sub in what was to be his 250th game. (Chapman would eventually replace Corey Enright when the veteran was injured).

The joint was rocking with an ebullient and confident local crowd celebrating having such an occasion in their region. It felt as though people were squeezed into parts of the stadium previously unused and the sound was different too – more guttural in its roar when we ran out.

We started well enough to open up a 20-point lead on the defensive Dockers early in the second quarter, but they were well-drilled and had big Aaron Sandilands standing in front of us every time we looked to move the ball.

Big Sandy always seemed to play well against us, and he started to dominate at stoppages as we began to tighten up. After Stevie Johnson had managed 12 first-quarter touches, the Dockers' chief niggler Ryan Crowley tightened up and restricted him to eight in the final three quarters. The Dockers also kept kicking regular goals, and we could not break their squeeze. Five unanswered goals saw them take a ten-point lead just before half-time, and although it was pretty much goal-for-goal through the third quarter, Fremantle dominated the last quarter, keeping us to just five behinds.

Stephen Hill sealed the deal when he came off the bench, took five bounces and goaled to stretch their lead to 16 points with less than 90 seconds remaining. To describe that loss as deflating would be an understatement. We had won our previous 14 at home, and 43 of our previous 44 matches at Kardinia Park, but lost our one and only final at the venue.

Port Adelaide, who had come off an impressive four-goal win over Collingwood in the elimination final, jumped us in the semi-final at the MCG and we trailed by 23 points at half-time. Just as we looked like being eliminated, we lifted to win by 16 points.

But the cost of playing an extra week was high, and our 2011 Norm Smith medallist and big-game dynamo Paul Chapman – who had played well in the semi-final win – was suspended for the preliminary final against the Hawks after arriving late to bump the Power's Robbie Gray.

We entered the preliminary final with a winning streak of 11 over the Hawks since the 2008 Grand Final and 'Chappy' had played in every one of those victories. Both he and the injured

Corey Enright were missing but our confidence was as high as it could be as we entered our sixth preliminary final in seven years. Hawthorn had lost a Grand Final and preliminary final in the previous two seasons and they now faced their worst nightmare.

We were professional and hardened but they had talent to burn in a match that remained tight until we kicked three goals in time-on in the third quarter to take a 20-point lead into the final break. We knew they would attack relentlessly, and of course they did. There were a few players – and I was one of them – who thought we needed to do something special for us to win as the Hawks continued to surge. It wasn't for any lack of effort or application, but we could not stop them. After Josh Caddy had goaled after seven minutes, we led by 19 points but there was still most of the quarter to play. With about six minutes to play Shaun Burgoyne put the Hawks in front.

The noise as his goal went through was deafening. We lost our composure for a couple of minutes after Shaun's goal, bombing the ball forward. I was watching helplessly from the bench, unable to get back on the ground until there was under two minutes left. Champion Data had me on the ground for 80 per cent of the last quarter, after 70 per cent in the third quarter. In the last seconds, we managed to create a scoring opportunity for Travis Varcoe, who pushed his kick wide for a behind after a timely attempt to smother from Brad Sewell. A goal would have tied the scores. The result – a five-point loss – was an absolute killer, simultaneously ending the Kennett curse and setting up the Hawks for what would become the first flag of their three-peat. I put my hands on my head and slumped to my knees then went on to all fours, exhausted.

In the rooms after the game, a comment was made that set the pattern for the ensuing years: 'Whatever happened at the end didn't cost us the game, the way we played cost us the game.'

After such a loss, I would check in, via text messages, on how teammates were travelling rather than me making any big statements. Emotions were high. We knew an opportunity had been lost. Nothing would be gained by mouthing off.

* * *

I'd arranged for Kathryn Cotsopoulos to attend the Brownlow medal with me the following Monday as a bit of fun, checking with her new boyfriend – now husband, Daniel De Lulio – that he wouldn't be fussed before I'd even asked Kathryn. He was fine but then poor Kathryn had to answer texts all night from friends watching the count on television, asking whether she and Daniel had broken up!

I didn't mind scrubbing up for the Brownlow medal and donning a Hugo Boss suit, but I wasn't at my best just days after a preliminary final loss. Once I started attending with Brit, I enjoyed the medal night more, but on this night, I was still thawing out. Such was my mood after finals losses, my friends would check with more relaxed teammates as to when it might be okay to resume contact!

The television broadcast focused on me a lot as I was polling well, keeping Gary Ablett honest as Stevie Johnson, who was ineligible because of a pair of suspensions through the season, kept pace with him. I did not consider myself a chance of winning so was not on the edge of my seat until the votes were called for rounds 20 and 21. I polled consecutive best on grounds to suddenly move from four votes behind Gary to two votes in the lead with just two games remaining.

All of a sudden, my palms were sweating. Kathryn had switched into work mode, jotting down some sponsors while Brian Cook jotted down a few thank yous. All in case of what might happen! The only sense before the night that I might be in the running had been via a phone call from the night's host, Bruce McAvaney, who was making sure he was prepared for anything by chatting to a bunch of contenders. Collingwood's Dane Swan and Stevie Johnson drew within striking distance polling votes in the final rounds. I was in the lead, with 27 votes, but Gary Ablett was just two votes behind.

It came down to the final round and all I could do was sit with a half-smile on my face. I thought I had a chance to gain a vote or two against the Lions, having had 25 disposals and scoring a goal in our victory but Mat Stokes, who had 35 disposals, took the two while I missed out altogether. As has been the way since Andrew Demetriou became CEO, the last match to be called was the Gold Coast–GWS Giants match. Gary Ablett, who had been named BOG in that game in all media, knew he would get votes but was clearly disappointed to not get two, knowing that three would edge me out. He spoke of that at the presentation: 'Joel deserves to be up here as much as I do,' he said. 'He's an ex-teammate and a very good friend and I was shattered I didn't get the two [in the last round].'

Winning the Brownlow would have been nice, but I was just disappointed to have experienced another close miss in four days. The top five in the medal that season carried something of a Geelong flavour with Gary Ablett winning from me, Dane Swan, Stevie Johnson and Patrick Dangerfield, who was then in Adelaide colours. It was the closest I would come to winning.

I finished my career with 214 Brownlow Votes, one shy of St Kilda champion Robert Harvey and Scott Pendlebury with only Gary Ablett (262), Gary Dempsey (246), Dangerfield (236) and Sam Mitchell (227) ahead of me in what has become a midfielders' medal.

My brother Troy polled one vote during his career at the Lions, in 2007 in a game against the Cats, a game in which Geelong led all night and won by 32 points after leading by 61 points midway through the last quarter. Demetriou even called out, 'J. Selwood one vote' on Brownlow night but the graphic showed it was awarded to Troy and it was officially registered as his vote. The least I could do was begrudgingly acknowledge it as being his vote, given all he had done for me. He has an equal career tally with my good friend Xavier Ellis and one more than my premiership teammate Tom Lonergan! Just for the record, Adam polled nine Brownlow votes and Scott 20 during their careers.

Chapter 13

In transition

AFTER THE PRELIMINARY final loss things looked grim for us, with so much experience having departed since the 2011 premiership: Joel Corey, (retired) Paul Chapman, (Essendon) Josh Hunt, (GWS) and James Podsiadly (Adelaide) joined recent departures Matthew Scarlett, David Wojcinski, Shannon Byrnes, (all 2012), Darren Milburn, Cam Mooney, Cameron Ling and Brad Ottens (all 2011).

Although I was kept at arm's length from list discussions, watching premiership teammates depart was emotional. A club-first approach is easy to say but harder to live with when necessary decisions are being made about teammates and you are their captain.

The decisions were always made by the list management committee. It was sometimes hard to keep my distance if teammates became emotional when they were not offered another contract. Although most of the decision-makers were good at taking the heat for their tough calls (even when some of those same decision-makers wanted the players to play forever), it did become taxing, because I would have loved them to continue to play forever, but I also knew everyone's time comes to an end eventually. We would miss them, of course, but there was no way I was accepting any potential slide.

Our first draft selections were in the teens and since Gold Coast's entry in 2011, and then the Giants in 2012, the expansion clubs had the call on the best young players. I was sure we could match and beat the system; there was no excuse to fall.

It was not as though all our talent had been drained. On the training track alongside me were my 2007 and 2008 draft mates, Hawk and Harry Taylor as well as hardened professionals Jimmy Bartel, Stevie Johnson, Corey Enright, James Kelly, Andrew Mackie, Tom Lonergan, Trav Varcoe and Mat Stokes. Fill a few holes here and there and fast-track the youngsters to play the Geelong way and we could contend again. That was our challenge.

As captain I decided I would need to show the way, to double down on my effort, to drive standards, to work harder than anyone, and to train as I always had, with ferocity and purpose. I would fill holes others might not be able to. If it meant putting the team on my back and carrying them to victory, I would do that as well.

During the pre-season, after a series of tortuous hill sprints on a December training camp in Coffs Harbour that ended with the group split into teams to compete up the hill, I literally did that when one of our rookies, Michael Luxford, an Australian under-17 basketball rep embarking on a new sporting career, cramped up 150 metres from the finish. Although he could blitz a yo-yo test he would buckle during long runs.

The poor bloke could not move but he had to, because he was on my team. There was only one option available, so I sprinted down the hill, picked him up, draped him on my shoulders and carried him up the hill and across the line. He was as stiff as a board and although I did not look up to see the group's reaction, I could tell many of them were a bit shocked at my competitiveness.

I still hated losing. It was black and white to me. Work hard. Learn good habits. Be selfless. Put the team's needs first. Success would follow.

That was the equation as we began the season in good enough form to win our first five games. I felt as though I was leading the way, with Stevie Johnson and Jimmy Bartel in good form too. Mitch Duncan and George Horlin-Smith had put in strong performances which was encouraging.

Then we spluttered, losing as much as we won, to drop to sixth on the ladder mid-season after Sydney thrashed us in round 11 by 110 points. It was the club's biggest loss since 1990 – when Hawthorn beat us by 115 points at Waverley Park – and the only 100+ point loss in my career. It was concerning but we refused to concede that internally or externally. After the game, Chris took the only practical response – to look ahead, not behind: 'We played poorly, the opposition were good, so our focus shifts really quickly to doing what we need to do to rectify it. If we were to walk through all the things that went wrong, it would be a very long list.'

The following week we bounced back against Carlton at Docklands. We were down by seven points in time-on, then

Horlin-Smith goaled and, with less than a minute to go, I kicked the winning goal. Carlton coach Mick Malthouse said I would be the player he would most love in his side while Chris Scott did not hold back either: 'Good players in big moments hang in there and Selwood finishing off is what we've come to expect from him.'

I was coming to expect just that as well, and the notion that I needed to play well or do something special for us to win tight games had crept into my head.

My intent was never in question but when you carry that view of leadership – that success was your responsibility – the danger is that when something goes wrong, you look to blame someone else. If you are not careful you can become a cop, rather than a teammate, and forget that the group that had won premierships had changed and other methods might be needed to give different – and new – individuals a prod.

I was pretty successful at hiding any frustration creeping into my mind from my teammates, but I wasn't sure, and some of the coaches were concerned that I would eventually burn out. They also wanted me to free my mind from concerns about what others might be doing or not doing to get better.

My personal response to any need, either mine or the team's, had been to do more, to push harder. I wasn't a big fan of what our conditioning staff called 'regeneration running' which was designed to assist with recovery. We would be asked to run at various percentages depending on our preparation. I struggled to see the sense in that. If I was running, then I was running hard which, I am sure, infuriated the staff trying to take us down that path. It was making me a better player, but the potential cost of that approach would have been obvious to the more seasoned operators around me. Although I did not share my thoughts to many, the captaincy demands felt rather big.

The club's leaders could only shift me so far because whatever lessons I needed to learn could only be learnt over time. Chris Scott, Tom Petroro, Harry Taylor, Tom Hawkins, Tom Lonergan, Jimmy Bartel, Corey Enright, Andrew Mackie, my brothers and Vic Fuller also all tried to be a sounding board for me.

My anxiety about our form may have been misplaced. After the Carlton victory, we won nine of our last 11 matches to finish top-four again. We won four of those games by under 10 points and although we weren't perfect, we had developed a fighting spirit that made us hard to edge out.

We finished third with 17 wins and approached the finals with some confidence. Unfortunately, in the qualifying final, Hawthorn had all the answers. Although we had won the round five clash, the Hawks had also been too good in round 22. Will Langford was sent my way, but I broke the shackles to kick the opening goal and finished the game with 31 touches, six tackles and nine clearances. It was not enough: we lost by six goals. The Kennett curse was well and truly over.

My mood was not great leading into the semi-final against North Melbourne – particularly with Stevie Johnson out with a foot injury – and it quickly became darker when the Kangaroos kicked seven of the first nine goals. I had only experienced two consecutive losses twice in my career to that point, yet we needed to make up a five-goal deficit to avoid a rapid exit from the finals.

We took too long to make a late charge towards victory with North keeping us goalless in the second quarter to take a four-goal lead at half-time. Halfway through the last quarter, the margin was 32 points. Then Hawk dominated, and we kicked the last four goals of the game – three to Hawk – with another disallowed due to a score review. The margin was just six points with less than three minutes left. We kept attacking but could not get closer. We were out, again.

The game had been brutal, with my jumper torn twice and a bandaged head testament to the battle I waged. North Melbourne's Brent Harvey risked missing the preliminary final when he leaped off the ground and cut my head. Despite me asking the umpire whether he had seen what Harvey had done, I adopted the players' code as soon as the siren sounded. The Match Review Panel found him guilty, but on appeal to the tribunal the charge was downgraded and he was free to play. To be honest I kept quiet a little begrudgingly as Harvey had been in a few altercations with my brothers at West Coast, so I knew he wasn't always squeaky-clean.

I was grumpy. I loved my teammates and my club but sometimes I wondered whether they cared as much as I did. It was taking me some time to learn that a person's immediate demeanour was not the only way to measure how much they cared.

At the best and fairest Chris Scott praised me but, concerned about protecting me so I did not burn out, said I probably did too much in an attempt to help the football club because I cared so much. I did but could you care too much? I didn't know what that meant. Probably, I still don't!

With our season over, I headed to Europe with my teammates George Horlin-Smith and George Burbury. The main question throughout the trip was the same one that drove me throughout my career: how do we get better?

While we were away, I would occasionally send a text to a new recruit or have a discussion with someone on list management about a potential trade. I could switch off and not talk football when we were being tourists, but I could not leave the game behind.

Chapter 14

A reality check

O N MY RETURN home from Europe, I met Brit Davis thanks to my teammate Taylor Hunt, who had been drafted to Geelong from the bayside region in 2008. He knew Brit from hanging out in the same bayside circles. He told me I should get to know her. Good advice.

I soon looked to impress her with a catch-up coffee at St Ali in South Melbourne. That went okay and soon enough I was making the long drive to where Brit lived in Parkdale, near her parents' place, once a week. I discovered that the journey up the Nepean Highway was a nightmare after 3 pm. It is probably no mystery why 2015 was the only year in my career that the Cats would miss the finals as I was driving 100-plus kilometres on weeknights, screaming at every red light I hit (I'm joking).

Growing our relationship was exciting and challenging all at the same time as I was not ready to forgo any of the time I devoted to the club. Brit didn't expect me to, but she also wasn't going to be taken for granted as her life was about to open up, as she was completing a degree in education while working in fashion.

Off the field things were sailing along, but football was about to test me in ways it had not done before.

* * *

I was finding it difficult managing the transition from being part of a tough and tight premiership-winning group to needing to teach an emerging group often struggling to find what was right for them. Connecting with people inside and outside the club required more of my energy, and the standards I set for myself were not always met by others.

Those whom I thought could help the team succeed in our next era copped it as I applied similar strategies to encourage them as the veterans in 2007 had deployed on me. Cam Guthrie and Mark Blicavs would often hear the urgency in my voice, and I was not afraid of giving the occasional bake. George Horlin-Smith remembers me berating him during one running session when he suggested to a teammate to push towards the front. I responded to his call: 'If it's that fucking easy, why don't you do it?'

One of my greatest strengths was my work ethic and my attention to detail but I was in danger of turning it into a weakness as the dynamics of the group changed.

Although my relationships with teammates were strong enough to avoid animosity, I began to sense I needed to adapt, or my message would stop resonating. What underpinned success for me was not necessarily the same as what drove others, and I was beginning to have conversations with people inside the club about how I could be a better leader. Horlin-Smith was an outstanding sounding board for me during this period, as was Cameron Ling who had returned to the club as a leadership consultant. Lingy encouraged me to relax and just 'hang' with my teammates for a while. Brian Cook could also see how much I involved myself in activities outside the club as well as community work. I was also doing plenty of unseen work. I used to call Brian 'boss' and he called me 'skipper' as we mulled over how my leadership could evolve. He wanted me to develop what he labelled 'influential skills' on top of my 'lead by example' policy. He could see the young players on our list requiring more of everyone's time.

I also had to ensure I made time away from the club for some players with whom I might otherwise only cross paths. That was critical because you had to catch up with people outside the locker room, away from the club, to really get to know them. By the final year of my career, after discussions with Anna Box, our newly appointed consulting psychologist, I had embraced an approach that had taken time for me to develop. As a leader there are some qualities you take for granted. Sometimes Anna would jot things down exactly as I said them, circle them a few times, and then share them back. We spoke about how I connect with teammates of different ages, styles and backgrounds, how I listen to their comments and that I was always happy to make those moments more about them than me. Anna circled my words and shared them back to me. While the words were not grammatically correct, they pretty much summed up my approach. 'They come different. I find their language, and then you know how to give 'em a bit of love'.

And if we were honest, at times the leadership group had messed up too. During the 2015 pre-season our conditioning coach, Scott Murphy, told us how we were going to build through the season then strike just at the right time. It would be as if we were equipped with a magical samurai sword to cut down the opposition. He told us we would go through many stages to build into a position to be, at the end, a samurai. When we heard that, the leadership group thought a samurai sword might be a good symbol for the team's approach to the season. Somehow, we managed to source a real samurai sword and had each player sign a flag committing ourselves to the season. The sword sat on display in a cabinet and the flag above it, with all our signatures, was next to my locker. It was hardly a magical sword; we slumped to 16th after four rounds and were only in the top eight for two rounds, just missing finals for the first, and only, time in my career. At some stage during the season, unbeknown to me, Steve Hocking told his assistant, Ben Waller, after a meeting that the samurai sword was to disappear by the end of the day. It did and has never been seen again!

Anyone watching me play through that season could detect an underlying annoyance as I fought what seemed like one-man wars with taggers. It felt as though my support crew had disappeared, with Stevie Johnson the only permanent midfielder left from our premiership era; Jimmy Bartel and James Kelly had been pushed to the wings in order to blood others.

My fight with Carlton's Ed Curnow in round eight was like Wrestlemania as he tried to shut me down a week after Sydney's

Ben McGlynn had done the same. My self-discipline was again tested and I went overboard, giving away silly free kicks and 50-metre penalties and then having a crack at teammates who did the same. I was certainly not a model of good on-field behaviour. I had also been having shots at opponents, like Fremantle's Nat Fyfe who recalled me telling him in round two: 'We will never tag you Fyfey, as you can't kick.' He finished the game with 36 touches – 25 contested – and kicked three goals, so the sledge obviously had a big effect on him! We also lost the match.

The season was becoming a reality check, but we kept fighting for a finals spot with regular losses punctuating wins. The lowest moment came when we dropped the round 12 match to Melbourne in 'Boris' Enright's 300th game. It was Demons' ruckman Max Gawn's breakout game. Our ruck stocks were light on with Rhys Stanley, our latest ruckmen, ruled out with a foot injury suffered the week before just as he was showing his worth following five seasons with St Kilda. We became overawed by the occasion and took our eyes off the ball. I was shattered about letting Boris down but he taught me a lesson in how to deal with such disappointment. At the function we had arranged at Geelong's Cunningham Pier the next night to celebrate his milestone, he wore a smile all night to set the tone for the group. To be honest though, the smile I wore was dripping with embarrassment.

I kept pushing teammates along, asking for advice and reflecting on whether I was being fair or not, as I desperately tried to nurture the talent around me. With free agency in place I was also scouring the competition, watching out for players from other clubs who might help us bounce back quickly.

After the bye, our round 14 game was cancelled due to the tragic death of Adelaide coach Phil Walsh who had been stabbed to death on the eve of the match. We did not even consider playing that game, no matter what it might mean to our place on the ladder.

We got on enough of a roll to win four in a row and briefly re-enter the eight after round 18. During that period, Sydney champion Adam Goodes travelled to play at Kardinia Park the week after he stood out of a game due to the incessant and disgusting booing he was being subjected to by crowds around the country. The AFL finally recognised the booing for what it was, and the clubs and the game made a concerted effort to end it then and there. The two clubs made a strong statement when we ran out on the ground together through a banner that marked my 200th game.

When Goodes won his first possessions, any booing was muted to the point of being irrelevant. It was a moment for me. 'That's why I am playing for this club,' I thought. We weren't perfect but we set a standard that we lived by. Goodes, one of the players I admired most, would play just six more games in his magnificent career, retiring after Sydney's loss to North Melbourne in the semi-final.

A loss to Hawthorn and a draw with St Kilda had us a game and a half outside the eight before a loss to Collingwood in the second-last round put us out of the race. Levi Greenwood shut me out of the game, which really reflected my year. As we headed into the final round, for the first and only time in my career, I would head into a game with the finals a mathematical impossibility. On top of that, three favourite sons of Geelong – and my friends – Stevie Johnson, Mathew Stokes and James Kelly were to depart. Three people who meant the world to me were not going to be around the next season. I understood they all wanted to keep playing for the Cats. Obviously, they believed they had more to offer, as did other clubs. Kel played two seasons and 40 games with Essendon, Stevie 40 games with the Giants, and Mat 11 with Essendon. Their departures weren't the only reasons I had a heavy heart. Unfair criticisms were being directed at Chris, who was just one of many people making these tough list calls in an attempt to keep us in contention.

The day was a great celebration of the trio's careers and Stevie's left-footed barrel a highlight, and a great memory at the end of his 253 games for the Cats. But the game came to a close on rather a strange note. With 20 seconds remaining Adelaide's Patrick Dangerfield marked inside the Crows forward 50. The moment was remarkable as Geelong's home crowd rose and clapped not for our impending victory, but for Paddy as he went back for his kick. He missed, but the fans were anticipating that the boy from Mogg's Creek was coming home. The media had been speculating for some weeks that Paddy would make the switch to Geelong and the crowd assumed the deal was done. He had confided his intentions with former Crows football manager David Noble, but he had not publicly declared he wanted a trade. The tiny beach community in Dangerfield country at Mogg's Creek was preparing for his return however and that meant every old salt on the surf coast was sure it would be happening.

Chapter 15

The danger man

IT'S NOT AN overstatement to say Paddy Dangerfield's arrival at Geelong transformed the football club and altered the trajectory of my career. The excited anticipation of the crowd in the last round of 2015 was right, and Paddy lobbed at the Cattery for the 2016 pre-season, alongside my brother Scott, who had returned to Victoria after 135 games and a best and fairest with West Coast. Carlton's Lachie Henderson and Gold Coast's Zac Smith also made the switch to Kardinia Park.

I had first broached the subject of Paddy joining Geelong during the 2014 International Series against Ireland, explaining to him how I thought he could make us better and how we could make him better too. He was intrigued and wanted to know about our program, our list and injured players he had not seen play. I told him to look out for Lincoln McCarthy who had only managed five senior games for the Cats at that stage. I told him the kid was special on and off the field. He was just one example I gave him.

Of course, Paddy had in his mind the possibility of one day returning to live on the surf coast at Mogg's Creek, where he grew up. Geelong were lucky we were the closest club to his hometown, and I was counting my lucky stars when he decided to join us.

I had no issue with him becoming our best player immediately. All I wanted was for the team to become better and I knew he would make that happen. If anything, I underestimated how good he would be and how much his performance would motivate me and others who had been at the club for a while to improve.

Throughout the difficult 2015 it became more obvious that we needed a lift to our midfield. Paddy and Scott would make a significant difference, while Lachie and Zac would fill positional gaps and holes in our list where 24- to 29-year-olds should have been.

Paddy had heard good things about me but wasn't sure if they were true. Mostly he remembered that I would greet him with a punch in the guts every time I lined up in the middle against him while he was at the Crows. I would also remind him – tongue-in-cheek – that it would be easier to play with me than against me.

When he arrived, I was rehabbing after a plantar fascia injury, which flared while I was overseas post-season. My injury meant it was going to be tough for me to make round one but I wasn't about to miss it. I told Paddy before Christmas I would be alongside him at the opening bounce after playing one VFL practice match in preparation. He nodded but I could sense his doubt. Even John Leyden, our rehab physio and my old mate from Bendigo, thought such a timeline for a return was too tight. John had studied his craft when he and Brock Bouch lived with me in 2009.

I didn't doubt it but it helped having Scott alongside me. He was also rehabbing from ankle surgery. Scott is an animal when it comes to cross-training. Trying to keep up with him on the rowing ergometer was nigh on impossible. Having the two of us in the same rehab group made life tough for John. No matter what instructions he gave us, the final minute of any exercise would turn into a race waged at 100 per cent intensity. I thought I was inducting Scott into the Geelong way but John was wary. He didn't want Scott to get dragged into doing work above and beyond – what he would see as doing it my way. John had to watch us like a hawk.

It was great having such a familiar sparring partner back. We resumed epic table tennis matches with our roars and screams of frustration often greeting anyone who joined us at my place in Barwon Heads. The house was not renovated then and the table was in a tin shed out the back with gym mats on the floor. It was a sweatbox. Each point between us became an epic battle of skill and will. These matches would start with the idea of playing the best of three sets and would turn into never-ending battles that would last for at least a couple of hours with racquets eventually thrown. We had delusions of grandeur. I was vulnerable to spin so he would try to slow the game down and force an error. He knew that taking the pace off the ball was my kryptonite. I had to concede he had my measure more often than not.

Often the night before a big game, Scott, Hawk and I would go to the club around 5 pm, have a spa and get in the pool, with the aim of being home after six. Unfortunately, one of us would pick up a table tennis bat more often than not and a game would start. We would be there for hours, sweat dripping off us, as one of us refused to leave until he had the chance to regain the lead. There we were, fighting each other with as much intensity as we would apply to our opponents the next day. It is this no-holds-barred fun that defines the best football clubs.

Scott also loosened me up without having to say anything. He became a great sounding board for me as he is an empathetic character who would give me direct feedback without a second thought. I could also trust him to be giving the right message to players on the fringe of selection as he understood what it was like to have lived in that difficult spot better than I did. If I was unable to cover that part of the list as effectively as I wanted to, I had faith that Scott was lending them his ear.

Then there was Paddy, the forever-grinning bull with a swagger only matched by his strength. A lot was made of how we would connect in the midfield but we never doubted it and two weeks out from the opening round, we hit the track together. People wondered what it would be like having two bulls in the one paddock. That was never an issue as we simply wanted Geelong to be the best we could be.

Paddy, who was 25 when he arrived, had his quirks but he went above and beyond when it came to performance. I was two years older than him and had reached the stage in my career where I looked to embrace those who were different. The lessons of the previous two years had taught me plenty.

Our preparation was different (he might have a surf the day before a game) but when we trained, Paddy and I went at each other as hard as it is possible to compete with a teammate. He loved beating me in one-on-ones and I loved being relentless in my approach in an attempt to grind him down.

I did make the opening round, and in our first match together he earned three Brownlow votes – after 43 disposals – and I polled two as we defeated Hawthorn, the winner of the previous three flags. He would poll three and me two four times that season and in one game I polled three and he grabbed two. I was the support act in a vicious one-two duo.

It was amazing to play alongside him as we were immediately on the same wavelength. He says it was the easiest football he has ever played because every time he looked up, I was where he needed me to be. I felt exactly the same way as we were rewarded for pushing the limits because we knew we had a teammate who was anticipating the other's move. We would not have to say much when we joined each other at centre bounces except how are you feeling? The rest became instinctive. He would fight on his knees for the ball before using his power to launch into motion like a Formula One car exiting pit lane. I could take on a tackler full of confidence, knowing he would be there to greet me on the other side. We trusted each other like a pair of trapeze artists.

Like Hawk, Paddy showed me there was another way to approach high performance and he would often take the mickey out of my pre-match speeches or laugh when he beat me in a one-on-one. I learnt from him, and I did not mind having the piss taken out of me. That's also what football clubs are about. In a club-produced video in 2017 Paddy asked me a question that had become standard locker room banter: 'Has it been hard to maintain a suntan these past 18 months living in my shadow?' I enjoyed his deadpan style and being on the receiving end of gags. When the leadership group began to stress after losing two matches in a row midway through the season, he didn't. He told Harry Taylor to come and talk to him if we lost six in a row, a losing stretch he had endured while at the Crows. His winning record at the Crows had been a perfectly respectable 60 per cent but his experiences had been varied. My winning percentage had been 77 per cent when he arrived and 2015 had been my first year out of finals. He had played in September four times in his eight seasons with Adelaide.

Paddy was also in the superstar stratosphere which made us laugh at him too, with boxes of boots arriving regularly and many media appearances sought from him. In previous eras we might have tried to pull him into line, but he was the best player in the game and he prepared assiduously, albeit in his own style. And, importantly, his values off the field were spot on; he was aligned to the club's senior leaders in every way. He went straight into our leadership group and provided great support. He was also on the AFL Players' Association board, and he became president in 2018.

The season was panning out perfectly as we entered the preliminary final against Sydney after eight consecutive wins, with all four of our recruits from other clubs playing. We'd had a week's rest after Isaac Smith missed a set shot after the siren to give us victory over Hawthorn in the qualifying final.

Within half an hour of the preliminary final starting, our season was over as the Swans kicked seven goals to zero in the first quarter and stretched the margin to 55 points just before half-time. The sudden nature of the mauling came as a shock. We were thrashed despite me and Paddy winning 39 disposals apiece. That loss hurt more than most in my career as I thought we were primed to deliver a flag and we were blown away by Sydney for the second time that season.

We did not know it then but finding one team better would become a recurring theme for the next five seasons as we continued to stumble just before reaching the summit. I sent a positive text to Paddy after our exit, telling him we needed to get better and we would. There were no recriminations, just a redoubling in desire.

It was no surprise when Paddy won the Brownlow by a whopping nine votes. His season was off the charts. I was happy to have run second to him in the best and fairest.

Chapter 16

History repeats

WE JUMPED BACK on the horse and won the first five games of 2017, before losses to Collingwood, Gold Coast and Essendon, the only time in my career the Cats dropped three games in a row. Paddy was still the best player in the game and his presence continued to help my performance. Zach Tuohy – who would prove to be one of the best value-for-money recruits of the era – arrived from the Blues to add another lively element to the changerooms, 24-year-old Tom Stewart made his debut, and we hoped that Mitch Duncan and Steven Motlop, each with over 100 games' experience, could take the next step.

I resumed training with intensity despite the disappointment of the previous season. I had established a set of habits over a long period, which meant I could respond to the challenge of fronting up after falling short. The VMOs and the touch sessions never stopped.

Adelaide set the pace at the top of the table but we were sweating on them every step of the way. Paddy and I made a statement when we beat the Crows in round 11 but I was again falling into the trap of making sure I was in the middle – with Paddy – whenever the game seemed up for grabs.

Paddy was in good form, earning 22 Brownlow votes in eight games mid-season. He led the team to victory in a thriller against the Dockers in the middle of that patch when I was knocked out in the opening minute. We overcame a 34-point deficit to win by two points when the Dockers' Michael Walters missed what would have been the match-winner.

Paddy's eight-match streak of dominance ended in Adelaide when the Crows reversed the earlier result, and the next week a sling tackle on Carlton's Matthew Kreuzer was classified as a two-match sanction by the Match Review Panel, reduced to a week with an early plea, ruling him out of a big match against Sydney. The club had wanted to contest the decision at the tribunal, but Paddy took his medicine despite the suspension meaning he would be ineligible for the Brownlow Medal. He did not want to risk missing two matches. The loss to the Swans saw us drop from second to fourth but we still believed we would retain the double chance. It was the first game Paddy had missed since arriving and we stumbled to lose by 46 points at home. That was bad enough, but I also left Kardinia Park on crutches after Buddy Franklin fell on my left ankle in a tackle. The diagnosis was a syndesmosis injury, and that surgery would allow me to return for the finals, a month away. I needed what is called a 'tightrope' operation on my ankle.

I've been told it was handy not being an explosive athlete when it comes to rehabilitating from injuries. I have a diesel engine, which tends to recover quicker but as I got older, it became more difficult and slower to recover, and recovering from such an injury was not easy. For the first eight days post-surgery I stayed away from the club to minimise any risk of infection. I was staying hydrated to assist my recovery but that saw me literally crawling from the bed to the toilet in the middle of the night. The ankle would freeze up and the pain was sometimes excruciating. I pushed it, icing the ankle around the clock for hour after hour with the ice machine on the bed. While I was following the club's rehabilitation process, I also threw in some homespun extras myself, including losing weight to ease the load on the ankle.

I was able to return for the first final against Richmond, but I wasn't right and in hindsight it would have been wise to have waited another week. Despite finishing above the Tigers, we played them on their home deck in front of 95,000 success-starved Richmond fans. We hung in there for three quarters before they blew us away.

We then defeated Sydney in the second semi due to Paddy Dangerfield's heroics up forward in an inspired move before we were eliminated by Adelaide in the preliminary final on the Adelaide Oval. It was tough for Paddy playing against his former club. I had a jab to settle the ankle but then was kicked in the sore spot early and limped to the bench. Our doctor, Drew Slimmon, strapped me up and told me to run along the boundary to assess my fitness before he would agree to send me out. I realised my popularity rating in Adelaide was not high as I heard words used to describe me that I had not heard before!

Drew said my trot up had been terrible and asked me to go again. I refused. I told him I wasn't going to subject myself to that abuse again. I ran back on to the ground thinking I'll have to tell Hawk what they had called me. I knew he would get a laugh out of it as we often discussed the absurdity of what was being said. He would even give it back to the crowd at times but I was not good at that. I just kept my head down and hoped none of my family and friends had heard the abuse. Booing was no different although I didn't think it was what real sports lovers did. In a radio interview in 2022, I described it as an 'ugly part of the sport'. Apart from what had been directed at Adam Goodes in 2015, most of the booing would be directed at the villain of the day and that was often me. It did not keep me awake at night.

After promising so much, we had again fallen in a preliminary final, this time by more than 10 goals. Chris Scott summed it up rather well: 'I hope that no-one associated with Geelong falls into the trap of thinking that we were close again, and have just got to improve a little bit to go the next step, because the cold, hard reality is we have got to go back to the start again. And there are some really good football teams with a lot of talent who didn't make the eight this year who I suspect will get better...we have got so much work in front of us to even make the finals.'

Chapter 17

Welcome back, Gaz

FOR SEVERAL YEARS there had been murmurings that Gary Ablett Junior wanted to return to the Cats. He had been close to making the move at the end of the 2016 season before Gold Coast officials ruled out any prospect of that happening.

By the end of 2017, the switch was on. Gaz was 33 and had been hampered by soft tissue and shoulder injuries in the final three of his seven seasons at the Suns. But he was a star and we wanted him back because we thought he could help us take another step forward. He came cheaply too, considering his ability.

I knew how good he was and how professional he would be. Chris Scott and I did not need to convince ourselves of the wisdom of the move, and we made sure those teammates who had not played with him previously, including Paddy Dangerfield, would understand how exciting it would be to share the field and locker room with him. Only nine of us had played with Gary before he left for the Suns.

Paddy, me and Gary were quickly dubbed The Holy Trinity but Paddy missed the first game with a hamstring injury. Chris showed he had a good sense of theatre however, starting Gary alongside me in the centre for the opening bounce. Gary was more relaxed the second time around and I was too as I was now pushing 30. His return showed our decision – and his – was a good one, as he polled three Brownlow votes in his first match back, while I polled two. It was a repeat of the round one Brownlow scorecard of 2016, when Paddy made his debut for us. We fell in against Melbourne but our form was an indicator of where we would eventually sit through that season.

Gary is a beautiful person and as competitive as anyone in the game, so I understood it was not going to be easy for him to play a different role among different teammates. My approach with such great players is to let the individual be. So he was left to run his own race. As a player he was still outstanding, and I sensed he would have been exhausted after being the main man at the Suns for seven seasons. We knew we could help alleviate that as the load would be shared.

He never fumbled and his disposals were more often than not perfectly executed, particularly when he somehow found space when none seemed to exist. But he now had played more than 300 games and had to be a little more careful in looking after his body.

We also unearthed Tim Kelly, who suited our game perfectly as he could lope from a stoppage at warp speed and direct low kicks to our forwards. He had first nominated for the draft in 2012, and how he had reached 23 before making his debut was beyond me. Our recruiters had been keen on him but were wondering whether it would be too big a risk to relocate him from Western Australia. Neither Tim Kelly nor Tom Stewart, who was 24 when he made his debut in 2017, wanted to waste any time given their relatively late starts at AFL level. They were put in the right positions that suited their strengths and kept growing in their roles.

We needed to rebuild our list, because defensive stalwarts Tom Lonergan and Andrew Mackie had retired at the end of 2017, and we also had seen a significant shift in the football department with Steve Hocking leaving to take the Football Operations role with the AFL. Hock had been there through my career and I knew intimately how valuable he was as a back-room operator. He did not mind hard conversations and he understood the foundations that Geelong's culture had been built upon. Simon Lloyd, who had been our director of coaching after a long career with Hawthorn, Collingwood and Fremantle, was a quality replacement, but Hock had left big shoes to fill.

The year turned into a struggle, with injuries meaning our line-up was constantly changing. We ended up using 40 players – the most since 1990 – even though most of our key players, bar Harry Taylor (7) and Lachie Henderson (8), played at least 19 matches.

We lost three games by less than a goal and won one after the siren when Zach Tuohy kicked straight against Melbourne in round 18. We managed to run that ball from deep in defence to Tuohy inside 20 seconds because our skills were so good. I was forever driving the coaches mad with requests for training to include game scenarios. I hated not having a plan in place. Skill wasn't our problem. Luck and continuity in certain sections of the ground evaded us, and we could only sneak into eighth place. It was not enough, and we were dismantled by Melbourne at the MCG in the elimination final, after failing to score a goal in the first quarter.

I had a bad night too, getting involved in a barney with Melbourne's Jake Melksham as we both headed to the bench. I was frustrated and angry and let it get the better of me as Hawk was lining up for goal. In the coach's box I was told later they could see what was unfolding and were screaming at me, but I was in the zone. When the umpire reversed the free kick, I sat on the bench feeling like I had all those years ago in Bendigo when Mark Ellis had ripped me off the ground for a similarly undisciplined act.

Another season of promise had ended early. It was the third year in a row we had been kept goalless in the opening quarter of a final, all after a week off and, on two occasions, after a relatively soft lead-in.

Travel with Brit was always on the agenda in the post-season and it was again as we headed to Portugal with friends Brenton and Yasmin Hall for Jarryn Geary's wedding to Emma Giles. I was better at organising team events than travel agendas but being away with Brit was a perfect way to relax before launching into another season.

* * *

We kept adding experience with Luke Dahlhaus and Gary Rohan joining the club and a young player with promise, Jordan Clark, was drafted with our first pick (pick 15). He was one of four players to make their debut for us in round one, along with Charlie Constable, Tom Atkins and Gryan Miers. Tim Kelly had wanted to go back to Western Australia for family reasons but a deal couldn't be completed to our satisfaction, so he remained. Our player development managers did a wonderful job at that time. I just asked them whether they needed any help to support Tim and his family.

The club had become busier too, with Geelong finally having an AFLW team. I was enthusiastic about the Cats having a women's team but we did not get it right immediately. I suspect we fell into the same trap as a lot of clubs, thinking that while it was great to have an AFLW team, the focus was still on the men's program performing well. That took time to shift but we have now adopted the right attitude as we chase overall club success, which means both programs support and learn from each other. The diverse viewpoints and the many different characters within the teams are making the organisation stronger.

The whole of 2019 was tough at a personal level as hamstring tendinitis got hold of me. I ended up sitting out on a wing while Tim Kelly continued to dominate in the middle. I could only run in a straight line and play at 70 to 80 per cent capacity, which turned the year into a nightmare.

Each week I would sit in team meetings with the hottest heat pack possible sitting underneath my hamstring in an attempt to 'burn' the tendon. Then I would rub heat cream into it before running out to train. It was the same on game day. After games or training I would hit the roof as the pain would peak while taking a shower. Rest was considered, and we looked at loading the hamstring with weights, but that was discarded as the rest of the body would end up sore. In the end, I just kept going.

I normally didn't dwell on injuries too much because I figured there was someone feeling worse than me. Thankfully, attitudes are changing. I also thought I was being paid a lot of money so had to put aside any niggles and just perform. I never believed you could come out and say: 'Look, I'm actually fucked.'

After all these years, my mindset was that I would get myself up to play regardless. Sometimes before a game I would think I might have preferred another 48 hours' rest but my football body clock was unbelievable. It would tick on time. After an anti-inflammatory, which worked most of the time, I'd go through a rigorous and highly tuned stretching regime and get to work. The truth was, I hated missing out, I loved the challenge and I didn't want to let down my teammates, the club or our supporters.

On reflection, it was unhealthy to think like that and it would not be until it was nearly too late that I understood and accepted that sometimes missing a week was the better option.

We were flying before the bye, winning 11 of our first 12 games, then we became like a draughts board, uncharacteristically losing every second game. That superb first half of the season did the job and we again finished on top, but again had to play our first final at the MCG, Collingwood's home ground. The match committee made the call to leave out Rhys Stanley and the Magpies jumped out to an early lead after we dropped marks in front of goal and missed sitters.

We could not make up the ground and the loss saw criticism of Chris Scott reaching fever pitch. It was unfair but predictable as we had now won just two finals in seven attempts over five seasons. Chris would take the blame even though the way we played was not down to him. He was no one-man show. Chris was hurting – as we all were – but we bounced back to beat the reigning premiers, West Coast, in the semi-final, after a five-goal to one opening quarter.

Unfortunately, my soul brother Tom Hawkins found a way to get suspended so he would miss the preliminary final against Richmond. It was a massive blow for the team and for Hawk, but it was not a time for recriminations. Chris summed it up well when he said the club owed Tom more than he owed the club, but I knew Hawk was hurting.

It was a time to be supportive of Hawk. He knew what my feelings had been when he had been suspended on other occasions during the home-and-away season, when a witty aside was often enough to send him a clear message. This time I made it clear I was in his corner, and I genuinely was. I wasn't afraid to hit someone between the eyes but that was not the way to go. It must have been hard for him and Mitch Duncan (who was injured) watching on as Richmond overran us in the second half.

I took longer than normal to recover from the loss. Brit was more concerned than usual with my reaction as I lay on the floor and binged on whatever TV series would keep me engaged. Brock Bouch visited with his children in an attempt to lighten my mood and he quickly realised I was yet to thaw out. I had prided myself on letting losses go but towards the end of my career that was becoming more difficult. My chances of winning another flag were dwindling. Doubts about our direction crept in and I questioned myself and whether I should continue as captain. I wondered whether I was doing the job effectively. As I turned the car out of the MCG and headed home I thought, 'I've had a good crack. Maybe it is time for someone else to have the captaincy.'

That year ended with more surgery. Julian Feller, an expert with hamstring issues, sliced my right hamstring tendon near my knee and liquid just poured out as the fluid build-up had been extreme. After he sewed me back up, I never had another issue, although the scar from the operation remains.

I can't remember raising the captaincy topic with anyone although I did subtly test the waters with Chris to see what he thought. He didn't realise what I was fishing for but gave me no sense he wanted a change.

As emotions died down, I was named captain again.

Chapter 18

Surviving COVID

2020 BEGAN IN the best possible way. In January, Brit and I were married and our brief honeymoon at Freycinet National Park in Tasmania had punctuated the pre-season nicely. Two months later, the whole world had changed as the dangers of the COVID-19 pandemic became clear.

Chris Scott had been aware that a crisis was looming and made noises about us being ready for whatever was coming, but the leaders in the playing group thought he may have been over-reacting. We sat in Chris's office and heard his message: that whatever happened Geelong would strive to be the best at managing COVID.

We travelled to Sydney on the same plane as Melbourne's AFLW team to play the Giants, lost the game and returned home to the news that Victoria was in lockdown. The next day, March 22, the AFL's chief executive, Gillon McLachlan, called a halt to the season, with the aim to play the remaining 144 games and finals once the position became clearer. May 30 was the suggested date for resumption. Being 'agile' and 'flexible' became regular descriptors of the path ahead.

It sounds ridiculous but my immediate thought was to accept the challenge this unprecedented situation would present and be ready when the game did resume. It didn't take long however for the extent of the crisis to dawn on me as I sat in on meetings with the Players' Association as it was outlined what may be ahead.

Relocation of teams was possible. The income of all players was in jeopardy. The whole industry was under pressure. I was clear that we needed to lace up to ensure the game would survive. Other people had other views on what expectations could be placed on players and their families, and I respected their thinking, but I also thought that when – if – the season resumed, then taking a positive approach to whatever we faced would give Geelong an advantage.

Chris, Simon Lloyd and I quickly realised how important it was to bring the partners of the players into the conversation, for them to communicate any issues to us and we would try to make things work. Everyone connected to players and staff was included.

There was no road map. Players just marched into the unknown, initially with that break from the club meaning it was up to each individual to stay in shape and keep their skills at a reasonable level. I enjoyed running, doing weights and going for a kick. I kept on doing that. I also recognised – as the club did – that we had to let people find their way through the period, given each player faced unique challenges. Getting treated for niggling injuries proved difficult. We introduced Zoom meetings that included quizzes and various bonding sessions just to keep some connection as well as updating teammates on what the AFL and the club were planning. We could only train with one teammate, so I tried to grab a young, hungry player to train with. Cooper Stephens was one player I trained with and Jordan Clark too from time to time. We kept the program loose, asking players to just do something, whether that be a four-kilometre or 10-kilometre run. None of us knew what lay ahead, so we weren't too prescriptive. The main message was: just don't get injured.

In May, the AFL announced the game would resume in the second week of June, but we would be playing in empty stadiums. When we returned to the club, we were testing ourselves for COVID in the car park before going inside to train in small groups while being diligent about hygiene. At least we had resumed our profession, a privilege we did not take for granted. The club was a strange and unfamiliar place as many of the staff had either been stood down or had to work from home. No player's family was unaffected.

We resumed on June 12 against Hawthorn at Kardinia Park. It was a strange feeling playing without a crowd and was not something any of us enjoyed. After a month of uncertainty, we were bundled onto a bus soon after beating the Gold Coast at home on 4 July. It had been my 300th and Gary Ablett's 350th game but was a muted affair in front of the empty stands. I had tried every avenue possible to get Brit and my parents into the ground to watch the game live but the state's COVID rules did not allow them to be there. They made a banner and stood in a park near their home to show their support for my milestone.

We headed north for what we were told would be a 30-day stay. Our first stop was at the Pullman Hotel in Sydney's Hyde Park. We beat the Lions at the SCG, then headed to the Crown Resort in Perth for three matches in Perth quarantine. Gary Ablett decamped from Perth to be at home with his wife, Jordan, and son, Levi, in a move everyone supported, the club having drinks the night before he left to acknowledge our milestones and to wish him well. As he returned to Victoria, at the end of July we decamped across the country again to settle in at the Mantra in Southport. The COVID cuts, as necessary as they were on a macro level, ripped the guts out of AFL clubs. Vic Fuller, who was at the footy club every day, doing whatever was needed, could not travel to the hub, the club's chef, Adrian Millman, one of my favourites, was gone as a result of the cutbacks. Along with Harry Taylor, they were my 'board members', my conscience, my psychiatrists, my sounding board, my eyes and ears but most of all my mates. As Chris had said before the season, we just had to remain positive, whatever we faced.

The AFL was setting up a base in Queensland, which was mainly COVID-free. We were able to find resort-style accommodation, filling rooms left deserted by the national travel bans.

The meetings the club was having with partners and families were often intense. The pressure people were feeling was real and colleagues had lost jobs or had been stood down. The maturity of our group and the trust we had built among families over the journey helped these discussions. But life at the Mantra still came as a shock. We had been spoiled at Crown, with a pool and chef-cooked meals ordered via our dietitian. Now we were back to a version of reality, albeit way better than what millions of people locked down in Victoria were experiencing. It was not what we had been used to – historically – when on the road. The Mantra was great but it did take some adjusting. We also contemplated, perhaps unfairly, how our partners might react to the different accommodation. I was also recuperating from a hamstring niggle after our loss to Collingwood in round seven.

There was no pool at the Mantra but there was a footy oval and we were allowed to move around, and the sun was shining. The food was pretty good too. Brit was able to join me in mid-August – the arrival of the first wave of partners and children gave us all a huge boost. We could go for walks and could swim in the ocean, but we could not sit in coffee shops or in restaurants as the AFL tried to keep everything on track and keep us all healthy. With the season having been compressed, with shorter breaks between matches, shortened games and constant travel, we had to keep focused. Playing at different venues didn't worry us as we had adopted a 'play anywhere' attitude, but by season's end, the Gabba had become our favourite venue as we knew how to win there.

It was all-hands-on-deck when it came to organising events. The agenda of meetings became rather unusual with mealtimes for children being discussed at one point as we realised pretty quickly that kids did not wait long past 5 pm before screaming for dinner. With the help of the hotel, mealtimes were staggered. We turned a function area into a games room and occasionally a band called The Roman Sandals – made up mostly of the medical team – would play with rookie Oscar Brownless on vocals. There was a rooftop where we set up a coffee shop which became our meeting place after breakfast. We stuck together and tried as hard as possible to look out for each other even if our responsibilities were different. Given we were able to keep playing, we knew we were fortunate in many ways and we kept emphasising that fact.

When the second wave of families arrived in the middle of September, there weren't enough rooms to accommodate everyone at the Mantra, so we were offered rooms at the RACV Royal Pines Hotel nearby. I had the unenviable task of telling the group that anyone with families might consider relocating to the Royal Pines, where the Western Bulldogs had been ensconced for most of the season. It was a very tentative presentation as I tried to ensure that everyone knew they weren't being forced to move. For many the shift came at a good time because looking after toddlers and newborn babies in a hotel room was difficult, even though we kept reminding ourselves how fortunate we were compared to those in lockdown.

During all the strangeness of our situation, we kept on winning. Our ability to communicate positively during games gave us an advantage; we had several de facto coaches in our team, and they knew exactly what we needed to do to win. To be honest, we had some teams beaten before the ball was bounced. We were desperate to keep winning and it seemed we were happier, in relative terms, than some other clubs.

My season wasn't stress-free as that slight hamstring strain was still niggling away behind my knee. I missed four matches after our 10-goal win over Port Adelaide in round 12. We won three of the four, in games at the Adelaide Oval, the Gabba and Carrara, with the loss to Richmond in the second-last round.

I was able to get a training block in and was back for the match against Sydney at Carrara on the Gold Coast a week before the finals.

We knew by then the Grand Final was going to be played outside Victoria for the first time and at the start of September, it was announced it would be played at night under lights at the Gabba, a truly history-making event. The game was scheduled for October 24 and we wanted to be there.

We missed top spot by a game, which left us fourth and in a qualifying final against top-of-the-table Port Adelaide on the Adelaide Oval, before a reduced attendance. The stadium was less than half full but that half was all Port Adelaide supporters! Our hit-and-run mission failed and we lost our 12th final in 16 attempts since the 2011 Grand Final. Hawk – who had just claimed his first Coleman Medal – had an off night in front of the sticks, managing five behinds.

I had an off night too as I dislocated my finger when it was caught in Travis Boak's jumper as I tried to strip him of the ball in a tackle. We did not have any guards with us, so I strapped some cardboard on my finger, but the finger kept slipping out. I had to play holding my middle finger and my thumb together which made the second half tough. That night when I went to bed it was still painful. The doctors took one look the next morning and sent me straight to Brisbane for an operation to have me ready for the semi-final against Collingwood nine days later.

Brit picked up me and our club doctor, Drew Slimmon, from the Brisbane airport and took us to the hospital. I was not feeling great as I had not eaten since the game because the doctors had recommended precautionary fasting in case the operation would be done that morning. By the time the operation started at 6 pm, I had gone more than 24 hours without eating. My first words to Brit when she visited me two hours later were 'don't touch me'. I felt nauseous due to a reaction I had to anaesthetic. I was so sick I had to stay in the hospital overnight.

Brit went back to Southport that night then returned the next morning to pick me up. I could not drive as I felt like I was about to vomit. It wasn't the first time I had felt like that after surgery but that did not make me feel any better because I knew it was not going to be a 24-hour feeling. The surgery was simple because they just had to tie up the knuckle, but the after-effects made me feel like death was a better option. I stayed in my room at the Mantra to avoid infection and then tried to train on Wednesday, two days out from the game. I was still sick, and it took me until Thursday to confirm I would play against the Magpies at the Gabba on Friday night. My footy brain was hard-wired to play, and any nausea was forgotten.

Collingwood was cooked after their epic one-point elimination final win over West Coast in Perth and the subsequent travel. We thrashed them, after a nine-goal to one first half. We then managed to account for the Brisbane Lions in the preliminary final with two goals from Gary Ablett just after half-time breaking the game open. My finger was no issue. I always thought the same way about injuries post-surgery: it's now fixed so go and do what you need to do.

We had just one more week to get through without any muck-ups. In the lead-up we caught up with my parents for a coffee at Mermaid Beach after they had arrived from a stint in quarantine at Howard Springs outside Darwin. We were standing around the cafe rather than walking together when Gillon McLachlan walked past. Poor Gillon had been carrying the weight of the world on his shoulders and was rightfully paranoid about anyone breaking the AFL's strict COVID rules. Brit feared the worst and thought the AFL might make an issue of what was, realistically, nothing. Happily, nothing came of it. Our paranoia was a sign of the times in a year that veered in unpredictable directions, often at a moment's notice.

Despite our loss to the Tigers in round 17, we thought we could beat them in the decider as it looked like they had spent a lot of tickets overcoming Port Adelaide by a goal at the Adelaide Oval in a classic encounter. We did have some sore bodies, including Paddy, who was battling a groin issue. We were confident we could control their chaotic game style.

Our plan was to slow up Richmond and control the ball as much as possible using Tom Stewart as a spare in defence. We believed if we could absorb their pressure and clear the ball from congestion and find space, we would gain an advantage.

Chris Scott is not one for emotional pre-match speeches, but this year had been so different from any other, it was appropriate his pre-game address made reference to the bonds we had created. 'It is the best feeling in life,' he said, 'to do something that is difficult but worthwhile with people you rate. You look around the room and there is no-one I would rather be with.'

In the first half we did all that we expected, despite Gary Ablett fracturing his shoulder in a mad minute that also saw Richmond defender Nick Vlastuin knocked out cold. Mitch Duncan and Tom Stewart were outstanding in their roles and we held a 21-point lead with 90 seconds of the first half remaining.

They were desperate to equalise numbers in their attacking zone but were struggling to do so, and we were showing more composure with the ball.

With under two minutes before the main break I was in defence, worrying about Dion Prestia while trying to identify where the most dangerous player might be lurking when a deep kick was spoiled in the direction of Dustin Martin. Alarms were flashing and I tried to support Jake Kolodjashnij who was being fended away. I was perhaps a metre short when Dustin flicked the ball on to his right foot and snapped a goal that few others could have achieved. I cursed myself but there was little I could have done. Our efforts to counter Dustin were total but we could not stop him.

Despite that late goal, we remained confident at the long break. I listened attentively to Chris Scott's words, with Mitch Duncan to my left and Mark Blicavs to my right. There was less than an hour left and it would decide our season. Chris stuck to our plan. 'We are going to play our game. It is contest versus chaos.'

Some commentators again criticised the coach – he was an easy target – for not moving Paddy Dangerfield into the middle earlier in the second half as the Tigers charged. He took the jibes on the chin when the fact was it would have been fine if Paddy had made the move himself. In the end Paddy was probably too compliant to our original plan, hoping he could snag one while up forward. Chris did order him into the middle midway through the third quarter after Dustin Martin kicked his second goal and the Tigers had turned a half-time deficit of 15 points into a three-point lead. Richmond was an outstanding team but

ABOVE: It took a while to be comfortable on captains day among the game's best but Gary Ablett's presence as Gold Coast captain helped ease any nerves. My number one priority as captain was to maintain high performance.
AFL PHOTOS

LEFT: I was not a natural speaker but I taught myself to become better at that aspect of the role as I knew it was part of the job of being captain.
AFL PHOTOS

TOP: Chris Scott is a great coach. We normally agreed but when we wanted the other to shift their position we found a little nudge in the right direction was all that was required to find common ground. AFL PHOTOS

RIGHT: Chaired off the ground after reaching my 150th game milestone in 2013. My mates Tom Hawkins and Harry Taylor helped carry their soaked teammate from the ground as Jimmy Bartel gives me a high-five. AFL PHOTOS

LEFT: It became a cliche for me to put a bandage around my head to stop blood from flowing. I had skin like crepe paper. AFL PHOTOS

BELOW: The syndesmosis injury in 2017 and the finger injury in 2020 were not much fun for me or Brit.

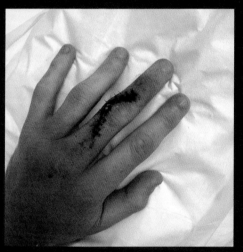

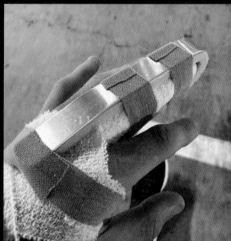

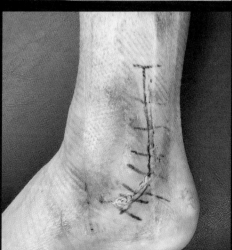

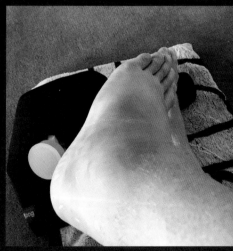

ABOVE: The 2011 Grand Final was the breakout moment for Tom Hawkins where he proved to the football world and to himself what a great player he was going to be. It was also Chris Scott's first premiership, in his first season as coach. AFL PHOTOS

BELOW: With Alastair Clarkson, coach of Australia, holding the cup after the 2014 International Rules match between Australia and Ireland in November 2014. AFL PHOTOS

ABOVE: A photo with the AFL and AFLW captains. Forming the AFLW team was great for our club and the community – it also provided me with some new insights. AFL PHOTOS

CENTRE LEFT: I took being an AFL Auskick ambassador very seriously, getting to know the children and their families. I enjoyed watching them grow into young adults. AFL PHOTOS

BOTTOM LEFT: I fell in love with Vic Fuller from the moment I walked into the club. His death rocked me and many at the club in 2021, not to mention his family. AFL PHOTOS

ABOVE: Grand Final day 2022 was the culmination of many years of hard work and resilience by outstanding people. AFL PHOTOS

RIGHT: I knew it would be a magic moment for Gary Ablett and his wife Jordan to see Levi run through the banner with me on Grand Final day. The gesture was to symbolise the club's respect for one of the game's greatest and his family. AFL PHOTOS

BELOW: It took until the last quarter of my last game for me to finally kick a goal I could brag about, a banana on the run from close to the 50-metre line. My emotions came to the fore immediately. AFL PHOTOS

LEFT: My good friend Sam Moorfoot helped make the Cats a better place. He deserved to celebrate the flag with us as he had contributed as much as anyone. Winning that flag was amazing and the day worked out perfectly but it also brought into the public arena many things we had been doing for years. AFL PHOTOS

CENTRE LEFT AND BELOW: I was determined to smile throughout 2022. I am not sure I stopped smiling all year. AFL PHOTOS

LEFT: Brit and I became closer during the IVF experience. It wasn't an easy road but our love for each other only strengthened and the joy that Joey's arrival has given us can't be described.

CENTRE LEFT: I owe so much to Mum (Maree), and Dad (Bryce), pictured here with the premiership cup, me and Brit. The biggest compliment I can give them is just to say that they have remained parents from start to finish, only concerned that I was kind to others and happy. AFL PHOTOS

BELOW: Family is the most important thing to Brit and I and we can't wait for what lies ahead with Joey. AFL PHOTOS

it was that one man, Dustin Martin, who was the difference. They now had their fast game up and were flowing through the middle and had also quelled Tom Stewart's influence in defence by evening up the numbers.

Halfway through the last quarter, Martin kicked his third, and their lead was now 22 points. Chris spoke to me on the phone, telling me we were going to attack the game through the middle. Our attitude has always been to just fight it out with the hope that we would catch fire and regain momentum. That means taking more risk which comes with either reward or disaster. We did not stop fighting but they were too good. It was disappointing to lose that one as we had actually given ourselves a really good shot but a 20-minute patch in the third quarter where we could not get the ball hurt us.

Gary Ablett bowed out without the third flag he so desperately craved but his dignified exit from the ground after the match, applauded by both sides, showed his status in the game. With his left arm hanging limply by his side due to the broken shoulder he sustained in the opening quarter (he kept playing), he raised his right hand to the crowd as every player and official stood to applaud him, the Tigers players even removing their premiership medallions as a mark of respect for the moment.

It was a sad moment but his three final years at Geelong had solidified my relationship with both Gary and his family, which made his return worthwhile alone. He had done everything in the game, winning eight All-Australians, two Brownlow medals, was a five-time winner of the AFLPA's MVP and three times won the AFL Coaches Association's Champion Player award. He also squeezed in six best and fairest trophies (four in his 110 games with the Suns and two in his 257 games with the Cats). I was fortunate to have played in two flag wins with him when he was in his prime and was clearly our best player.

In the nine seasons since the 2011 flag, we had finished lower than fourth just four times and missed the finals just once. We kept believing we were good enough but it seemed we always found one better. Whether it was a lack of midfield depth or a lack of cross-the-field depth or whether our best players were not at their best at the end it all amounted to the same thing. Through all those years I wondered whether we had entered the finals on a less than full tank, having spent more chips than we could afford to gain the double chance. There were also times, on reflection, we decided not to rest an important player because we felt the prospects of winning the next game would be reduced. This thinking was an inexact science and was hard to measure until the season was run and won. Even then a definitive answer was impossible. The post-season medicals gave an indication of who needed surgery or what sort of break might be necessary. Even our GPS results could tell different stories, depending on the style of game you were involved in. We evaluated everything but that did not mean an answer would spit out.

In 2020 I thought we had timed our run to peak at the right time but that loss to Port Adelaide in the qualifying final used up a little bit of gas. In other seasons we were found wanting as we tried to fill holes that we knew existed and sometimes the burden fell on players taking on roles they were not suited to.

Chapter 19

New, old blood

I HAD SENSED BEFOREHAND that the Grand Final would be Harry Taylor's last game. He had not told me as he did not want any fanfare or distraction as we headed to the match. But we had a moment together before the game and I told him, with more emphasis than usual, I would be giving everything I had to play in another premiership with him. He had no doubt as to the meaning of my message.

From his first day in Geelong when I took him on a tour to the surf coast and throughout his great career, we had been through plenty. But it wasn't until days after the loss when we found time one-on-one to sit down over a meal and a couple of beers at the Main Beach Surf Club in Southport that he told me he was finishing up and heading back to Western Australia to be close to his and his wife Michelle's extended family. In his 280 games he had become my man, a partner in leadership, the vice-captain I needed.

We could yell at each other on the field, me telling Harry to tighten up on his man and him asking me if there was any danger that we might stop the ball coming out of the centre so easily. We would immediately forget about our on-field banter post-game. Most of the time we spent talking about football was about reflecting, analysing and becoming better at what we were doing.

In the end we hardly needed to talk to know what the other person would be thinking. Along with a few others, Harry had been my footballing sounding board, both on and off the field. I was going to miss him more than I imagined. He once wrote a letter to me to mark a milestone; this had become a club ritual that had started when Corey Enright reached his 300th in 2015. Teammates would express their thoughts about their teammate on paper, which not only meant a lot in the moment, but would become important keepsakes. As is Harry's style, he went further, and enclosed a compass along with the words: 'This gift from me, in recognition of your ability to both motivate and inspire and set the course for others. You are the compass of the AFL.'

The year had ended without a flag, but as a team we had got through to the final week of an extended, fractured and unprecedented season and our bonds had tightened. Hub life had been like a school camp. Our resolve to do it better than the rest had kept us positive and motivated. Cam Guthrie, who won the best and fairest in a breakout season, summed up that enhanced camaraderie when he said on the night before we checked out of the hotel that we all wanted to go home but we didn't really want to have to leave each other.

* * *

Despite the Grand Final loss, we felt like we had been a team on the way up in 2020. Sam De Koning might not have played a senior game but had shown plenty of talent at training and obviously had a good temperament, while 23-year-old Brad Close, who had played eight games in his debut season, was a mature player with a future. After 19 games in 2019, Jordan Clark had battled to get a game in his second season, but I still believed in him and was working closely with him to get through a tough patch. Sam Simpson, another father–son recruit, now in his third season, had made giant strides before being concussed in the Grand Final.

At the top, we were changing presidents, with the calm presence of Colin Carter departing at the end of 12 years' service and Craig Drummond taking over. It was a seamless transition. Colin had been an outstanding servant of the club and Craig, who had been a club director since 2011, was a successful businessman continually searching for a winning edge.

The thinking throughout the club was that we were set to contend again in 2021. Not only were the young players showing they would make it, but several high-quality players were coming to Kardinia Park. Jeremy Cameron had told the Giants on the Monday before the Grand Final he wanted to join the Cats as a free agent. Hawthorn's Isaac Smith was also interested as was my old Vic Country teammate Shaun Higgins.

When Cameron's name was first mentioned, we were more than a little excited about the prospect of him joining the Cats, though we thought the odds were long despite his family being from Dartmoor on Victoria's west coast. We thought he would perfectly complement Hawk, who had no issue whatsoever with sharing the limelight. It was a bold play a long time in the making. I had a couple of conversations with him over the phone, once when Jeremy was up north fishing. To be honest if I had known Jezza then as I do now, I would not have interrupted him with the call. He is as relaxed as they come. He wanted a change and luckily for us, part of his plan was to buy a farm. The time was right for the switch.

We thought we might be able to keep the average age below the pension zone too, as we also had picks 11, 13 and 18 after we had traded Tim Kelly to the Eagles at the end of 2019. That seemed too good to be true and so it turned out when the Giants forced us to trade our three picks inside 20 to gain Jeremy but, importantly, the list management team grabbed a couple of second-round picks in the transaction.

On draft night those second-round picks gave the recruiting team the confidence to trade out a future first-round pick to Richmond and nab a relatively unknown quantity in Max Holmes at pick 20 just weeks after 31-year-old former Saint Jack Steven had decided to retire after just one season with us and a year remaining on his contract.

Jack's retirement call didn't give commentators much faith in our strategy of recruiting Isaac Smith and Shaun Higgins, given both were on the wrong side of 30. It meant we would still have 10 players on the list who were 30 in 2021 and three players turning 30. We knew the risks but I also believed in our approach and understood the strategy behind it.

I knew Shaun would be an asset on and off the field as he is a terrific person while Isaac, an old sparring partner at the Hawks, proved to be a revelation. We knew he could play the role we wanted from him as his endurance and willingness to work is elite. Isaac is happy-go-lucky most of the time and, along with Jezza, lightened up the locker room in the pre-season. On top of that both knew when to switch on and were mentally tough. They also had smart footy minds, while it soon became clear that Jezza carried attributes only few players possess.

Isaac still loved the Hawks, as he should, given the three flags he won there and the friendships he formed, but the relaxed professionalism the club espoused gave all the players – particularly experienced ones – control over their preparation. This made Geelong just right for him and his family to make the move after his 210 games with Hawthorn.

Chapter 20

A Fuller life

Iᴛ's ɪᴍᴘᴏssɪʙʟᴇ ᴛᴏ predict who will influence you most. Often your biggest heroes are close to home.

Vic Fuller was authentic before that description became a buzzword and we expected him to be around forever. With Adrian Millman a casualty of the COVID cuts and Harry Taylor having returned to Western Australia, Vic was the only one of my trio of 'board members' still at the club. Vic's famous opening line to anyone who walked through the door for the first time was legend: 'I was here when you got here, and I will be here when you leave.' It was his reminder that no-one was bigger than the club. It was great to have him back as we'd missed his presence at the hub in Queensland and he had missed us.

As he was a volunteer with us since the mid-1970s, he could say exactly what he thought without fear or favour. We loved his intransigence. Watching Vic rebuke someone if they did not wipe their plate clean after eating one of Adrian's meals and then put it in the right place for Vic to put it in the dishwasher was both hilarious for the non-offending players and a quick lesson in respect. He made us laugh, and we didn't want it to stop him playing his vital role. Vic reminded everyone that the luxuries they were enjoying were only due to the hard work of others.

His assessment of anyone's performance could be brutal. 'Not good enough' was a phrase he used freely, and no-one was spared of such a brutal appraisal, from the CEO to the senior coach to the veteran, to the rookie. He also wasn't afraid to share his opinion widely. Vic's annual list management suggestions were legendary. Those running the VFL program would start at player number one and ask Vic for his assessment of the entire list. By the time they worked their way down to Mark Blicavs at number 46, there were very few players left on Vic's list. They would remind Vic they had to field a football not a netball team so they could not implement all his recommendations. Happily, I was never part of Vic's purge.

The night before Vic died, aged 79, on February 22, we had exchanged text messages. My brother Troy, who was working as a recruiter at the club after playing with and managing the VFL team, had alerted me to the fact Vic had not turned up to the VFL training session that day so I wanted to check in and, as was our way with each other, rib him gently for his absence.

We both knew he must be a bit off-colour because Vic was at the football club every day, and would be the one turning out the lights. He was more than a part of the furniture at the Cats. He was its beating heart.

I sent him a text:

'Are you Ok, Vic? Doc results?'

He responded with a message.

> **Hi mate Had a bit of polymalga! In my arms and hands, but medication worked well.! Still hoping to clear up info, when advised about my blood test.! Thanks for asking, see you tmoro! Cheers Vic**

I couldn't resist a jibe in response:

> **I'll bloody need to help you with the drinks more if that's the case. See you tomorrow vic.**

As I went past Vic on the way onto the track that February morning, he was filling up the drinks as usual and I asked him again if he was really okay. He dismissed my concern saying: 'Yeah yeah, get out there' and training started. In the warm-up, Shaun Higgins ran over to me and told me in a worried voice that Vic had collapsed and the doctors were attending to him.

He had fallen next to the race, so we all had to move to the other side of the ground and training ceased immediately. We stood there in silence for 20 minutes. The doctors worked on Vic while they waited for an ambulance. He could not be saved.

All I could think in my shock was a phrase he would normally say to me: 'C'mon you arsehole, get through it.' I eventually retreated to my locker, stunned. All I could think was how unfair it was for Vic. He had just returned to the footy club, doing what he loved, and a massive heart attack had knocked him down. He had just got his life back. Then in a flash he was gone.

I went up to Brian Cook's office and started contacting past players, and Balmey, Hock, Bomber – people who loved Vic. I wanted them to know before the news broke.

Soon after, Chris Scott gathered the group in the locker room and spoke briefly. He got it completely right when he spoke to a very raw, emotional bunch. He was as shattered as we were and expressed how sad Vic's death made us all feel and confirmed that there would be no more training that day. He told us the club would send out updates.

It had been my worst day, and the next morning I didn't feel like going back to the club, but I knew Vic wouldn't forgive me if I hadn't. I knew I would hear his voice rebounding through the corridors – something I would sense for the rest of my time at the club. I gathered a few of his belongings – the big Cats coat that kept him warm at VFL matches, the packets of Allen's red frogs he kept by the thousands, his blue clipboard with at least 60 pens – and bundled them all up.

Harry Taylor would later wear that big coat of Vic's to honour Vic in his farewell lap of honour before a game at Kardinia Park the following April, but at that moment he was in Western Australia and doing it hard too. Vic and Harry had a special relationship, with Harry sending Vic the Geelong jumper he had worn in his last game, the 2020 Grand Final.

Before training the club – players, administrators, everyone – gathered on the grass as I thought it was important that we should gather as a group. I said: 'Yesterday was really tough for a lot of people. He touched people in many different ways. He was a hell of a person. He'll live on in this footy club. He did not want things to be about him until it was about him. He will be laughing all the way to heaven.' I didn't find talking about him hard. Vic made time for everyone. He had what I called 'Cats manners'. I was just so sad. We had a minute's silence to reflect. When the moment had ended, I declared, 'Vic would want the show to keep on going.' We trained with his face overlooking us on the big screen. I had glassy eyes for days.

Not too many people knew how to approach me after Vic's death, and I didn't share too much with others. It wasn't that I thought doing so was a sign of weakness or vulnerability. I just felt like I had to care for others during the time, pick myself up, dust myself off and get going again. I was shattered but just couldn't let myself fall apart as the season was fast approaching. Vic would have wanted us to keep rolling, and in the AFL, you often seem to have little choice.

I focused on getting the eulogy for Vic right. I had to nail that. I called on Troy and Hamish McLachlan to help write these difficult words, words which I found even more tough to read. Hamish was spot-on in everything he suggested, which helped. Inside my locker, I put up a photo of Vic with a big grin on his face, pulling the drinks cart while I annoyed him by grabbing at the tray. I surrounded the pic with his words: 'I was here when you got here, and I will be here when you leave. Get back to work, you arseholes!'

I loved Vic Fuller as much as I loved any man. I hope he knew that but I still wish I told him that more, even though it makes me laugh to imagine what his response would have been. Too often things are left unsaid. I've found expressing your feelings removes doubt and has people feeling safe and connected and assured. That's ultimately what we all want.

Chapter 21

Life goes on

WE DID GET back to work but not in the way anyone expected, with an upset loss to Adelaide in round one. We started the season without Jeremy Cameron due to a hamstring strain he had suffered in January, and then lost Paddy Dangerfield for three matches after round one when he was suspended for a bump that left Adelaide's Jake Kelly concussed.

We were on the right side of the umpiring in a thriller against the Lions in round two, when Mark Blicavs should have been penalised for holding the ball in the dying seconds with our lead of two behinds.

It was the night Chris Scott and Chris Fagan had exchanged words at quarter-time as Chris stuck up for Gary Rohan who was being sledged by opposition players. I had to tap Chris on the shoulder to refocus him on his job as he was angry at what the Lions were saying. The vision made headlines and he copped a $10,000 suspended fine in the aftermath. These things sometimes happen in the heat of the battle.

In round five against North Melbourne we lost Paddy again, this time to a syndesmosis injury that required surgery on his right ankle. We then copped a poor decision against the Swans at the SCG in round seven, when Jezza – who had played his first game for the Cats in round six – marked a kick that was deemed to have travelled less than 15 metres, another incorrect call. Chris was furious at the umpires that night as we ended up losing by two points but had calmed down before his media conference, so he didn't say anything he would later regret. He always supported umpires and constantly reminded us that umpiring is a tough job. He thought it was important to relay that message publicly too but that didn't mean his disappointment wasn't real.

I was angry too. In the cold light of day, I could see we had been lucky against the Lions and unlucky against the Swans but we needed a win, and I just thought it was a win we had been denied. Perhaps that attitude of needing a win reflected our mindset that season, as at times we were probably focused too much on the scoreboard and the ladder.

We were still winning plenty of games and having big moments too. Our 10-goal win over Richmond in round eight, when Jezza kicked six goals, was a reminder we were contenders. In the short time he had been with us I put Jezza in the same class as Gary Ablett Junior when it came to their ability to do freakish things on the footy field. He could not only make the footy talk but seemed to talk to the footy. He doesn't just squeeze the footy for show when lining up for goal. He is assessing which end of the football is the better end to kick. Like Gary, he could sum up quicker than most the chance of pulling off something outlandish and once they decided to have a crack, they committed to it 100 per cent. The touch and attention to detail this unique pair brought to the game is elite and although they would know when to play the percentages, the boundaries they play within stretch much wider than most because they know what is possible for them.

We won the next five but there were signs we were just going if you looked hard enough, especially when a calf injury forced Mitch Duncan out just as Paddy Dangerfield returned.

St Kilda might have beaten us in round nine if Max King had not kicked 1.5 and then Gary Rohan kicked a miracle post-siren goal from the boundary to snatch a win against the Bulldogs, our sixth straight. Jezza hurt his hamstring again in round 16, and we were battling everywhere except in the win-loss column. Apart from Hawk, who was All-Australian again, Tom Stewart and our only real improver for the season, Jack Henry, no-one was in great form. Our most damaging players were inconsistent. Paddy was playing sore so his explosiveness was missing and our youngsters were either not ready or just having a minor impact. Despite all this, after beating the Kangaroos in round 20 we were half a game clear in second spot, and a top-four finish was ours for the taking.

Then Tom Stewart hurt his Lisfranc when his foot was stood on – at training of all things – after our round 21 home-ground defeat by GWS. If we were honest, his loss was going to be too hard to cover.

Despite that loss, we were still on the verge of taking top spot in the final round of the season when we led Melbourne by 39 points at half-time, and they still trailed by that margin in time-on in the third quarter. They were brave and kicked the first five scores of the last quarter to draw within seven points, but even though most of the quarter was still to be played, we still should have won. When Bayley Fritsch goaled to bring the margin to two points, there was still plenty of time left but it took until the final minute for it to all fall apart for us as we clung to a two-point lead. First Cam Guthrie kicked out on the full on the wing and Brad Close punched the ball away to concede a 50-metre penalty. That series of blunders led to the ball going back inside 50, allowing Demons' captain Max Gawn to mark and kick the winning goal after the siren. The Demons took top spot and we dropped to third. Instead of playing the Lions at a neutral venue we again had to face Port Adelaide in Adelaide in the qualifying final. We didn't know it at the time but, on reflection, that second half fadeout against the Demons might have rocked our confidence.

As we left Geelong on the bus taking us to the airport to catch a plane to Adelaide before the qualifying final, I took the opportunity to give Craig Drummond an idea of what I was feeling about the club's direction. Brian Cook was leaving as CEO after 20 years and external voices were becoming emboldened about a need to change our coach who had one more year left on his contract. I knew those voices would only become louder if we did not win the flag.

What I said to Craig was short but very clear: 'You have to back the coach.' My main thrust was that the board and the club needed to show him some love rather than entertain the doubters. No matter how the season ended, changing the coach at this point was not the path to success.

Craig immediately sought the thoughts of a couple of other key leaders around the club about what was needed to give Chris the best chance of continued success. Chris had a ridiculous winning record that was still hovering around 70 percent and Craig recognised that Chris had been left as the voice of the club on a range of issues during COVID, which affected external perceptions of him and had also added unreasonably to his workload. He also understood it was time for other senior voices of the club – including members of the board – to take on those responsibilities. The program needed some adjusting because after two years of COVID people were tired and some nerve endings were frayed. I knew as well as anyone what Chris did and thought on a range of issues, and it was time the president knew that I was in the coach's corner. Chris had been exceptional for two years, trying to accommodate everyone's needs, and it was time that was recognised internally.

He *is* a great coach. His tactical nous is unsurpassed and his communication with the leaders among the playing group has been outstanding. We were all aligned with him and made sure any of his messages permeated through the group. His other strength, which is a rare thing, is to see the opportunities in our program to keep us fresh. He is a master at tweaking the overall program or varying individual loads so the team peaks on game day more often than not. That did not mean we won every big game – even Bart Cummings lost some Melbourne Cups – but his overall winning record over 12 seasons at 70.28 per cent remains ridiculously underappreciated.

What I had also come to appreciate about his coaching was the environment he fostered which helped bring out elements in me that I may have kept hidden if under a different coach. I was as competitive as anyone but also had an empathetic side and he wanted Geelong to be a place where players could play with ferocity but then pursue whatever floats their boat away from the club. Under Chris – and me – no-one had to worry about feeling pressured to fit into an old-fashioned and unhealthy stereotype of how a footballer should act away from their responsibilities at, and to, the club. He knew I enjoyed being involved in community activities and supporting people when I could because it gave me a purpose outside the game and allowed me to engage with people from all over the place. He let me be me.

For all that, I was conscious not to set myself up as an exemplar of how life as a professional footballer should be lived. Over time, my thinking evolved as I listened and learnt from Tom Hawkins, Harry Taylor, Dangerfield, Mark Blicavs, Isaac Smith, Cam Guthrie, Shaun Higgins and Mitch Duncan. Footy was a tough game but it did not mean kindness had no place in it. I often found the opposite to be true.

Craig brought his own style to the presidency. He is a successful businessman who loves football and he was certainly interested in my views on football and had sounded me out about potential chief executives earlier in the year, when we sat together at the Lord of the Isles, a hotel near our ground in Geelong. I admitted my bias but said he had to consider Steve Hocking who had been running Footy Ops at the AFL for four years. I knew he had an ability to put the right people in the right seats and get the best out of them. Hock's emotional intelligence was higher than anyone I had met in football.

All that discussion happened under the spotlight of intense scrutiny and assessment as to whether our game style was too slow. There was plenty of robust discussion among the leadership group and the coaches about selection and tactics. One of our biggest problems could be over-compliance. If the plan was to increase the number of uncontested marks to keep the ball off the opposition, we might take 160 marks. We also knew that keeping the ball off the other side helped our defence and we knew defence won premierships. We needed to find a better balance and we needed the players who could help us do that.

* * *

This was all happening while we were still meeting all the COVID protocols imposed on all teams. In Adelaide the security had been rigid. Only four people were allowed in a lift and any food, which was set, was dropped outside our door. Butter chicken wasn't my usual pre-game meal. We had to ring through for water. We tried to open the doors and speak to each other from our tiny rooms but when the authorities cottoned on to that this ploy was banned too.

After Port Adelaide shut us down to win the qualifying final, we went to a hub in Perth, staying at the Tradewinds Hotel in East Fremantle. We tried to replicate the atmosphere from the hub the year before but it wasn't the same. Something was missing, although a victory over the Giants had us playing Melbourne for a spot in the Grand Final at Optus Stadium.

We were also a bit carefree, with the spa becoming increasingly dirty during our two-week stay. It was a four-person spa not really designed for six footballers at a time. Jezza would either be sleeping or wandering about in his jocks, jump in the spa and pool and go back to his room.

It was probably no surprise that a virus – not COVID – ripped through the hotel on the eve of the preliminary final. Jezza was confined to bed as was Brad Close. There were seven players on the morning of the game looking less than likely to play and we were considering lobbying the AFL to postpone the match, a ludicrous but not unreasonable request. The boys were genuinely crook, so I admired them for putting their hands up to play. Lachie Henderson had also nicked his hamstring at training but he had to play. I then felt my calf tightening during the warm-up.

When we got to the top of the race to run on to the ground, I said to Isaac Smith, 'We've got to win this in the first 20 minutes or else we're fucked.' When I looked the boys in the eyes as we circled pre-match, Jezza was white. He was part of our walking dead.

Melbourne jumped us, kicking five unanswered goals after Jezza had kicked the first. We had no answers and they handed us our worst finals loss for 52 years. After beating us for the second time in four weeks, they deserved their spot in the Grand Final. We had fallen just short again and despite the illnesses we faced leading up to the preliminary final, we had rarely played like a premiership team during the season. The reality was we were exhausted, mentally and physically, from two years of travel and uncertainty. There was little the coaching staff or club leaders could do. Post-premiership, in early 2023, Chris Scott would be able to say that for many of the years between flags, we had limped into finals and then copped some bad luck. It was only with the flag won that people really heard that reality.

Chris hid the depth of his disappointment well post-game when he said, 'While it hurts at the moment, the easy response is to say we're going to fight and work really hard as quickly as we can. That would be missing the fact that the last two years have been really hard on people in the game. Our players deserve a break and what they will get this time is enough time to regroup. We've fallen short and we're bitterly disappointed at that.' He also referred to the club's rebound after the 2010 preliminary final when Collingwood beat us by 41 points after leading by 81 points in the third quarter.

Everyone was tired and although many tight bonds had been built among the players and their families over these two COVID seasons, we had also sacrificed plenty. It was hard to complain because we understood (and had regular reminders when we saw the effect of the pandemic on friends and family) that our position during COVID had been privileged. Sometimes it didn't feel that way. Football clubs had been decimated with people losing their jobs in every department. The incomes of people who remained had been slashed and uncertainty was the only certainty. None of the restrictive demands placed on us had been reduced and falling short again left people frayed.

Amid our disappointment at not reaching the pinnacle, we braced for the inevitable criticism about how old our list was and what we had to do to contend. I had become desensitised to that narrative but still needed to address whatever it was that was making us second-, third- or fourth-best every bloody year.

The footy questions kept coming. We knew we were in for significant change in the football department with a new chief executive in Steve Hocking – my old football manager – returning with bold ideas to shake up the place after Brian Cook decided to keep his career as a club executive going at Carlton after his club-saving work at the Cats came to an end after 23 years.

Chapter 22

IVF begins

A S WELL AS the on-field disappointments of 2020 and 2021, Brit and I had been dealing with a very personal challenge that had, to some extent, been put on hold until the end of the 2020 season. We had decided during the year to find out why we weren't able to become pregnant as we realised things weren't happening naturally for us. We longed to have children and we were impatient to find out what was causing our difficulties.

Only a few people knew our issue, which had consumed much of our thinking and energy in the final part of 2020. It wasn't an easy time as we were surrounded by toddlers and family reunions in the hub. We loved the energy that the families brought to the place, but it was sometimes difficult given our situation, particularly for Brit who was around mums and their children most of the day and didn't have football as a release. That was no-one's fault. She loved children and particularly her friends' children, just as much as I did.

We needed to undertake testing but had to wait until football in 2020 had finished. The tests showed I had a low morphology sperm count. In simple terms, sperm morphology is the size and shape of sperm. Look it up! We were given clear options: to keep trying or to enter an IVF program. After much thought we chose to undertake IVF under the direction of Dr Lynn Burmeister at the No.1 Fertility clinic in East Melbourne.

We soon learnt that Lynn is an outgoing character. Her style put us at ease, and she filled us with confidence about our prospects of success. We respected her intelligence and expertise yet her loud high heels, red flowing hair and penchant for wearing pink was an added bonus. Her flamboyance made us feel comfortable in an environment that induces anxiety.

Given we were still restricted by COVID, our first consultation was by telephone. Brit and I sat opposite each other and put the phone on speaker so we could talk to a counsellor about the IVF process.

BRIT: We did the phone consultation in a meeting room in the footy department at GMHBA Stadium to fit it in with Joel's schedule. It probably wasn't the right place to do it because I think I got a bit frustrated, angry even, that I had to meet him at his workplace, and I was the one who had to take the day off work for the call.

I wasn't really sure how I would fit the IVF process into our lives because we both worked full-time and the clinic was in Melbourne. But I knew that I would have to make the time. I think I was just frustrated then because I knew the whole process basically falls to the woman and I was overwhelmed!

We are the ones having to go through all the treatments, book all the appointments, make and take all the phone calls to nurses/scientists/whoever, go to the appointments, put on alarms and organise when we needed to take medication and at what times etc, etc. To name just a few!

I think Joel was a bit shocked but I just needed him to know I never wanted to hear footy would get in the way and that I would need him throughout this process. I'm pretty independent and I didn't want to admit I needed help.

I admit I was taken aback by Brit's comments. It was not her intention to make me sit up and take notice, but her words were something of a verbal shirtfront. My first reaction was to become defensive. I thought surely, she knew I would be there for her and would always be there for her. Perhaps that was an assumption I was not entitled to make.

As much as she loved footy and fully supported my commitment to the game, she also knew the practical reality: football could be a selfish game and sometimes those lucky enough to make it to the AFL can justify being really selfish. We were already on a footy clock from week to week. Now we had another clock to follow: the IVF clock.

I can only imagine the expression I had on my face as Brit made her point. I quickly understood that my life would need to change. I couldn't imagine then how the total IVF experience – as arduous as it would be, or perhaps because of that – would eventually make me both a better person and captain. It did change my approach to football and to many of the people around me. It opened up my mind to what else was going on in the world and what others might be going through. We knew others would also be facing the trials and tribulations of IVF, for a start.

The first realisation I had was that I would need to be with Brit every step of the way, respecting and prioritising her needs, understanding the minutiae of the IVF as best I could, what she was being asked to do and to be as committed as she was to achieving a pregnancy.

This was not something that would come easily for me. I always connected effort to outcomes, accepted any challenges and strived to meet them head-on. Generally, that approach led to success too, at least in my chosen sport. Mine was a busy but habitual life: there were daily exercises, travel, training, teammates, meetings, games, catch-ups with my sponsors, connecting to Cats' supporters as well as friends and, of course, Brit.

Our marriage did not change that much because most of our personal challenges until that point had not interrupted our professional lives. Brit knew my approach to my profession was total and she respected me for it. As I did respect her commitment to teaching. But it was also clear to her – and me – that us undertaking IVF meant I needed to be more flexible.

We were also well aware that our financial circumstances were better than many other couples who had to jump into the same boat, an important reality we would never lose sight of. But this was going to be *our* experience, although we knew there would be common ground with others undergoing the IVF process, and other areas in which our experience would differ.

One thing we would not do was tell everyone what was happening. Brit wanted the process to remain as private as possible but she understood that we needed to trust key people. In February 2021, I told Chris Scott and Simon Lloyd that I would need to take some days and some mornings off due to IVF, but I did not want others to know the reason why. They did not ask me one more question over the next 18 months other than the occasional informal check to ask how I was going. Brit also received similar unqualified support from Libby Gatgens, the principal at the Nelson Park School where she worked. Her work with special needs children sustained her through many flat spots during the year. She calls it her happy place. The satisfaction she had gained from that work helping her recover from disappointment. Her approach sustained me too.

BRIT: It's important to note that everyone's IVF process is different so the experiences and understanding of those involved can vary. The basic IVF process is to undergo a variety of injections/medications to stimulate follicles in a woman's ovaries, in order to produce multiple eggs which are then gathered at an egg collection procedure. At around day 10 of my cycle and course of injections/medications, I would need to have a scan to see how I was responding to the medication and how the eggs were growing and what size they were.

I was lucky I could do these scans locally at Geelong's Epworth Hospital rather than having to travel to the clinic in East Melbourne. On roughly day 14 of your cycle the eggs are gathered under anaesthetic. The eggs are inspected under a microscope and the best are collected. Depending on your partner's sperm (and whether it was a fresh collection or frozen) the eggs and sperm would then be taken to the lab on the same day to start the fertilisation process – that is, the making of an embryo.

Throughout the four- to five-day process you would be regularly informed as to how the process was tracking. If there was a viable embryo you would have a transfer of the embryo to the uterus. If there were any leftovers, they would be frozen and stored.

Our initial test results didn't show any major concerns. The egg count was high, blood tests were normal, there were no underlying medical conditions and our general health was good. The only issue was that Brit had a scarred cervix from previous procedures related to abnormal cells in the uterus.

BRIT: Our first egg collection was incredibly successful. I responded extremely well to all my medication and my scans showed I had a high number of follicles ready for the egg collection. I went in for the procedure and 22 eggs were collected, resulting in 12 viable embryos. We went to do a fresh embryo transfer but ran into complications with my cervix. Because it was so scarred, Lynn was unable to insert a catheter to complete the transfer. All 12 of our embryos were frozen. A few days later I went in for a second procedure to widen my cervix for future transfers.

Brit strictly adhered to the regime and she became pregnant, confirmed by a blood test, after the first embryo transfer which occurred after some early hiccups during our third IVF cycle. A nurse from the fertility clinic called us with the good news as we were driving to Marvel Stadium for the round nine match against St Kilda, in May 2021. I told John Leyden to look out for me on the bench as I was naturally a little euphoric. I'm guessing he guessed what I was on about. Although he did not know about the IVF program, he knew we were trying to have a baby. Every time I came to the bench, he asked me if I wanted to sit for a little longer. Brit and I were both rapt, of course, but on reflection we were also naive. We just assumed everything was okay. But it wasn't.

> **BRIT:** I went in for an eight-week viability scan by myself (because of COVID restrictions). The scan revealed there was no heartbeat. I had miscarried the baby. The scan outlined that the baby stopped growing at seven weeks.
> I decided to have a dilation and curettage procedure to remove the foetus, as I had not passed the baby naturally.

We were devastated, and my response was more suited to football than what we had been through. Positive to a fault – a trait that would sometimes annoy Brit – my initial thought was: 'Well, you were pregnant, that's a start. We can just do that again, right?' It wasn't that I was not concerned or not trying to be caring but such a message was not needed at that stage. I should have shown more sympathy for Brit. Thankfully, I would get better at that over the next 18 months.

I told Hawk about the miscarriage because I just needed someone to know why I was so flat. He had stepped up to help but then went to another level. Both our parents knew. I also told Simon Lloyd.

With Brit's blessing I travelled to Adelaide to play Port Adelaide in round 13. It was a significant occasion, as it was to be the 753rd AFL game by a Selwood, breaking the record of most games by brothers set by Terry, Neale, Anthony and Chris Daniher.

That small time when I was away – Victoria was still in lockdown and we were stuck in a mini-hub in Adelaide – was harder for Brit, being alone, than she had imagined it would be. I was glad to get back.

By this stage we were talking through each situation as Brit was living by a rigid IVF timetable. Her efforts to make that work for me too went beyond reasonable. She would check with the fertility clinic whether what she needed to do would fit in with my footy schedule. If there were any clashes, I would work it out to make sure I was by her side.

We had to find ways to keep a smile on our faces. The sound of Dr Lynn's high heels as we sat in the clinic would make us laugh as we tried to guess how many zeroes were on the price tag of her designer shoes. Was it four or five? Silly things that weren't really funny lightened the emotional weight we were carrying. When we went to the chemist with a prescription, we would play medication bingo, guessing how much each visit would cost.

I learnt too, not to describe IVF as 'our journey'. Brit had bluntly pointed out that doing blood tests – she would eventually do more than 100 – or having injections was not 'a journey'. It was bloody hard. I also resolved not to look at my watch or check for time when we were at the clinic. Sometimes the incredibly busy doctors would be running behind time, but I put the thought of missing a main training session or a football-related appointment to one side. I was lucky to have credits in the bank at the club. Brit eventually became more anxious about time than me as she did not want to miss her teaching. Being with the kids was, she would tell me, her happy place.

There were also times things just didn't work for a range of reasons. I was far from in the right place at the right time every time but Brit knew my priorities and bloody hell, I would soon find out how mentally and physically strong she was – and is. At times one of us would feel grumpy, tired, anxious, frustrated, despite our best intentions.

Sometimes after an appointment I would drop her off at school even though I would have preferred her to be at home, resting. She had been cleared to work and was determined to do so. It wasn't my place to demand otherwise. That sounds easier than it was because the drugs she was prescribed did have an impact on her physically. I could see that with my own eyes. The emotional toll was also relentless.

Meanwhile tests showed a rare chromosome abnormality – Trisomy 4 – had caused the miscarriage, so we pushed forward again. The next frozen embryo transfer was promising and we had our hopes up again when Brit had a blood test before we played the Saints in round 22. However, the pregnancy had not developed.

BRIT: This transfer turned out to be a biochemical pregnancy, which is a pregnancy and the embryo implants but at two to three weeks it results in a miscarriage. The nurses initially told us that we were pregnant, but I needed to have a follow up blood test in three days' time. The wait took place over the weekend of round 22, when Geelong was to play St Kilda. Our second tests results, on the Monday, came back with low hCG levels, meaning that the pregnancy hadn't developed.

As I headed on the road to participate in another finals series inside hubs – this time in South Australia and Western Australia – we decided to have another embryo transfer. Football in the hub had delayed us in 2020 and Brit was determined, in her words, to 'not let footy get in the way of the process again', so Brit's friend Morgan Hill, my brother Scott's girlfriend, drove her to have the embryo transfer while I was on the road.

BRIT: Morgan drove me to Melbourne during lockdown for the third embryo transfer. After this transfer I got really nervous. I was waiting on my pregnancy blood tests results (which is always a 12-day wait), I was in Vic lockdown without Joel and it was an unknown when he would be returning. I had to take these horrible clexane injections (an anticoagulant) and I struggled to do them by myself because they were painful.

A few times I got Joel's best mate to give me the injections or my acupuncturist would do it for me when I was seeing her. After a few days I just learnt to give them myself (like all my other needles) because the alternatives were becoming a hassle.

I was desperately trying to make my way across to WA as my mental health wasn't great. I had received numerous recommendation letters from my therapists, my GP and my fertility doctor to be reunited with my husband in Perth. We knew the implications of doing another cycle during this time, but it didn't really sink in how much it would impact me until this point, when I realised I could potentially have had three failed transfers. Joel was somewhat sheltered from my desperate attempts to make it over there, as I didn't want to stress him out.

After many attempts at applying for a G2G pass to travel to WA, I received a phone call from the head of the WA police. He said there was never a chance of me being accepted as they knew my partner was a football player and that this was not a genuine enough circumstance.

Brit's attitude had always been that if I was away, I was away but after the disappointments we had endured, for her to be alone at this time seemed too much for her to contemplate. But there was no way she wanted me to miss the finals. She never went down that path. Partners of elite sportspeople sure are resilient – the sacrifices they make are so real. Life on the road can be tough at times for sportspeople but even tougher for their partners. Couples from non-Victorian clubs spend the most time apart but good or bad luck can play a part in what impact your absence has. COVID exacerbated the stress.

Things were a little crazy as Brit considered whether she had the option of reaching me via Darwin as I prepared for the preliminary final against Melbourne. That was not going to work. She wanted us to win but losing wasn't going to be the worst result for her either. It was simply a tough time. I knew Brit would not want me to return to be with her as she not only wanted what was going on in our lives to remain private, but she loved football and didn't want to get in my way. I don't recall whether I specifically asked her if she wanted me to come home because I not only knew the answer would be no, I also suspected asking the question was unfair because she had every right to say yes.

BRIT: Geelong won the semi-final against GWS which put them into another preliminary final. I was so emotionally drained by this point, and I had to watch Joel make another milestone on the TV (most games played for Geelong) and I wasn't able to be at the game with him. I was about four days past my transfer and I was going through all the usual stresses of the IVF two-week wait.

I also had the stress of wanting Joel to succeed, but then I came to the realisation that if Geelong won the prelim, we wouldn't be allowed to go to Perth for the Grand Final. It also meant I would find out the results of my pregnancy test six or seven days before the Grand Final as the AFL had announced in late August there would be a fortnight's break between the preliminary final and the Grand Final in 2021. I was trying very hard to not let Joel know how much I was struggling at this point. I was very lucky I was still working full-time with my students (special needs teachers and students were able to be onsite). It meant I was around a few staff members and friends during this period. Although I never shared what I was going through with them, it was a nice distraction.

It had been a long two seasons under COVID and the things that often sustain you when sacrificing time together – such as milestone games or celebrations together after wins – had disappeared. Brit missed my 300th and again when I broke the club's games record in the semi-final. Each moment was minor in the context of all that was happening but sometimes when stress hits, the sting of small disappointments remain.

The ground I was on could not have been more foreign. This was a fresh and bucking beast we were on. I could not control what was happening and that was new. Delegating tasks to others had made me realise the notion that I had to do everything for it to be done had been misplaced. I also stopped to think before judging others' actions. Although I had prided myself on my emotional intelligence, my approach to issues had been very black and white for much of my career.

I flew home immediately after our preliminary final loss. I was disappointed but the silver lining was I could be with Brit when we again received bad news that the latest embryo transfer had resulted in a second biochemical pregnancy.

BRIT: We received a phone call from my nurse at my clinic, telling me we had another biochemical pregnancy. We were struggling to understand why it wasn't working. It was a hard time. Our clinic was also really puzzled when everything looked great on paper. It was a relief that the season was over because the next few months were quite tough and consumed both of us. I was in constant fear of being exposed to COVID (if I got COVID, I wouldn't be able to do IVF for three months) and there were cancellations of IVF procedures from the government due to COVID. During this time, we decided to get our nine leftover embryos genetically tested. The results came back in early November and showed that all our embryos were genetically normal.

This period was more than a grind. We held on but not without bouts of anguish. We maintained complete confidence in Dr Lynn but I must admit I sometimes found it disconcerting when they told us the answer to our issue was not staring them in the face.

The commentary around the preliminary final result and what it meant for Geelong – that we were at the end of our cycle of success, and that our list was too old – didn't rankle. Scrutiny of my performance affected me even less. I had never resented what was being said. In truth a part of me thought at the end of 2021: 'If only you knew what was really happening in my life when you made that comment.' But that was to put things in perspective for me rather than to denigrate the commentariat. They could only ever know half the story.

BRIT: We ended 2021 with seven IVF cycles, three procedures, five embryo transfers, and three miscarriages (all in 10 months) and had no real explanations as to why we weren't having success.

We realised we could not do this alone and organised to have a support nurse assigned to us. We got lucky when Caron Filetti, from No.1 Fertility, took on the role. Suddenly Brit and I had someone we could liaise with when we had questions that needed answering. We were pulling out all stops, trying things many couples in our position would find impossible due to the expense. We took advice and acted. Finding ways to make things easier for couples undergoing IVF is something I would love to support down the track.

> **BRIT:** After discussing the different options with Dr Lynn, we decided to go in for a small procedure in mid-January 2022, to check that everything was still looking okay and to have a solution washed through my uterus as a bit of a clean-out. This surgery got cancelled due to the Victorian government cancelling IVF procedures; they were deemed 'elective surgery'. We had about a week of panic trying to work out our next option. That changed a number of times during the week but after a few days, the government decided to reverse its call and IVF procedures were back, but on a limited capacity. I ended up going in for the suggested procedure and everything looked fine.

That week when surgery was cancelled had us on the brink, a mix of anger and frustration combined with some rationality and positive thoughts made for a combustible mix. The sense that our reality was one few could understand had been highlighted by the government's hasty decision.

While I remained a key part of the process, Brit needed me to stick with her direction – not in a domineering manner; it was just a practical reality. She needed me more than anything that might be happening at the football club. I was not a professional when it came to IVF. Neither was Brit although she was expected to learn quickly and would endure 1000 more challenges than me. We had one more transfer using the tested embryos in storage. It was our sixth transfer and eighth cycle.

Chapter 23

Bring the love

SOMEHOW, I WAS still able to segment my life. Although the IVF process was obviously at the forefront of my mind, there was still that constant footy issue that had to be resolved. How could we get better? Since the 2011 Grand Final win, we had now played in 22 finals and had won only seven. And I had been captain through all those disappointments. The only footy question that occupied me during the 2022 pre-season was how do we get some love back into the place?

The COVID years had exhausted us all and playing AFL while simultaneously dealing with the anxiety that accompanies IVF had taken a further toll on me. I liked being in control, but I could not control much of what Brit and I had confronted through 2021. Like everyone, I'd have good days and bad days as personal issues arise. Rarely did I share how I was feeling but those who knew me best could detect an occasional surliness in my mood.

COVID's impact had been real and I could only imagine how others were feeling. Something integral to the place had been lost during the shutdown and the cuts that followed. Brutal decisions inevitably caused strain and what had made Geelong a great club and so competitive was in danger of disappearing as we tried to settle into a new normal ahead of season 2022, as COVID restrictions had eased. My admiration for those who had shared the COVID journey in 2020 and 2021 was total but by the end of a second disrupted season the club had started to skim over a few issues and little cracks became bigger cracks. We needed to put our work boots on to eliminate those failings.

I put my thoughts to Steve Hocking. He had taken over from Brian Cook in November and hadn't been at the club since 2017. I told him we needed Geelong people at the club, people who could bring that love. To his credit, Hock rapidly picked up on the need and recruited the exact characters we needed in James Kelly, Shannon Byrnes and Matt Egan. The move to engage Harry Taylor, who would have to drag his family back from WA just a year after he had sold up and headed home, was supported by me. Kelly, Byrnes, Egan and Taylor were all true Geelong people. Just what we needed.

There was no doubting Matty Knights (who coached at the club for 10 years), Matt Scarlett and Corey Enright's love for the Cats was as strong as any of their replacements but they needed a change in environment as much as we needed to change the environment. They had recognised that themselves, putting the club first as always. Scarlo stepped away from football while Boris Enright joined the Saints, his first experience at a club other than Geelong, and Knighta went west to the Eagles.

* * *

My early pre-season training had been strong but in January I was reminded of my footballing mortality when I joined Mark O'Connor and first-year player Mitch Knevitt in a conditioning running drill called 'bow tie'. It requires you to run for 60 metres between cones then diagonally forward to another cone, jogging for 60 metres and striding for 170 metres. As I laboured between cones, I soon realised I was two gears behind that duo (both of them among the club's top five runners). One of them yelled: 'Have we got six or eight run-throughs to go?' I yelled 'six' hoping I was shooting the eight question out of the sky.

I then took a shortcut on those remaining six. I had *never* taken a shortcut. Walking back to the car afterwards I thought, cheekily and unkindly: 'When are Brandan Parfitt and Paddy Dangerfield back?' I was searching for some teammates I could keep pace with.

It wasn't the first time I had battled through a session but normally I'd be able to identify the reason why. I always considered myself a top-10 runner at the club but a few power-based, conditioning runs had thrown up a few queries. Had I eaten properly? Had I needed the morning off? Was I recovering from something? But none of that existed. It was my first sense that footy was getting harder for me.

Tom Petroro and I had discussed during the summer whether 2022 might be my last year, but any conversations we had had been vague although they were very honest. He just gave me a sense of what he believed the Cats were thinking and how we might manage the season. Having your manager intimately involved in such an important decision might seem strange to outsiders but it pointed to the strength of our relationship as well as his understanding of the way the Cats worked. It's also indicative of the ways of modern football, with managers and clubs needing to be constantly in dialogue about a range of issues relating to their players. Brit was open-minded and selfless, ready to support whatever decision I reached, happy for me to keep going if that was what we decided; but she was well aware the end was in sight.

* * *

Anna Box, a consulting psychologist who also started with the Cats in November, was beginning to talk with me too. Our focus was to give me a greater understanding about myself, my values and my emotions as I entered my final years. Our discussions had started with a walk around Albert Park and something about her style made me open up. It had not previously been my go, but I warmed to her immediately.

One of the phrases we came up with early was 'Connect to WIFI' with WIFI an acronym for 'What If, Fuck It' which would help me attack what was ahead of me with a sense of freedom. The phrase came to life for me when we thrashed Essendon in the opening round. I took two bounces inside the MCG's centre square, the hard patch normally the domain of speedsters. I had never done that before, but I was filled with a boyish wonder as I cantered through the middle, one bounce – why not two? I was connected to WIFI.

The win over the Bombers revealed we were going to play with speed and to look to get the ball to our forwards quickly.

We had enough players ready to embrace this style, with endurance beasts on the wings and high half forwards ready to peak. Ty Stengle was an unsung addition who kicked four and looked classy. Off the field he was quiet, and I searched for a way to connect with him. My nickname for him would not be 'Bruz' as some of his closest teammates called him. Eventually we settled on it being 'Sis' and our relationship would develop as his humour and skill began to shine through.

The next week was the Buddy Franklin 1000-goal match, which we lost. We were the Washington Generals for a night. The mayhem that followed his goal when the crowd invaded the ground to surround Buddy was memorable and play stopped for close to 40 minutes to clear the ground with their lead 38 points. I was near the bench, so I did not get caught in the crowd. Zach Tuohy showed his class when he returned to the centre of the mob to give a spectator back his wallet after the supporter dropped it when Zach inadvertently shirtfronted him as he rushed in the opposite direction to the surging crowd. It was a miracle we all made it back to the safety of the rooms unscathed but the euphoria made the moment memorable. For the first time in my career I told my teammates to avoid injury in the final five minutes when play restarted.

The next morning, I had to catch a 6 am flight out of Sydney to pick up Brit and take her to the hospital for another egg collection. Brit was nervous about whether I would make it, but I was adamant I would be there and was up at 4.30 am after having little sleep. She backed me in but was relieved when I arrived at the Pullman Hotel in East Melbourne with plenty of time to spare, depending on whether you regard 15 minutes as plenty of time. I was never going to miss such an important appointment; I would have driven overnight if I needed to but fortunately all went to plan. Brit had a fresh embryo transfer five days later. We had decided it was time for another egg collection because the results from the first batch had been disappointing. Again, a fresh 22 eggs were collected, which fertilised 11 embryos.

BRIT: I had a fresh embryo transfer five days later with a perfect embryo which started to hatch, but it turned out to be another unsuccessful transfer.

That weekend I was due to lead the club for the 227th time and break Carlton great Stephen 'Sticks' Kernahan's record for most games as captain. I had a head cold leading into the match against Collingwood but too much had been arranged for me to miss, so I rolled into the game. Sticks paid me a great honour when he turned up to speak before the game to congratulate me. I was very average on the field, and so were we for three quarters. We conceded nine goals to three in the third quarter and fell 37 points behind, but somehow, were able to rally. Through Jeremy Cameron, who kicked four of our last eight goals, we lifted to win by 13 points after keeping Collingwood to one behind in the last quarter. With Brit and family, Tom Petroro and Kathryn De Lulio (she had married Daniel), Vic Fuller's wife, Nola, my close mates from Bendigo in the stands watching on, the win was one to savour.

I was also glad that the focus was now off me, as I set myself for another tough encounter against the Brisbane Lions in round four. I was determined to immediately bounce back from my average round three performance. It was not to be. I was home relaxing with Brit, when an unexpected message from Chris Scott popped up on my phone asking whether this week might be a good time to have a rest. Brit noticed my reaction without me knowing I had even responded, and she asked me what was on the text.

I just replied: 'I'm not playing this week'

'Is that how you found out?' Brit said.

'Yeah, I'll speak to them tomorrow.'

Brit and I would talk footy but she knew that it was my workplace and she respected that. The silence that followed was a little uncomfortable. My mind was racing. We were playing a top-four team and we had won two and lost one. This was a massive match and surely, I did not need to be rested after just three games? If they believed they had told me that was to be our policy, then the message had not been delivered clearly enough. Sure, the senior players knew they were going to be rested from time to time throughout the season but the exact games we would miss were left to management decisions, depending on circumstances. In other years we had often looked at the fixture and the ladder before a final decision would be reached.

The discussion about when to rest and not rest players had been part of club dialogue for as long as Chris had been at the club. In his first season as coach, no player had played every game on our way to the flag. As time went on things continued informally, with selectors responding to situations as they arose. Often the quality of the opposition had played a role in whether a player took a break for a week. However, in 2022 the club was determined to hold its nerve and give a player a break when they deemed it necessary. The depth of the squad gave the coaches confidence that any player could be covered.

The professional in me had wanted to be part of this discussion. How was I to use the break? What was my program during the break? How often would this occur? And I wanted to hear the news directly from the coach. That was unfair but I wasn't thinking about how busy football clubs are during the week or that the senior coach's office is the busiest place in the building. As players we often forget that and think the senior coach should know exactly how each individual is feeling about any decision he might make.

I was uncomfortable with Chris's method of communication, and I made that clear to him the next morning. I wanted to hear such news from him directly, I said, not by text. Nothing should be assumed. It was another reminder to the coach – as if he needed one – that doubts are never far from the surface of any player's mind, even from those he doesn't expect to have such thoughts.

He said he had not made the decision without thought for me nor was he being flippant with his method of communication. He had hoped to keep the tone breezy, thinking that would help me take the idea in my stride. Chris suspected a reaction was likely from me and was impressed rather than disappointed in the way I had expressed my thoughts in response. The two of us generally reached agreement on important decisions over time as we nudged rather than bludgeoned each other. He always resisted the temptation to needle me into performing because he thought that would be unhelpful in the long-term as well as being unfair on me. Sometimes I thought I didn't need coaching; Chris knew how to coach me, how to get the best out of me.

Chris was calm but reminded me that I was a big part of his plan. I asked him whether Mark O'Connor would be taking my spot. He told me I was an automatic selection in our best 22 and would be for the rest of the season. But even after our conversation I looked at our team and thought: 'Gee, it's pretty strong. Is there really a spot there for me?'

The embryo transfer failure news arrived in the same week. I knew where my priorities were but my emotional band was being stretched close to breaking point as I feared the club was looking to move past me. Another part of me was excited by that view of our list. We looked so strong on paper.

On reflection, I wasn't acting in a manner consistent with my philosophy as a leader. My reaction was emotional. That didn't mean my response wasn't understandable or reasonable in the circumstances. It was just hard on others.

I didn't attend the Brisbane game. Not out of spite but the illness I had before the Collingwood game was lingering and Brit and I needed some time alone together. We were tight but we were confronting difficult questions. Despite IVF being different from anything either of us had experienced, I just thought we could, and would, find a way through. But maybe there wasn't one?

I did watch the match on television and did not yell at the screen once. Apart from a few anxious moments early I could see us playing exactly as planned. We held off the resilient Lions by 10 points. As captain I was proud of the team's professional approach and although I already knew they could win without me, they had proved that decisively against a very good side. It was a long way from the thoughts I'd been having in past years.

I felt the benefits of the week off the following week although we lost to Hawthorn at the MCG. We then beat North Melbourne easily in Hobart before having a frustrating three-point loss to Fremantle at home. We now sat seventh on the ladder with a 4-3 record.

I was not in a good mood after the loss to the Dockers. I snatched my towel and headed towards the pool to recover. I was wondering how we had let that game slip when I stopped to chat to James Kelly, expecting him to feed my anger with possible recriminations.

'It wasn't good, but we will be okay,' Kel said reassuringly. He had a measured approach in everything he did and was a firm believer in the process.

I kept walking while his assessment sank in. 'Wow, that was different.' That sort of thinking was not what I had been used to. As I gingerly lowered my aching body into the pool, a thought entered my mind: 'You know what? Maybe he's right.'

On the following Monday, in the players' cafe, I discussed the Freo loss with Tom Stewart and Paddy Dangerfield. We realised our immediate reaction to the result had not been good. We had done plenty right in the match but our pressure dropped off in the third quarter and we were unable to convert our field position. Max Holmes had been subbed off, robbing us of run but we had set up the ground well and we were in the contest. We had performed well in general play but our moves forward had been too easily intercepted. The Dockers had edged us out, but there was a deeper issue we had to discuss. After much chat, we resolved that if we wanted to win together, then we had to lose together too. It wasn't a decision we communicated to the group but one we resolved to stick to, so the road ahead would become flat rather than our season becoming another rollercoaster ride.

Throughout my career, I had been more pissed off about results than anyone but where had that got us? I tried to hide those emotions around Brit and my teammates but only they could say whether I had been successful. I had to change because my reaction to losses had been the same in 2021 and 2020 and the year before that. And, ultimately, that approach had worked momentarily but did it have us peaking at the right time? The only answer was no.

We spoke about the impression we were giving young players such as Max Holmes and Sam De Koning when we lost. They had only seen us go on about detail: whether we could have been better in the ruck or could have helped our backs by exiting the defensive 50 wider or wondering why forward tackles were down. I was beginning to wonder whether that approach might have been a self-defeating one. I was even more determined to enter Kardinia Park with a smile on my face – whatever our results – for the rest of what could, in reality, be my last season.

That resolve was tested sooner than expected when St Kilda beat us at Docklands despite us dominating most of the game. In a short third-quarter burst they kicked seven goals to two to overrun us with a 10-point win that moved them above us on the ladder. I stuck with the view that 'If we're gunna win together, we're gunna lose together'. We sat behind closed doors deep in the rooms, vowing to stick together as a playing group. We had a giggle and eventually we realised that 20 minutes of bad football had cost us. The players and coaching staff reminded each other we were building a new game style so to expect perfection was unrealistic. High expectations were mandatory but perfection close to impossible.

We still thought our style was right. We just had to keep working on it.

* * *

Delegating has never been a natural thing for me. I would either rail against the thought of handing over responsibility to another, or think if a job needed doing, then I was the one to do it.

In 2022, at least off the field, things changed. As I prioritised Brit and IVF, I started handing jobs to others. Gryan Miers was charged with organising St Patrick's Day so we all wore Irish County jumpers. I asked Mark Blicavs and Jack Henry to set up a quiz for the boys. Brad Close organised golf days. They all thrived on the opportunity and my mind was freer, but it had taken some time for me to get there. It also signalled my shifting back to Geelong being a place I enjoyed walking into every day, with fun and connection at its heart.

The team had also to give Tom Atkins and Max Holmes more responsibility in the middle and that move was making us better. I needed to give them the chance to call the shots at centre bounces or leave the job to them when games were finely balanced.

We were winning but I was battling at times to get my head around the shifts happening in the midfield space. I was still looking too much for perfection and needed to relax a little more and let the boys keep growing.

Chapter 24

Joy and trepidation

ICONTINUED TO WALK into the club with a smile on my face and that was okay for me but watching Brit go through so many painful tests was tough. My admiration for Brit grew every minute. During pre-game warm-ups I would check to see where Brit was sitting. Being around too many children was difficult for Brit as she just wanted her night at the footy to be a switch-off. When games were at the MCG, I organised for Brit and a friend to sit in a mate's corporate box.

BRIT: The clinic recommended I do an ERA (Endometrial Receptivity Analysis) test. It meant I would do another full IVF cycle and, on the day that I would usually have had an embryo transferred, they would instead do the ERA test to see if it was in fact the right time for transfers during my cycle. My cervix had closed up again and I needed a green whistle (a pain relief inhaler) at the hospital to finish the test. This test came back with perfect results, meaning we had been transferring embryos on the correct day, but it meant we still had no real answers as to why we weren't getting pregnant. In the meantime, my clinic had sent me to Dr Peter Ellims, a haematologist, who put me on a drug called hydroxychloroquine (yes, Donald Trump's COVID 'cure') in the hope that it would change my fertility issues. I had to be on this drug for six weeks prior to a transfer. That was good timing as we were waiting on genetic testing results that take about 3-4 weeks from the 10 embryos we had in storage. We eventually received those results and all of our 10 embryos were considered 'genetically normal'. We decided to go ahead for our eighth embryo transfer.

* * *

After the loss to St Kilda we had good wins over Port Adelaide, Adelaide and the Bulldogs, and after the bye we headed to Perth to play the battling West Coast. It was an afternoon game, which meant a 40-hour round trip and even though restrictions had been eased, I told Brit to stay at home. We won a scrappy game before flying back that night and were due to arrive back in Geelong about 2.30 am. I knew something was up, when I received a text from Brit well after midnight. It read: 'Is the bus back?' I suspected she might be pregnant. Why else would she want to know when I was to walk in the door?

BRIT: I did have my eighth embryo transfer and my eleventh IVF cycle. Joel was away for two nights and was to return home late on the third night. It was around the time when it was too early for pregnancy blood tests, but I would be sneaky and do an at-home pregnancy test. Results of at-home pregnancy tests aren't reliable during IVF as you can have false positives due to the drugs you are on, but I always did these tests and could understand them very well due to my history.

The Friday before Joel's Saturday game, I messaged Caron, my nurse, whom I had become close to and was allowed to have message contact with. I told her I had received three positive pregnancy tests, two on the Thursday and one again on Friday morning (the lines were also getting stronger). She didn't want to get my hopes up and kept me level-headed. At this point I hadn't said anything to Joel because he was playing the next day and I didn't want to upset him or get his hopes up before the game.

On the Saturday morning (game day) I had another positive at-home pregnancy test. Caron actually messaged me before I had woken up and asked what the results were. Again, she was very hopeful but said we need to wait until Monday for a blood test. I had done six tests by this point and, as the hours and days went on, all of the lines were getting darker. I was silently confident that I was pregnant and couldn't wait for Joel to come home that night.
I couldn't sleep and waited up for him to come home. He knew something was up because I texted him around 30 minutes before he got home.

Brit was on the couch with a big smile on her face when I arrived around 3 am. The news was positive. How good. We contained ourselves – just – because we knew we had to wait until daylight for official confirmation. The blood test confirmed Brit's home test was right. We tried to stay level-headed given what could happen – what *had* happened so often through so many cycles – but we were also beyond excited.

> **BRIT:** It was such a special moment and we both knew what it meant to each other. Although we never really got too excited it was a relief that we had made some progress and we were quietly celebrating to ourselves.

That didn't mean we weren't anxious. Given what we had been through, we did not let our minds wander nine months into the future. We held our breath for the first 12 to 16 weeks before we began to let ourselves relax and enjoy the experience.

We followed the West Coast win with a big win over Richmond in Jezza's 200th, although only his 29th with us. It was one of the games of the season with Tom Atkins winning the vital match-winning centre clearance with less than two minutes left, followed by a goal by Jack Henry to win by three points. Unfortunately, Tom Stewart was suspended for four weeks for a bump on Dion Prestia. Tom took his medicine for getting his timing wrong. I drew on my own experience when I had been suspended in 2011 and told him that year had worked out okay. I also suggested he might gain pride and satisfaction with our group if the team could keep winning without him.

All through the week, the much-anticipated top-of-the-table round 17 clash against Melbourne had been the talk of the town. Everyone, it seemed, had been talking about this match, because it would indicate whether Geelong had gone past the reigning premiers. But on match day, footy was the furthest thing from my mind.

I wasn't preparing for footy in any way. I was with Brit in the maternity services section of Geelong's Epworth Hospital, the stoic expression on my face a brave attempt to hide my anxiety. After so many emotionally draining setbacks, Brit was now six weeks' pregnant and the joy we had shared at the positive news less than a month earlier suddenly felt, if not rash, then irrelevant, given the number of times we had been thwarted in our quest. One phone call from Brit changed all our optimism. She was straight to the point: 'I'm pretty scared.' She told me that after some exercise, the first she had done for a couple of months, she had noticed some bleeding.

After we asked each other what we should do, we knew there was only one answer. We had to get it checked out, for Brit to undergo yet another scan. She arrived at Geelong's Epworth Hospital at 11 am with me joining her about 20 minutes later after an anxious drive from Barwon Heads.

The first scan showed nothing because the embryo was at such an early stage, so we had to go downstairs to make use of another, more powerful scanning machine. Again, we waited, wondering what might lie ahead, a nervous couple faced with uncertainty, trying to stay positive.

Four hours passed before we received the all-clear from Epworth's empathetic professionals. I had learnt over the journey not to look at my watch although this was a very different experience. Whenever we could we tried to find an excuse to laugh, to distract our mind, but this time, jokes were hard to find.

Brit played sudoku on her phone. My mobile stayed unusually quiet. Brit kept telling me to go and get food and to stay hydrated, but I was not going anywhere. We just stayed put, in a private consulting room, alone yet together in our thoughts.

Once we received the positive news, Brit made me smile when she asked the doctor whether she would be able to go to the footy that night. He did not take long to answer: 'Nuh, you're going home.' I could tell by the look on his face he was only ever going to give Brit one such response. I dropped Brit back home, both of us emotionally drained but so relieved. At 4.30, way earlier than normal, I packed my bags and said: 'I'm going to the footy club.' I needed a release before the group arrived.

I swam for about 40 minutes then just sat in the spa. I guess I was dehydrated after the strain of the morning and afternoon. I had also failed to eat much during the day as it had not been front of mind. Having had the previous week off I had been feeling in great shape, but the stress of the day had taken its toll. That didn't worry me too much – many times I had rocked up to games feeling exhausted but had told myself I would get through. Muscle memory would kick in and I would perform. That was both good and dangerous because despite the myths sport likes to create, everyone has their limits. I just had not passed mine.

My mood shifted when I realised in the team meeting that I was to start on the bench. I have a good poker face, so my expression didn't change but I wasn't happy that no-one had told me beforehand. I didn't speak to anyone about what I thought was something of a slight given I had not played in the previous match. No-one knew my boiling inner thoughts as I took my place on the bench alongside Sam Menegola, Tom Atkins and Gryan Miers.

Not knowing the final line-up before running out was not unusual. Sometimes we would only be certain at the warm-up as the coaching staff literally like to leave such calls to the last second. But it isn't ideal for some as generally such decisions are easier to accept in the lead-up than when you are looking for your name on the whiteboard pre-game. That's footy, I suppose.

My annoyance stemmed from the fact I had woken up feeling so fresh after a week off. I had been rested for the previous match against North Melbourne as there were only five days between rounds 16 and 17.

Looking back, it was good timing as after the events of the day I just needed to get through the match. But I still spoke to Anna Box about how I might express my thoughts to Shaun Grigg. I had discussed my new role in the midfield with Grigga regularly and he was, I assumed, the key to the call for me to start on the pine. I was impressed with Grigga as a young coach, particularly as it is difficult coaching people you have played with or against. I did not want my thoughts to bruise him but I had to tell him how I felt. He just said: 'You should have told me your feelings, and I would have started you on the ground, no big deal.' It had been an issue to me however. Talking with Anna had revealed it challenged my sense of belonging, my sense of what a captain's role was, even though no-one apart from me viewed it in that way. They had known I would do anything for the team so were probably as surprised as I was by my reaction. I could see my thoughts had tightened up a bit and the feelings followed. My acceptance of this role would make me a better captain. I now realised I did not have to see myself as the main man.

My move to the bench lasted the rest of the season. We had been tinkering with it during Paddy Dangerfield and Brandan Parfitt's absence, but the centre square combination gelled when Tom Atkins became a permanent member of the midfield. We veterans had been good solid runners but, if we were honest, we had not kept up with the younger opponents for long enough when it mattered. Max Holmes, an incredible athlete, could run up and down his wing for 90 per cent of the game while Zach Tuohy, Isaac Smith, Gryan Miers and Brad Close were endurance machines. Around the ground we were able to use our rotations, with Mark Blicavs complementing it all as the ultimate hybrid: ruck, midfielder, defender. His impact is amazing. He doesn't need to touch the ball; he is just always in the road; he is football's ultimate disruptor.

Starting on the bench did take some adjusting. It can become frustrating watching minutes tick by while sitting on your bum when the ball gets caught on the opposite side of the ground. I struggle to sit still at home, let alone when a game of football is unfolding in front of me. It wasn't easy for me or Paddy, who would also have several starts on the bench, but we learnt to trust our teammates. Importantly, they learnt that we actually *did* trust them. In the end the recipe was almost, albeit not quite, perfect.

We defeated Melbourne in a hard-fought match by 28 points to grab top spot for the first time that season. Despite their midfield stars, we won the clearance count by 18 with Tom Atkins and a rejuvenated Paddy Dangerfield starring in the middle. Although I played less game time than any of my teammates my impact was high with 10 score involvements.

Was this going to be another close but not quite year? Or was it shaping up differently?

* * *

With all that was happening, I needed to unscramble my mind, so I again went to Anna Box for a serious chat. We began catching up fortnightly in the Cotton On corporate box at Kardinia Park, sometimes to riff, sometimes to address a specific issue. I explained my emotions around what was occurring, actually opening up to an expert for the first time in my life. Not long into our conversation, I thought, 'She gets it.' We would riff about everything happening in my life from IVF to football.

During these chats I was able to outline my definition of what success looked like for me and the answers were a long way from winning a Brownlow. It became clear that the five aspects of life I valued could apply and went beyond football. They were: simple pleasures, making a legitimate difference, respectful relationships, leaving a place better than I found it and a happy home.

I had always considered myself mentally tough and self-aware but this year was so different, and when Anna spoke about mental fitness and we explored what underpinned my thinking, it made sense. Another valuable layer of support had been added to my life at just the right time.

By the time of my 350th in round 20 we were a game clear on top and suddenly we were being spoken about as premiership contenders ... again. My form was okay but over the last few seasons, age had been catching up with me. I had been reaching the end of seasons gassed, feeling the effects of playing so much because I hadn't missed many games, or because of an unfortunately timed injury.

The Bulldogs' Tom Liberatore spent the first quarter of my 350th just bashing into my back every time he had a chance. Every time I rose from the bench or was being tackled, I thought: 'Something is up with my back.'

After our win I waved to the crowd as I ran a lap of the centre square post-game. I thought that was important because it was a cold night, and everyone had stayed to watch me being chaired off. I had to say thank you in some way. I could feel a twinge each time I lifted my arm to wave to fans and my friends and key people in my life who were all at the game. Even Kathryn De Lulio was there, less than a week after having a baby through caesarean section. I had told her not to come. She came anyway.

I had a scan later that week which revealed I had a small crack in my back. No-one seemed too concerned, however. Only Brad Close picked up on it when he saw me lifting weights well below my capacity and questioned me. 'This is all I've got today,' I said. Brad was quick with his response, accompanied by a smirk: 'Remember, you have to get better every day.' He had heard me parrot that phrase enough times; I deserved the gentle rebuke.

I missed the following week – a scheduled rest – against St Kilda. By the time I returned to play against the Gold Coast, I was sore but better than usual for that time of the year. The Queensland sunshine helped.

Chapter 25

Decision time

O N T H E M O N D A Y before the last round, I sat with Tom Petroro at the back of A Pillar of Salt cafe in Church Street, Richmond to make some sort of decision on my playing future.

Hawk and Paddy had each asked me whether I was going around again while we chatted either over coffee with Paddy or in the sauna with Hawk and I had said 'probably' without committing. I had already sounded out Harry Taylor for what I knew would be frank advice. He knew how to be honest, raising the topic on a Pilates mat in the warm-up room during the week leading into round 22. He was making sure I was thinking clearly about the topic and followed me all the way to my locker to continue the conversation. His suggestion, subtly, was that sometimes you just need to be told. The words were similar to the ones I had used with him in 2020, conveying a message without saying the words directly.

Chris's approach was perfect. I knew he would have supported me and kept playing me. He left it to me to work out whether playing on in 2023 was the right call. We trusted each other.

Now it was Tom Petroro's turn. He was someone I could rely on to poke me when others just wouldn't. He had my respect and was prepared to challenge my thinking to ensure what occurred was best for me.

Tom and I spoke for two hours. He asked the right questions and told me he was getting vibes from the club – the conversations were mainly between him and Steve Hocking – that the decision would be mine, but they weren't pushing for me to stay. We tossed around questions about whether I could play without being captain or perhaps play only 15 or so games. He was honest, telling me he thought I had 10 good games in me but he didn't think that was enough to justify continuing. The conversation was hard for Tom. We had such a special relationship that went way beyond the average manager–player connection. He had a responsibility to tell me his view, whether it was right or wrong. He later admitted he lay awake wondering what to say and decided he could only be honest.

Despite his thoughts I walked away from that meeting still thinking I probably wanted to play on in 2023 more than I wanted to stop, but I wasn't definite. The drive home was a great chance to percolate Tom's view. I got the sense that Tom and the football club were protecting me from myself.

A mid-year conversation I had with Port Adelaide coach Ken Hinkley before our round 10 game at home had stuck. He asked me what I was doing in 2023 before saying, in an offhand manner, that he had noticed a decline in my contest and clearance work. 'I guess you are missing your one wood defensively,' he said.

'Yeah,' I replied, 'but I still have my irons.'

'But you can only use them for so long,' he said.

I had so much respect for Ken – we had formed a close relationship during his time as an assistant at Geelong in my early years. Initially I wasn't too impressed with his opinion but I knew how good a judge he was, and that he wouldn't tell me his thoughts for his own enjoyment.

Tom Petroro and I had spoken about Nathan Jones's challenging experience the season before when he became only a spiritual figure in Melbourne's premiership push. Jonesy, who had been drafted a year earlier than me, had been squeezed out of the team just as the club pushed towards the premiership, a success he had played a major role in setting up. I admired the way he had handled the situation.

I thought being challenged like that might be a good test of my character. I could tell by the look on Tom's face he didn't think I needed to go through what Jonesy had endured. As I drove home all those thoughts were going through my head. Eventually the fact Tom didn't think I should play on and the logic that lay behind that thought finally sank in.

I rang Tom from the car and told him I wanted to catch up with Hock that week. Such decisions are normally list management decisions, but no-one thought the responsibility for discussing my future should rest with the list manager, my premiership teammate Andrew Mackie.

Such a call was the responsibility of Steve Hocking and Chris. A little-known fact about Chris regarding his view on list management was that he would almost always want his senior players to have another year. Often it was a collective decision that would end a player's career, but at times the senior coach would have to face the player solo to deliver the bad news – eyeball to eyeball. It was, and is, an antiquated system.

That made Steve Hocking the key man.

Hock's diary was full, so I suggested he come around for dinner on Thursday night. As soon as he accepted, I thought: 'Okay, I know where this is going'. Then I thought: 'Do I? Maybe not. Maybe he is going to tell me how desperate he is for me to continue.'

Brit made chicken and pumpkin salad, a dish she pulls out when we are trying to get on someone's good side. Hock sat down after a big day on AFL-related matters and we made small talk as we ate dinner before we cut to the chase.

'Okay, so what are we doing?' I said.

Hock responded, mate to mate: 'What more do you need to do?' I could tell he could see me enjoying 2022. Now was the time to finish.

That's all I needed to hear. There was no animosity. On the contrary, there was just respect.

Hock, Brit and I spoke for three hours. I was only half-joking when I said to Hock: 'How can you boot me out when the team is finally in the spot that I have wanted it to be for so long? Footy is actually the easiest it has been for ages and I am walking away.'

'But isn't that beautiful?' he said.

'Absolutely,' I said.

I knew it was the right thing to do.

I then turned to Brit and said: 'I came in winning one and I am going to go out winning one.'

There had been little public discussion about me as the futures of Buddy Franklin and Dusty Martin kept newsrooms busy with speculation about those two greats. That was a relief as I wanted to leave the ultimate decision late enough to not have to reconsider or worse, to lose my focus. This was more of a risk now than it had ever been as I focused on Brit and our growing baby.

Brit was great. She was like me in not wanting the ride to end, because we both loved the club so much. But when Hock shut the door that night, Brit said to me: 'It's the right time you know.' That didn't mean we would not keep asking each other questions as to whether it was, in fact, the right time but the initial thought did help my thinking.

I was also rapt to leave the club in a position where several teammates were more than ready to take over from me as captain and my spot on the field could be filled. The wise heads such as Chris Scott, Steve Hocking and Craig Drummond saw that as a true measure of leadership and although it took me time to recognise that, it had become clearer to me throughout 2022.

I needed to grab Chris before training the next day. I'd asked Hock when he left to let Chris know so I presumed he was on top of the news. We bumped into each other near the computers and I signalled for him to join me in his office. His office has frosted windows now but the door is normally open. I shut the door behind us.

I sat down and before he had a chance to do the same. I said: 'I'm okay.'

He stood there looking at me, a confused expression on his face. He said: 'I don't know what you are talking about.'

When I told him that Hock had joined me for dinner the night before, he twigged but he said: 'You had better tell me the details because I am not yet across what has gone on.' We became teary as I explained I had decided to finish up. I went to walk out and then did a U-turn and we embraced. I reminded him it was a secret as I did not want to cause any distraction. 'Let's fucking do this,' I said. Then I left it for him to walk out and address the group ahead of Paddy's 300th.

It wasn't the best address Chris has ever given as we sat on the Cats emblem covering the blue floor in the rooms. Chris is usually extremely good when celebrating an individual's milestone but all he could muster for Paddy was: 'I'm not going to say anything about you mate, because you know.' I was a bit taken aback because I thought the moment had been stolen from Paddy. Thankfully Chris circled back to tell him how special he was to the group but the meeting, in truth, was flat and uninspired.

Hock had called me at 8 am to check if I was okay. I asked him the same question and he took a while to answer. I could tell he was finding it hard.

He also told me I should tell Mum and Dad of my decision, so I drove to their unit in Highton and waited impatiently for them to return home. I was booked to have a haircut at 3 pm. Dad moseyed in from lawn bowls just as Mum arrived after dropping in to get a Tatts ticket on the way home. They saw no need to rush and they only caught me in the driveway as I was about to leave.

'Make sure you enjoy tomorrow night because it will be my last game at home,' I said. They were taken aback. 'But you're going okay, aren't you?' Mum said. They didn't want the journey to end either. They had been watching one of their sons playing in the AFL for nearly 20 years. They had watched me play in pretty well every game since I was eight and had never veered into coaching. They were perfect parents. I left their stunned looks behind to get to my haircut before I rang them to tell them to keep it a secret. When Troy paid a visit soon after I had left, they found it hard to keep their emotions in check.

Nigel Lappin, an understated person who had a great influence on me, had told me all year to take in each week as you never know when the end was coming. This time I knew that the end was soon to come, give or take finals' results.

Brit and I headed off to the twilight game against West Coast. Driving across the Latrobe Terrace bridge we saw Kardinia Park loom. The moment hit me. I played the game against the Eagles with glassy eyes, but I managed to pick up 28 touches. The umpires liked what they saw, because they gave me two Brownlow votes.

Post-game I battled to contain my emotions as I looked around the packed stadium and saw Brit with my parents. I sensed too, by the look on his face, Chris was feeling reflective as well. He had called down to the bench in the last quarter to see whether I was okay to finish the game on the ground. He could see me taking the scene in and he did the same as the club song rang out. It was a special and amazing feeling.

I wanted to hide but had to act natural and found solace in talking casually to the Guthrie boys in the race. Then Paddy's son, five-year-old George, saved me as he came running towards me. I thought: 'Well done George', scooped him up and let him take the attention. I had let myself become emotional that week but with finals ahead and the decision made, my shoulders felt lighter by the week's end.

Chris embraced Brit as he entered the rooms, which was enough to raise Hawk's antenna. The next week I told Hawk we were pregnant. His initial thoughts had been that the hug was because I was giving it away. The signals he thought he'd picked up had become scrambled. Now he was unsure, again.

Chapter 26

Getting it right

OUR RECORD IN qualifying finals had not been good, there is no way to avoid that. Our only victory since 2011 had been in 2016 when the-then Hawk Isaac Smith missed a set shot for goal after the siren. We didn't really need Isaac – now a Cat – noting loudly that everyone seemed a bit tight as we began the build-up. We had, after all, won 13 straight since the St Kilda loss. We had certainly been winning together!

The pressure had been piling on Gary Rohan when he fronted the media at the open media session held in the week leading into the game and he came across as defensive about his finals record. Chris had backed him to the hilt in a sometimes-fiery appearance on *Footy Classified* in the week before the final. 'I just don't buy that there's pressure on him. I don't think anyone who knows footy is thinking, "For Geelong to win, Gary Rohan has got to dominate".' Chris said. 'I get a bit defensive of my players and I'll wear that as a badge of honour.'

This was another example of why we loved Chris. For years he had shouldered the blame for a loss while we took the credit when we won. Again, he was setting up that reaction. His approach also said something about his character. He was prepared to persist with a player even when the critics had that player in their sights.

Collingwood had been on an unprecedented run – with just one loss, to Sydney, in their previous 12 – and we knew they would be hard to beat. But we were ready and in good form. I would start the game on the bench alongside Paddy Dangerfield. By then, I was starting to embrace the idea.

We started slowly as Collingwood's pressure was unbelievable. They forced mistakes, and we gave away free kicks we had not normally conceded. We were rattled. We could not hear each other due to the noise from the massive crowd, and with not many goals kicked and much of the play happening on the Shane Warne wing (opposite the bench), staying connected with the coach's box became difficult.

The ball whizzed around and the Magpies were winning the loose ball. Jezza kept us in touch with brilliant goals at the end of the first quarter and the end of the third when he kicked a goal from the boundary line (his 100th for Geelong) very few players could. In between the Magpies stifled our ball movement from end to end and although we began winning ground balls, our scoring relied on interceptions.

We were in a dogfight and Collingwood were playing better than we were. They deserved to be two goals up two minutes into the last quarter when Jordan De Goey goaled.

At the next centre bounce Tom Atkins gathered the loose ball and handballed to me and Jezza marked my high up and under and goaled. The freshest players always started the last quarter in the middle at Geelong, which meant I was in the action.

We had spoken about handling the grind during the year, so I remained confident. I resisted focusing on what I needed to do to create a win. I had habitually asked myself that question when such tight situations arose but this year, I went to the centre bounce focusing more on the collective. My question was: how do we set up to give ourselves a 60 per cent chance of winning the clearance?

There had been a change of mindset for us at centre bounces as we rotated different foursomes through the middle. Could we get the ball to a spot where we could have more players near the ball? Were we positioned according to our strengths? Could we work our man over so our teammate would have space? It remained my favourite part of the game. Four vs four – a cage fight.

In previous years my thinking would have been I have to get on the charge as the ball is bounced. It looked great if it worked and if I happened to shark the ball at pace, but it had a strike rate of about 15 per cent while also giving the opposition a chance to exploit me. I had worked hard on ground ball work to increase my chances of making the percentage play work.

This year was about setting up properly. It doesn't guarantee anything of course, as luck is as vital as experience.

We had that combination of luck and experience when Brad Close put us back in front after Jezza gathered a hot ball on the wing. He handballed to Hawk who flipped it over to me in space. Paddy was forward so Collingwood defender Nathan Murphy had to follow him as he charged towards the pocket to create space for Ty Stengle with Brad behind him. All I had to do was execute a short 45-degree kick to Ty who handballed to Brad. He slammed the goal through, giving us a one-point lead, with half the quarter gone.

The sequence worked but it was such a fine line, with all the interconnecting parts needing crucial decisions to lead to that moment. We had learnt to dance together under the most extreme pressure. We trusted each other and hung in there and executed a basic play that had been refined through training. We did not seek individual brilliance but relied on skills we had trained to execute when the pressure was on.

Collingwood were never going to stop and again took the lead after another De Goey goal. It took a huge Gary Rohan mark and goal to put us a point in front again. Gary had joined a list of unfairly maligned Geelong players to stand up when needed in a big final. He had positively cemented his place in our club's history.

Scores were then level with 150 seconds remaining after Jack Crisp scored a behind. Then Max Holmes kicked the clincher as a result of hard running on the fat side after we turned grim defence into attack. The final 100 seconds were hard work as we looked to create stoppage after stoppage. I lifted my arms in relief when the siren sounded with us six points in front. It was a similar pose to that when we had outlasted a brave Collingwood 15 years earlier in the 2007 preliminary final.

As I entered the rooms, I knew we would learn enough lessons from that game to be hard to beat no matter who was ahead of us. I also knew that missing the odd game throughout the year had improved my ability to contribute in that tense last quarter.

Other than the sub, Mark O'Connor and Jake Kolodjashnij who was injured I had played fewer minutes in the match than any other Geelong player but had picked up the most disposals, at least in our side.

In the preliminary final against Brisbane, Paddy started in the centre square. We had accepted the reasons for him starting on the bench in the qualifying final, but we were adamant he would start in the square for the next final. I was happy to start on the pine. Paddy kicked a goal within the first minute as he pushed forward and we were away to a flier.

With Jake Kolodjashnij playing a blinder, we blew the Lions apart in the third quarter to stretch a five-goal lead to 63 points at the final break, setting us up for a berth in another Grand Final, my sixth. We had outscored the Lions by 59 points from intercept possessions and would head into the Grand Final on the back of 15 straight wins. The only downside was a hamstring injury to our speedster Max Holmes in the third quarter. Max had earned his spot in our best team after a brilliant season and had been one of our standout performers on the night. Unfortunately for Max the decision to leave him out of the Grand Final side, one Chris Scott would later describe as 'brutal', was made the night before the game.

* * *

The Grand Final went according to script. Winning in 2022 was the culmination of years of hard work and sticking together even as the doubters became louder and the criticism more consistent. When the siren sounded with us 81 points ahead, I knew immediately I had made the right decision to end my career.

Those watching closely would have seen the hugs with big Hawk and Chris Scott linger just that bit longer. Hawk reckons if anyone wanted a measure of how frustrating the years of near misses had been, then they only had to look at that hug between us.

The lap of honour after the Grand Final is so uplifting. To see the happiness on the faces of our fans makes all the hard work so worthwhile. So, here I was, wandering around the boundary on cloud nine with the medal Auskicker Archie Stockdale had hung around my neck when I saw Sam Moorfoot hanging over the fence, his face alight with a beautiful big smile.

Sam has been such an important part of our group and a good friend to all at the club, so I didn't think twice when I asked him if he would like to jump onto the ground with me. Whether he was allowed on the ground or not under AFL rules, was never a consideration, although I did catch the eye of Lindy, his mum, to make sure she was fine with him joining the mayhem.

The moment was captured on TV and went viral, with eight million views on the AFL social media channels and coverage extending to America's ESPN. We lost count of the number of interviews Sam did after the game; we had created a media megastar! Months later, Hawk and I took him to a pub appearance with us and more people wanted photos with Sam than with either of us.

I didn't think the moment was going to be as special or give so much joy as it eventually did but anyone could see by the smile on my face what Sam means to me, and to the club.

Sam and I have been good mates since he began working at the club in 2015 after Lindy and Sam wrote to the club asking whether there might be any employment opportunities at the place he adored.

Lindy did not have high expectations as Sam has Down Syndrome and finding employment can be hard, but the club saw an opportunity for him to work part-time in the Cats Bistro and Cats Shop; he has done the rest.

My brother Troy, who was then working with our VFL team, was the first to connect with Sam and reckoned he could contribute more. Troy and our VFL co-ordinator, Nathan Tweddle, arranged for Sam to be interviewed for a job in our football department. As soon as we saw his impact, we made him hydration manager at training. He told us it was the best job in the world; little did we know he would become the best hydration manager in the world!

With two older brothers, Jack and Tom, close in age and spirit, and parents, Lindy and Dale, who let him be him regardless of where he finds himself, he was used to the banter that comes with all football clubs, so he fit into the environment immediately. Lindy tells me he never repeats any of what he hears – he understands the trust inherent in the relationship.

He is high functioning, with a positive energy that never dims. It was soon clear he could connect with everyone and anyone, regardless of where they stood in the club. I love that attitude and I enjoyed how it rubbed off on the group. He became a connector, especially when he would walk by when Chris Scott was deep in an important discussion when he probably should have kept his distance. Sam's presence would often disarm Chris in such moments and would lighten everyone's mood.

It became pretty clear very early that he enjoyed being around us and we enjoyed being around him and it has remained the same as our friendship has developed with the WhatsApp group I have with him, Hawk and my brother Scott, now an assistant coach at Collingwood. It's my busiest.

The reaction to me interacting with Sam and that moment when I carried Levi Ablett through the banner was interesting, because it put on public display something I have valued right through my time at the club.

Expressing my sensitive side was something that has taken time. The media can go pretty hard if the performance doesn't follow. I was comfortable with what transpired on Grand Final day because I had been doing the same things all my career. I knew I was being true to myself regardless of the result. But would the reaction have been as positive had the Cats lost?

That question is impossible to answer, but what the club understood is you can combine a killer, competitive instinct on the field with a caring nature off it.

Vic Fuller, the heart and soul of the club, embodied that outlook; his cheeky greeting to everyone who arrived at the Cats, reinforcing the sentiment. 'I was here when you got here, and I will be here when you leave,' he said. When reading his eulogy, I said that I fell in love with Vic Fuller the day I met him. His approach to life was spot on - leave the ego at the door and you might learn something. Bloody hell, did I learn something along the way?

The club fostered my belief that if you are open enough to listen you can learn from anyone. It's part of why jumping in the car with a first-year player to attend a school visit was never a chore for me. They might give up a little bit of dirt on their teammates to me, or reveal a dry sense of humour in a different setting.

Lessons bobbed up everywhere I looked; from coffee with Frank Costa on Geelong's waterfront to a conversation with a teammate's partner to a quiet beer with Tom Hawkins and Harry Taylor. No agenda; just a catch up to talk about things that might matter to you, to them, to anyone.

Vic's love for family and football gave me a degree in life. Nigel Austin's ambition for Geelong and his business Cotton On and his never ending quest to get better inspired me.

Mum and Dad's humility allowed them to always be Mum and Dad even though Dad would occasionally follow a compliment with a quizzical question: 'Why don't you move the ball a bit quicker?'

I admired AFL CEO Gillon McLachlan for getting the game through COVID and dropped off a bottle of wine to let him know. Chris Scott's resilience under fire made me proud and I told him that.

As for Lynn Burmeister's desire to make babies. Wow, she was a star. The fact that her clinic went from wearing pink to blue for Grand Final Day showed the lengths she went to for her people. We were so grateful for the care and expertise our obstetrician Michael Shembrey and his staff displayed. We let these people know our gratitude. Why wouldn't we?

Brit understood how much I loved doing what I did and backed me to do that to its full extent. I loved my old schoolmates and my brothers too because they were here when I got here and will also be here when I leave.

Every teammate had a story. It took until the Grand Final celebrations before my premiership teammate Tys Stengle told me his one. That's his to share but my respect for him only grew.

As for my manager Tom Petroro, I needed someone who told me the truth, who kept me thinking, who challenged me, who simply wanted the best for me.

Everyone has a list though, if they think about it. Eventually, I recognised that passing on such lessons to others was enjoyable for me too.

Glynn Harvey is a local fruit and vegetable wholesaler running the family store Harvey's of Highton in Geelong. Glynn is vigilant in ensuring high standards are maintained. The shelves are stacked with care to show fresh produce, the floors are clean and the interaction between staff is kind and respectful. I liked taking the players to their warehouse to help them understand what 50 years of high performance looked like, emphasising how important hard work, attention to detail and genuine care was to achieving that result.

Footy created so many opportunities to connect with everyone from business icons to teammates to Cats' supporters and staff to chance encounters with people who just want a chat and I took up most of them.

Every interaction was an opportunity that a boy from Bendigo relished. All you had to do was be real and more often than not the people you were with would shine.

I suspect a few teammates eventually picked up on my attitude and eventually it began to permeate through the Cats. Mates of mine and mates of teammates were always welcome in my world, as were partners and parents and children and brothers and sisters, as were high achievers in their chosen world. All in.

That's why being captain was something I cherished because I have a theory that leaders make it look easy and for me most of the time it wasn't that hard.

Some people can work themselves up way too much. They think you need to do this, or you need to read that. I keep it simple: what about just generally being half a decent person? Have your eye out a little bit for everyone and make sure you have a bit of fun along the way. That was the basis of everything I strived to do.

Being part of the Geelong community drove home to me how important that outlook was, whether that be at a pre-season community camp or at a clinic or during a hospital visit. I was lucky I enjoy interacting with others and am comfortable in most environments, whether it be around children or in a hospital with a very sick person or with people with disabilities. I seem to know what to do and what to say. I get great energy from kids and teenagers and love hearing other people's stories. Not only am I genuinely interested in their experiences, it is also a part of my personality that needs nourishing.

I'm often asked where that characteristic comes from, and apart from the influences of two great parents and an attitude that comes from living in a country town, I have no answer. Anna Box reckoned after our many sessions that my lens on the world is to ask: what is needed? That means entering a room and subconsciously noticing who is on the outside, who needs to be included, who needs some love? It's instinctive and explains why my own sense of belonging can be surprisingly challenged at times. It's also why knowing people's names is so important to me as it helps me connect.

I understood that wasn't the case with all my teammates, so the club instituted a couple of things to ensure all player experiences outside of the club were positive. It is no shame to not be comfortable when visiting a hospital as it is often confronting. It was better to put players in places that suited their personality or interests.

I saw community visits as an opportunity to connect not only with the people we were interacting with but also with young teammates. I would show them what was needed and at the same time get into real conversations about issues that were more often than not unrelated to footy. Those sorts of discussions rarely occurred within the walls of the club. On the road or over a bite to eat away from the club people were more likely to open up.

It was at one of these community camps, when children were asking questions, I discovered that Quinton Narkle had been a prefect at his school. That sort of unexpected insight was commonplace on these trips. It was also good for young players to see how important this part of their history, culture, or upbringing was to the captain.

Sometimes the lessons delivered I was less proud of. It was on a drive back from the community camp in Warrnambool in 2017, with Ryan Gardner in the passenger seat, that I was pulled over for exceeding the speed limit. That misdemeanour was enough to cost us a TAC Cup sponsorship, something that had been teetering on the edge for a while. I could understand the TAC's decision but I was embarrassed. At least it emphasised to others I was as capable of making mistakes as they were.

It is obvious to me the impact I could have on someone with a simple gesture. It did not have to be grand, just authentic and part of that was keeping the interaction between me and the person rather than making a big deal out of it publicly.

The number of people I was able to connect with was a privilege for me and inspired me as I watched how they dealt with hardship and joy in equal measure. They knew I was in their corner; often I was blown away when told of the impact a simple message from me would have. It would be disingenuous to say it wasn't an honour, on Brownlow Medal night, to receive the Jim Stynes Community Leadership Award 'For dedication and commitment to community engagement'. It was a very proud moment, and perhaps it described who I am and how I thought about myself: I wasn't just a footballer. I could be good at something else.

The fact is I like making people feel good, and I thought Geelong and its players could, and should, do that. My family had taught me that despite the privilege of being an AFL player, and all that comes with it, it was, and is, important to me to never lose touch with the real world. Within the club I wanted everyone to feel that the position they held was really important – because it was – and helped our teams succeed. That meant building relationships and that meant taking the time to do so.

It was only on Grand Final day in 2022 many saw that side of me on display, but I did allow myself a little indulgence at my retirement media conference when I said: 'I am pretty soft at times … I think the boys know that side of me … a lot more, too.'

It was funny. Many people have told me their perception of me changed after the Grand Final but what happened away from footy was as familiar to me as playing the game. I had been doing the same things all my life that people saw me do over four hours on Grand Final day.

Brit and I drove home from the Grand Final celebrations on a high, just saying to each other: 'Can you believe how that all turned out?'

Chapter 27

What is next?

B Y THE TIME the best and fairest wound up at Crown Casino a week later, Brit and I were exhausted. The club had shown their love with a great farewell that left me humbled and then eventually ready to scream out: 'Enough.' Brit finished the school year knowing she would not return at the start of 2023 and we kept healthy and happy. We had a trip to Hawaii but I found it hard to sit still. Back home, we spent unrushed time together and prepared for our baby's arrival.

I thought I might have withdrawals when Geelong resumed their pre-season, but all I missed was regular contact with lifelong friends.

The summer was filled with a new job in a leadership role at Melbourne Storm that satisfied the competitor within as well as letting me see how another great club operated. My first impression of Storm's football manager, Frank Ponissi, and legendary coach Craig Bellamy was so positive I could not say no. Their attitude permeated the club. I was looking forward to learning how a new sport managed their routines, culture, relationships, while providing my experience in leadership.

A couple of days a week at the Storm was enough as I took a break from the pre-season and the Cats for the first time. Hawk reckoned I was driving him a bit crazy with constant phone calls but I thought he was the one more often ringing me! He suspected I could not really let go – I needed to know how things were going at the club while making sure I kept in touch with everyone. To be honest, we missed each other. I was rapt to hear Paddy had been named captain with Tom Stewart his vice-captain. It will be great to see how Paddy leads because he will be different from me and I love that. He was the person who got me enjoying football again when he arrived and became a magnificent support. I'm excited to see what direction the team takes, and I hope Paddy enjoys it as much as I did. Tom is such a dedicated player who wants to get the best out of himself. He will keep playing good football for such a long time.

I'm guessing I'll be involved in AFL footy at some point in some way again, but I wanted to spend my first year outside the game, unbound from the clock and the fixture, with a mid-year trip to London planned during a European summer.

All the while, Brit and I prepared to become first-time parents.

BRIT: I had a wonderful pregnancy. I feel I had someone looking over me and had given me the gift of a lovely, enjoyable pregnancy. This pregnancy was always going to be considered high-risk due to my experience with IVF. My obstetric group was incredible and gave me all the care and reassurance I needed. I don't think they could really believe what we had been through and were very considerate and caring during the whole process. I had mobile numbers if I needed to contact them (which only ever happened once) and I saw them every two weeks until the pregnancy was around 14 weeks. After that I was considered to be having a 'standard pregnancy' which was probably the most amazing news I'd heard. Everything was going great and it continued that way. I was even riding my bike until the day before Joey was born!

Then during a hot summer Wednesday, the magical day arrived. At 5.31 pm on 22 February 2023, Joey Victor Selwood entered our world weighing a healthy 3.1 kilograms and stretching 48 centimetres.

He peed everywhere as he was held aloft, the little devil, as he showed us he was here to party. Brit was exhausted but we were both excited beyond description as we realised life was all about the three of us now.

As the paediatrician checked Joey's hips she recognised me and congratulated me for the Cats' efforts. All I could think was Brit had better not hear her. My mind was only focused on two things: the beautiful Joey and how Brit was feeling.

When we revealed the news to the world, Brit spoke for us both on social media. 'The world just got a whole lot better. Joey Victor Selwood, your Mum and Dad are so in love with you.'

We were heading home to Barwon Heads as a family.

We chose the name Joey because we liked it and Victor was obviously a nod to the great Vic Fuller. It was not lost on anyone that Joey was born exactly two years to the day since Vic had died. Unlike Mum and Dad's decision to name me after a rock star, there was nothing behind Joey – we both just liked the name. It didn't take long however for my friends to suggest I had just mucked up the spelling of Joel. That made me laugh.

Smiles came easily – our hearts were full of our love for the bundle we were holding and for each other. The gratitude we felt as we became parents was a little overwhelming knowing the emotions we had been through and the commitment and genius of others through the IVF process that led us to the maternity ward at Geelong's Epworth Hospital.

As Brit expressed when she announced in September – it was the week before the preliminary final – that we were expecting a baby, we also felt empathy for those couples experiencing fertility issues or loss hoping our tale, as unique as it is, might lend hope to others and raise awareness so people's experiences are not forgotten.

On Instagram Brit wrote: 'We couldn't do this announcement without acknowledging those who are struggling with infertility or loss. I know how much my heart would break every time I saw a pregnancy post and my heart truly goes out to you if that is what you are feeling right now. These past few years have changed me forever. For anyone who has lost hope right now I have been there and I'm thinking of you and I hope one day you get your miracle.' My thoughts were the same. On the same day I wrote: 'What I have worked out through the process is that women are amazing, and my wife is a superwoman. In a journey that hasn't been easy, we have found a way, through great support and Brit staying positive.' I must have forgotten Brit's rebuke when she had reminded me during the long path to pregnancy that it was no 'journey', but I did remember her comments at our first discussion with our consultant, that success depended on her commitment.

About 24 hours after our miracle was born, I was holding Joey in my lap as the Cats played Hawthorn, but my eyes were on Joey way more than on the footy as he twitched and yawned and slept and cried. He was our dream come true.

Now that we were entering a new phase in our lives, I could only reflect on how fortunate we had been with so many amazing experiences already behind us. Sure, there had been some hard work and some testing times – which I was reminded of when I went back to the club to see what was happening with my back. Medical records showed I was having my 94th and 95th scans since 2011 – but I had enjoyed a huge amount of luck to be surrounded by great people and great friends within communities that always made me feel at home.

Brit and I stopped to grab a coffee as we drove home from the hospital. I ran into the Pane Di Matteo coffee shop in Highton and told the barista our baby was in the car. A cheeky smirk appeared on his face when he said: 'Now you've made it.' I could only say: 'Yeah I have.' I had wanted to be a dad all along and that quick exchange felt so good. I told Brit what he had said when I got back to the car and we could not get the smiles off our faces.

We knew keenly that Geelong – a club I loved before they knew I existed – had got us to that point. I had such good fortune to join the Cats at the start of such a successful era.

My good fortune had extended to a meeting with our local member, Richard Marles, about retaining the maternity ward at Geelong's Epworth Hospital. I didn't realise he was then the acting prime minister while Anthony Albanese was in India. If you had told me at 20 I was going to be putting the case for a maternity health ward to the acting prime minister nearly 15 years later I would have said: 'No way' but football can take you to some crazy places.

It was all so worthwhile. I enjoyed driving the bus at times, enjoyed sitting in the middle and then being at the back while others were at the wheel. I realised you can lead from any position and it was nice to take some different vantage points while still being captain. I didn't need to be up front all the time. I just loved going to work, having fun and representing Geelong.

Now, I move on. A couple of years ago, I imagined my future would mean immersing myself in a football club trying to make it as good as it could be as an ex-player in an off-field role. Then I had expressed doubts about what might lay ahead as it seemed that playing football might be the only thing I could be really good at. Fortunately, right now that's not my thinking as I can see so many experiences ahead of me.

Wherever I find myself I know one philosophy won't change.

I will be all in.

James Braund

Milestones and statistics

Joel Selwood

Date of birth: 26 May 1988

Junior clubs: St Therese's, Kennington-Sandhurst, Bendigo Pioneers

Draft: Selection No.7 2006 AFL National Draft

Debut: round 1, 2007 v Western Bulldogs, Docklands Stadium

AFL Games: 355 (259 wins – 1 draw – 95 losses)

AFL Goals: 175

Winning percentage: 73.10%

Games at Kardinia Park/GMBHA Stadium: 111 (97 wins, 14 losses)

AFL RECORDS

Most games as captain: 239 games as Geelong captain 2012–2022

Most finals: 40 (22 wins, 18 losses)

First player to win AFL Rising Star and premiership in first season

Most games by siblings: 786 games (Joel 355, Adam 187, Scott 169, Troy 75)

GEELONG CLUB RECORDS

Most games: 355 (when retired end of 2022)

First Geelong player to play in four premierships, 2007, 2009, 2011, 2022

NOTABLE RECORDS

305 games as teammate alongside Tom Hawkins

Fourth on list of most wins as an AFL player when retired: 259 wins

PLAYER HONOURS

Premierships: 2007, 2009, 2011, 2022

Grand Finals: 2007, 2008, 2009, 2011, 2020, 2022

Geelong Club best and fairest: 2010, 2013, 2014

Runner-up Brownlow medal: 2013

All-Australian: 2009, 2010, 2013, 2014, 2016, 2017

All-Australian captain: 2013, 2014, 2016

AFL Rising Star Award: 2007

AFL Coaches Association best young player: 2008

AFL Players' Association best captain: 2013

AFL Players' Association most courageous: 2009, 2012, 2013, 2014

AFL Players' Association best first year player: 2007

Michael Tuck medal (best on ground pre-season premiership): 2009

Pre-season premiership: 2009

Geelong best clubman: 2011, 2013

Peter Badcoe VC Medal (player who exemplifies Anzac spirit): 2016, 2018

Geelong Club community champion award: 2011, 2020, 2022

Jim Stynes community leadership award: 2022

Victorian representative: 2008

International rules v Ireland: 2014 (captain), 2017

AFL Life Member

Geelong Life Member

Bendigo Sports Star award: 2009

JUNIOR CAREER

All-Australian: 2005

TAC Cup team of year: 2005

Captain AIS/Academy tour of Ireland: 2005

Ron Barassi medal (best Australian player on Irish tour AIS/Academy representative) 2005

MILESTONE GAMES

AFL Debut

Western Bulldogs 113 v Geelong 93

Round 1, 2007

50th AFL Game

Geelong 126 v Brisbane Lions 33

Round 5, 2009

100th AFL Game

Collingwood 62 v Geelong 65

Round 8, 2011

150th AFL Game

Geelong 98 v Melbourne 30

Round 16, 2013

200th AFL Game

Geelong 95 v Sydney 63

Round 19, 2015

250th AFL Game

Melbourne 94 v Geelong 97

Round 1, 2018

300th AFL Game

Geelong 89 v Gold Coast 52

Round 5, 2020

350th AFL Game

Geelong 94 v Western Bulldogs 66

Round 20, 2022

Acknowledgements

When sitting down and writing this book I didn't know how much enjoyment I would get reflecting on my journey.

The experience was made even better by the many kind people who took the time to share stories of the challenges and amazing times we had as I strived to fulfil my dreams. I am forever grateful.

Thanks to Brit, who was pregnant with Joey when the book was being written; for her patience, input, and insight on all matters. Her preparedness to share her IVF experience purely because it might benefit others revealed her care and empathy for others.

My family (Mum, Dad, Troy, Adam and Scott), friends, teammates, colleagues and other special people in my life for their ongoing support and the openness they showed in allowing me to tell many stories of the journey we've had.

To the team at Hardie Grant for taking a chance and guiding me through the process with care as well as the editor who did such a great job shaping the words into a book. For those who read the draft and made such valuable contributions at such short notice, a sincere thanks.

A special thanks to Peter Ryan, the journalist I reached out to midway through last year, to help tell my tale. He understood the assignment and put in the work to get the whole story and a little more.

He was also ALL IN.

And to all those who have made the journey so special, the supporters, football lovers young and old, my opponents, and most of all the Geelong Football Club, thank you.